Medical Library Service

College of Physicians and Surgeons of British Columbia

Child Health Assessment

A Handbook of Measurement Techniques

James R. Rodrigue
University of Florida Health Science Center

Gary R. Geffken
University of Florida Health Science Center

Randi M. Streisand
University of Florida Health Science Center

FOREWORD BY
Anthony Spirito
Brown University School of Medicine

Allyn and Bacon
Boston • London • Toronto • Sydney • Tokyo • Singapore

This book is dedicated to my son, Nicholas.
JRR

To my wife, Sandy.
GRG

I dedicate this book to my family.
RMS

Executive Editor: Becky Pascal
Series Editorial Assistant: Susan Hutchinson
Manufacturing Buyer: Suzanne Lareau
Marketing Manager: Joyce Nilsen

Copyright © 2000 by Allyn & Bacon
A Pearson Education Company
Needham Heights, MA 02494

Internet: www.abacon.com

All rights reserved. No part of the material protected by this copyright notice may be reproduced or utilized in any form or by any means, electronic or mechanical, including photocopying, recording, or by any information storage and retrieval system, without written permission from the copyright owner.

Library of Congress Cataloging-in-Publication Data

Rodrigue, James R.
    Child health assessment : a handbook of measurement techniques / James R. Rodrigue, Gary R. Geffken, Randi M. Streisand.
       p.   cm.
    Includes bibliographical references and index.
    ISBN 0-205-19832-5
     1. Children—Medical examinations handbooks, manuals, etc.
2. Child development—Testing Handbooks, manuals, etc.   3. Medical screening Handbooks, manuals, etc.   I. Geffken, Gary R.
II. Streisand, Randi M.   III. Title.
    [DNLM: 1. Pediatrics—methods. 2. Pediatrics—standards.
3. Questionnaires.   WS 200 R696c 2000]
RJ50.R625   2000
618.92'0075—dc21
DNLM/DLC
for Library of Congress   99-21430
                                                                        CIP

Printed in the United States of America

10 9 8 7 6 5 4 3 2 1   03 02 01 00 99

Contents

Assessment Instruments by Child Health Domain   vi

Foreword   xi

Preface   xiii

PART I   *Introduction*

1   Instrument Selection and Review   1
by James R. Rodrigue
Selection of Instruments   2
Format of this Handbook   3
Approach to the Reviews   4
References   6

2   Methods of Evaluation and Psychometric Issues   7
by Gary R. Geffken
Norm-Referenced Tests   7
Psychometric Issues   9
Interviews   12
Observational Assessment of Behavior   13
Informal Assessment   14
References   14

3   Selecting and Administering Child Health Instruments   16
by Randi M. Streisand
Clinical Assessment   16
Summary and Clinical Case Example   21

Assessment in Research   22
References   25

PART II   *Child Health Instruments*

4   General and Illness-Specific Adjustment   **27**
by Gary R. Geffken and Randi M. Streisand
Reviews   29
General Observations and Recommendations   63
References   64

5   Stress and Coping   **65**
by Randi M. Streisand
Reviews   67
General Observations and Recommendations   89
References   90

6   Attitudes and Beliefs   **91**
by Randi M. Streisand
Reviews   93
General Observations and Recommendations   128
References   128

7   Pediatric Pain and Childhood Injury   **130**
by James R. Rodrigue
Pediatric Pain   130
Childhood Injury   132
Reviews   134
General Observations and Recommendations   167
References   168

8   Quality of Life   **170**
by James R. Rodrigue
Reviews   172
General Observations and Recommendations   194
References   195

9   Health-Related Knowledge and Adherence to Medical Regimens   **196**
by Gary R. Geffken and James R. Rodrigue
Reviews   198
General Observations and Recommendations   213
References   214

10 Parent, Family, and Health Care Professional   216
by Gary R. Geffken
Reviews   218
General Observations and Recommendations   247
References   248

PART III   *Summary and Recommendations*

11 Reflections and a Glance Toward the Future   249
by James R. Rodrigue
Child Health Assessment: Recommendations for Instrument Development   251

Index   254

Assessment Instruments by Child Health Domain

Domain	Instrument	
General and Illness-Specific Adjustment	Acceptance of Illness Scale (AIS)	29
	Behavioral Profile Rating Scale (BPRS)	30
	Behavioral Upset in Medical Patients-Revised (BUMP-R)	32
	Children's Eating Behavior Inventory (CEBI)	34
	Children's Physical Self-Concept Scale (CPSS)	35
	Children's Somatization Inventory (CSI)	37
	Deasy-Spinetta School Behavior Questionnaire (DSBQ)	40
	Diabetes Adjustment Scale (DAS)	41
	Hospitalization Self-Report Instrument (HSRI)-Memories of Hospitalization Questionnaire (MHQ)	42
	Living with a Chronic Illness (LCI)	44
	Negative Behavioral Changes (NBC)	46
	Negative Events Related to Short Stature (NERSS)	47
	Nurse's Rating Form (NRF)	49
	Pediatric Behavior Scale (PBS)	50
	Pediatric Inpatient Behavior Scale (PIBS)	53
	Pediatric Symptom Checklist (PSC)	55
	Perceived Illness Experience Scale (PIE)-Child Version	58

Domain	Instrument	
	Personal Adjustment and Role Skills Scale (PARS-III)	59
	Post-Hospitalization Behavior Questionnaire (PHBQ)	61
Stress and Coping	Children's Concern Scale (CCS)	67
	Coping Health Inventory for Children (CHIC)	68
	Coping Strategies Inventory (CSI)	70
	Fear Faces Scale (Fear Self-Report Scale, or Fear, SR)	72
	Hospital Fears Questionnaire (HFQ)	73
	Hospital Fears Rating Scale (HFRS)	75
	Hospital Stress Scale (HSS)	76
	Kidcope	78
	Life Events Checklist (LEC)	80
	Medical Experiences Questionnaire (MEQ)	82
	Medical Fear Questionnaire (MFQ)	83
	Role-Play Inventory of Situations and Coping Strategies (RISCS)	85
	Waldron/Varni Pediatric Pain Coping Inventory (PPCI)	87
Attitudes and Beliefs	Asthma Attitudes Questionnaire (AAQ)	93
	Attitude Toward Disabled Persons Scale (ATDP)	94
	Attitudes for AIDS Prevention	95
	Body Attitude Scale (BAS)	97
	Chedoke-McMaster Attitudes Toward Children with Handicaps (CATCH) Scale	99
	Child Attitudes Toward Illness Scale (CATIS)	101
	Child Satisfaction Questionnaire (CSQ)	103
	Child Vulnerability Scale (CVS)	105
	Children's Eating Attitudes Test (ChEAT)	107
	Children's Health Care Attitudes Questionnaire (CHCAQ)	109
	Children's Health Locus of Control Scale (CHLC)	111
	Children's Hope Scale (CHS)	112
	Death Anxiety Questionnaire (DAQ)	114
	Diabetes Opinion Survey (DOS)	115
	Enuresis Nuisance and Tolerance Scales	118

Domain	Instrument	
	Intentions to Engage in AIDS-Risk Situations	119
	Parent Participation Attitude Scale (PPAS)	121
	Parental Attitudes Toward Children with Handicaps (PATCH) Questionnaire	122
	Parental Health Beliefs Scale	124
	Perceptions of Asthma Medication Scale (PAM)	125
Pediatric Pain and Childhood Injury	Behavioral Approach-Avoidance and Distress Scale (BAADS)	134
	Charleston Pediatric Pain Pictures (CPPP)	135
	Child-Adult Medical Procedure Interaction Scale-Revised (CAMPIS-R)	137
	Child Behavior Observation Rating Scale (CBORS)	140
	Children's Hospital of Eastern Ontario Pain Scale (CHEOPS)	142
	Children's Pain Inventory (CPI)	143
	Faces Pain Scale (FPS)	145
	Headache Symptom Questionnaire-Revised (HSQ-R)	146
	Injury Behavior Checklist (IBC)	148
	Minor Injury Severity Scale (MISS)	150
	Modified Behavioral Pain Scale (MBPS)	152
	Neonatal Infant Pain Scale (NIPS)	153
	Observation Scale of Behavioral Distress (OSBD)—Revised	155
	Oucher Scale	157
	Pediatric Pain Questionnaire (PPQ)	159
	Perception of Procedures Questionnaire (PPQ)	161
	Scare Scale (SS)	164
	Toddler-Preschooler Postoperative Pain Scale (TPPPS)	165
Quality of Life	Child Health and Illness Profile— Adolescent Edition (CHIP-AE)	172
	Child Health Assessment Inventory (CHAI)	174
	Child Health Questionnaire (CHQ) Child Form	176

Assessment Instruments by Child Health Domain

Domain	Instrument	
	Child Health Questionnaire (CHQ) Parent Form	178
	Functional Disability Inventory (FDI)	181
	Functional Status Questionnaire (FSQ)	183
	Functional Status II(R)	185
	Health Status Measure for Children (HSMC)	188
	Pediatric Oncology Quality of Life Scale (POQOLS)	190
	Quality of Well-Being (QWB) Scale	192
Health-Related Knowledge and Adherence to Medical Regimens	Adaptiveness Rating Scale (ARS)	198
	Diabetes Mismanagement Questionnaire (DMQ)	199
	Family Asthma Management System Scale (FAMSS)	200
	Medical Compliance Incomplete Stories Test (MCIST)	202
	Preschool Health and Safety Knowledge Assessment (PHASKA)	204
	Self-Care Adherence Interview (SCAI)	205
	Skin Cancer Knowledge Questionnaire (SCKQ) for Parents	207
	Test of Diabetes Knowledge (TDK)	209
	The 24-Hour Recall Interview	211
Parent, Family, and Health Care Professional	Bereaved Extended Family Members Support Group Evaluation (BEFMSGE)	218
	Chronicity Impact and Coping Instrument: Parent Questionnaire (CICI: PQ)	219
	Coping Health Inventory for Parents (CHIP)	221
	Diabetes Family Behavior Checklist (DFBC)	223
	Diabetes Family Responsibility Questionnaire (DFRQ)	224
	Family APGAR-Revised	226
	Family Coping Scale (FCS)	227
	Family Inventory of Resources for Management (FIRM)	228
	Health Resources Inventory for Parents (HRIP)	230
	Impact on Family Scale (IFS)	232

Domain	Instrument	
	Interview Schedule on Impact of Cystic Fibrosis on Families	234
	Parent Perception Inventory (PPI)	235
	Parent Protection Scale (PPS)	236
	Parental Coping Scale: Pediatric Intensive Care Unit (PCS: PICU)	239
	Parental Stressor Scale: Neonatal Intensive Care Unit (PSS: NICU)	240
	Parents of Children with Disabilities Inventory (PCDI)	242
	Pediatric Oncology Nurse Stressor Questionnaire (PONSQ)	244
	Perceived Illness Experience Scale (PIE)	245

Foreword

Child health has emerged as a distinct subspecialty within many professional disciplines. Within a relatively short period of time, texts, handbooks, and several professional journals devoted entirely to the subject have emerged. When fields are relatively young, such as child health psychology, the process of measurement and the meaningfulness of research designs are significantly affected by the availability of appropriate measures. Many investigators have developed measures for use in child health specialties. Although admirable and important to the advancement of children's health, the resultant measures are not always well-developed or suitable for use in new studies by different investigators. All too often adult measures have been adapted to children with not enough attention paid to developmental differences or to psychometrics. When the measures are relatively well-developed, they are often not widely known or available. Consequently, similar but differentially developed measures of the same construct are common, with continued refinement of a measure's initial psychometrics rare.

In a developing field, there is a need for a broad array of measures, especially those that can be used to evaluate change in functioning over time. In child health, this need for a wide array of measures is particularly problematic. In addition to generic measures, disease-specific measures are necessary to measure factors within groups that are related to health status and health-related adjustment changes, some of which would be missed by relying on generic measures. Also, widely accepted generic measures may be compromised when applied to a specific disease population due to confounds between item content and medical conditions.

The cataloguing of measures is an important advance in any scientific field after the first few decades of systematic study. Up until now, the scattering of assessment tools in child health professions has made it virtually impossible to keep tabs on the development of measures. Even more problematic, without comparison to other measures, the decision making of researchers and practitioners alike in regard to which measures are most suitable and best developed has been affected. Thus, this handbook makes a valuable contribution to the emerging field by describing, in a comprehensive and practical manner, the measures available across a broad range of child health.

The authors of this handbook should be commended for gathering a wide range of measures and then classifying them according to the major domains of children's health: general and illness-specific adjustment, stress and coping, attitudes and beliefs, pediatric pain and childhood injury, quality of life, health-related knowledge, and adherence to medical regimens. This first attempt at a summary of the assessment measures in the field brings together information on over 100 instruments for practitioners to consult and researchers to scrutinize. This handbook is full of user-friendly information with enough detail for the reader to make decisions regarding the usefulness of any given measure. This volume should be an essential resource in the offices of all child health professionals, whether they provide evaluations and treatment or conduct clinical research.

The practice of children's health care depends on the availability of empirically supported assessment measures. This handbook makes an important contribution by informing the field of the measures currently available and their validation status. If this handbook serves as a catalyst for more in-depth studies of the psychometrics of measures used in the field, it will play an important role in the further refinement of assessment in child health. If this handbook results in greater attention to and study of assessment measures that are able to detect change over time, then the field will advance because the underpinnings of child health assessment and treatment will be considerably strengthened.

Anthony Spirito, Ph.D.
Brown University School of Medicine

Preface

The growth in child health professions has led to increased awareness regarding the need for new assessment technology. Consequently, the child health literature is burgeoning with new measurement techniques that vary considerably in type, quality, and focus. Assessment instruments have been developed for purposes of measuring child and adolescent psychological adaptation (general and illness-specific), pain complaints, quality of life, health-related knowledge, coping with illness, adherence to medical recommendations, and family functioning, among other topic areas. To date, there exists no single reference that provides a comprehensive listing and summary of available instruments specific to the field of child health. Indeed, these instruments are widely scattered throughout the literature, thus making it difficult for clinicians and researchers to identify, review, and evaluate assessment tools that potentially meet their clinical and research needs. In this handbook, we present and review a collection of assessment tools that have been developed to assess various aspects of children's health.

This handbook was written for child health professionals who conduct assessments as part of their clinical activity or research programs, including child health psychologists, psychiatrists, pediatricians, nurses, health educators, and social workers. Also, students in child health fields who are considering outcome measurements for future use in clinical practice or research projects should find this handbook to be particularly useful. The primary objective of this handbook is to make information about child health assessment instruments more accessible to child health professionals and students. We provide relevant information about the specific purpose of each instrument, for whom its use is appropriate, basic administration and scoring procedures, sample items whenever possible, psychometric information, pertinent references, and how to obtain copies or permission for use. Also provided is our summary impressions of each instrument and its relative strengths and limitations.

We have organized this handbook into three parts. Part I consists of three chapters and provides the reader with a more complete description of the organization of this book, highly relevant information necessary for evaluating the psychometric characteristics of child health instruments, and a review of issues and guidelines to assist child health professionals in the selection of appropriate instruments for use in clinical practice and research. Part II has seven chapters and is the central showpiece of the book. Here, we review over 100 child health instruments in the published literature. In Part III, we describe our summary impressions and conclusions regarding the status of child health assessment, and provide specific recommendations for its continued advancement.

We extend our warm thanks and gratitude to several people who provided valuable assistance and support throughout the preparation of this handbook, including Ken Tercyak, Phil Eisenberg, Stacey Carmichael, Melanie Jones, Kathy MacNaughton, Tony Spirito, and members of the R Club. We also thank the reviewers of this manuscript for their helpful comments: Pamela J. Bachanas, Emory University School of Medicine; Ronald T. Brown, Medical University of South Carolina; and Elissa Jelalian, Brown University School of Medicine.

Chapter 1

Instrument Selection and Review

JAMES R. RODRIGUE

As child health psychologists, we have found ourselves often searching for assessment tools designed to measure constructs of interest in our clinical and research activities. Discussions with our many psychologist, pediatrician, nursing, psychiatry, social work, and health educator colleagues suggest that others, too, spend considerable time searching for instruments to assess their patients' knowledge about health, pain-coping strategies, adherence behaviors, family interactions around health-related matters, attitudes toward their illness, and perceived quality of life, among other domains of functioning. In general, we have found that many child health clinicians and researchers are unaware of the vast array of assessment tools that have been developed to measure various aspects of adjustment, stress and coping, attitudes and beliefs, adherence behaviors, health-related knowledge, quality of life, pain, and family adaptation. The purpose of this handbook is to assist child health professionals in identifying available child health measurement instruments, evaluating their strengths and limitations, and determining their potential utility with clinical and research populations of interest to them.

In the following chapters we provide reviews of over 100 assessment tools designed to measure specific child health domains. It is our hope that readers will find these reviews helpful in selecting instruments that meet their specific clinical or research objectives. Each chapter begins with a brief summary of the key assessment issues facing child health clinicians and researchers in the particular domain under review and ends with a brief summary of our observations of the assessment instruments. Although the actual measures are not included, we have attempted to make the reviews sufficiently detailed to highlight each instrument's particular format, and we have provided up-to-date information on how to obtain the instruments. Whenever possible, our reviews were sent to the instrument's developers for comments, accuracy check, and provision of any additional psychometric information. In the end, however, we made the final decisions about what to include in the reviews.

Selection of Instruments

Although we provide reviews for over 100 child health instruments, there are others that are not included in this handbook. We had to be selective in our approach for many reasons, not the least of which is the fact that there are too many instruments and assessment devices in the child health literature to review in one volume. We struggled over whether to include measures that are not as comprehensively developed and validated as other instruments within a particular domain. Although we did eliminate some measures on the basis of insufficient development or psychometric inferiority, we included some less well-developed but promising instruments because researchers may wish to examine these tools further to determine their eventual utility for the field of child health.

We finally had to narrow our choices, which we did in several ways. First, we focused only on instruments for which published information exists. Second, we decided to include instruments that are in preliminary or early stages of development, although we recognize that our descriptions may soon be out of date. In so doing, we alert readers to the existence of a particular measurement tool and encourage them to review recent literature or contact the developers directly for more current development and psychometric information. Third, we omitted measurement tools that were not developed specifically for use with pediatric populations, children and adolescents in health care settings, or family members of children with health-related concerns. Though the majority of such instruments (e.g., Child Behavior Checklist, Conners' Parent Rating Scale, State-Trait Anxiety Inventory for Children, Personality Inventory for Children) are used frequently in child health clinical and research settings, they have been reviewed extensively by others (e.g., Goldman, Stein, & Guerry, 1983; Mash & Terdal, 1997) and there is considerable debate over their suitability for children with physical health conditions (Perrin, Stein, & Drotar, 1991). Fourth, we focused specifically on the seven domains included in this handbook (general and illness-specific adjustment; stress and coping; attitudes and beliefs; pediatric pain and childhood injury; quality of life; adherence to medical regimens and health-related knowledge; parent, family, and health care professional) and therefore did not include instruments that assess other important child health behaviors, such as tobacco use, drug abuse, or sexual activity. Within the seven domains, we continued to be selective and reviewed primarily those measures for which reliability and validity data are available. In some instances, the original developers may not have provided such data, but others reporting use of the measure included reliability and validity data in their study descriptions.

In light of the time lag between manuscript development and publication, we recognize that many of the instruments reviewed herein will have been further validated during the publication process. Moreover, several new instruments will have been published since our completion of the original manuscript (March, 1998). If this handbook meets an emerging resource need in the child health domain, as we suspect it does, it is our intention to publish periodic updates. To this end, we welcome all comments that will facilitate enhancing the utility of future editions of this handbook.

Format of This Handbook

Several excellent books exist in which assessment indices have been comprehensively reviewed (Corcoran & Fischer, 1987; Goldman et al., 1983; McDowell & Newell, 1996). We acknowledge these colleagues whose efforts we have found most useful in our own work as clinicians and researchers. Because this handbook is intended for child health professionals representing several different disciplines, Chapters 2 and 3 provide useful information about psychometric components of assessment (test development, reliability, validity, etc.) and a framework to guide clinicians and researchers in their selection of instruments for clinical practice and scientific inquiry.

Chapters 4 through 10 include our reviews of the instruments within each of the seven child health domains. Some domains have been the focus of considerable empirical attention, and consequently, the assessment tools are more sophisticated and well developed. In such instances, there is ample evidence of a measure's reliability and validity, and parameters surrounding the measure's use are well delineated and described. In contrast, other domains, though highly relevant to the developing field of child health, have been the focus of less scientific study. The development of measures in these areas has occurred less frequently, and in some instances, there are significantly fewer assessment tools from which the clinician or researcher can select (e.g., health-related knowledge). Each of the chapters in this section begins with a brief summary of the key measurement issues in the particular domain reviewed and closes with a summary listing of our observations about the assessment tools available in the area. We should emphasize here that although most instruments clearly fit into one of the identified domains (e.g., health-related knowledge), a few instruments may be appropriately placed into more than one domain (e.g., pediatric pain and childhood injury *and* stress and coping). In the latter instance, our decision about where to place the instrument was based primarily on the original developer's intended purpose in creating the measure.

Frequently, we are asked by other health professionals who work in health care settings and by students interested in conducting child health research how they should develop assessment tools to measure the constructs of interest to them. In some instances, these requests come from those interested in examining some aspect of clinical service delivery (e.g., satisfaction with health care). At other times, graduate students in clinical psychology or nursing, for example, may ask for a brief assessment instrument to include as part of a research protocol. We hope that these individuals first turn to this handbook for a review of available instruments and for direction in the selection of one that meets their specific needs. Given the development of the child health field and the relative newness of assessment methodology in the domains reviewed in this handbook, it is likely that new questionnaires and measurement tools will continue to be developed and evaluated. Indeed, we expect that the increasingly prominent and necessary focus on outcomes assessment will lead to an exponential increase in the number of child health assessment tools in the next several years. Consequently, in Chapter 11 we provide our conclusions and recommendations to guide those who will continue to develop and evaluate the tools that will advance the field.

Approach to the Reviews

Our approach to writing the reviews was rather straightforward. We attempted to provide the reader with a short summary of the instrument or assessment method, its intended use and applications, and psychometric data as reported by the authors during scale development. If additional psychometric data have been reported, we provide this information in summary form as well and include a few relevant references. Our own comments and opinions regarding the assessment instruments are limited to the Comment section of the review.

We followed the same format in writing reviews for each assessment tool. Although each review was written by one of the handbook authors, the other two authors examined the reviews for completeness. Also, as previously mentioned, the majority of the reviews were sent to the original developers of the instruments as a check for accuracy and completeness. In some cases, instruments were further examined by experts in the field. Each review presents the following information: title, manual and address for obtaining the instrument, purpose, instrument format, administration, and scoring procedures, psychometric information, and our comments.

Title

We provide the title of the instrument reviewed, followed by its original developer and the date of first publication. We recognize that many instruments have been developed by a team of researchers; however, we have chosen to list only the principal author of the initial publication reporting the instrument's development. In some instances, measures were revised and renamed by either the original developer(s) or subsequent researchers. To assist the reader in quickly identifying the measure, we used the title most commonly referenced in the published literature.

Manual and Address Information

If a manual exists, we provide information about its publication and how to obtain it. Most assessment tools, however, are not accompanied by user manuals, so we have indicated how to contact the developer(s) for more information and to inform them of your interest in using their instrument. Readers are strongly encouraged to contact the developer(s) for the most current version of the instrument and scoring guidelines, permission for use, and any new psychometric information. We have attempted to provide the most current address information for instrument developers, although we recognize that address changes may have occurred since the publication of this handbook.

Purpose

For quick reader reference, we have provided a very brief description of the instrument's purpose as intended by its original developer(s).

Format, Administration, and Scoring

This section presents information about the instrument's administration format (e.g., child- or parent-completed questionnaire, nurse observation, etc.) and scaling properties, for whom it is intended, and scoring procedures. We have also included sample items, whenever possible, as well as brief descriptions of the different subscales for which sufficient information exists. Approximate administration times are included, although the reader is cautioned that instruments may require different lengths of time to complete depending on the developmental level and reading abilities of the child.

Psychometric Information

Reliability and validity information is presented in this section. In most instances, the focus is on the data provided by the original developer(s), although these data are supplemented by subsequent psychometric information published by other researchers. Some instruments have been used in several studies, and we chose not to include detailed psychometric information from every study. Rather, a range of reliability and validity summary statistics or information is presented, and relevant references are provided in the last section of the review. Also, we included information about the original samples on which the instruments were first used and any noteworthy sample characteristics of subsequent studies reported in the literature.

Comment

Our specific comments about the strengths and limitations of each instrument are presented in this section. We provided our own evaluative statements and recommendations for future development and use, as well as any cautionary comments made by the original developer(s). Also, we attended carefully to the instrument's cultural sensitivity and cost-effectiveness in reviewing the instruments and in many instances made comments relative to these two important assessment issues.

Relevant References

In addition to the publication originally reporting the instrument's development, additional published reports of reliability and/or validity data also are cited. We have been selective in our listing of relevant references, and readers are cautioned that our list is not intended to be comprehensive.

References

Corcoran, K., & Fischer, J. (1987). *Measures for clinical practice: A sourcebook.* New York: The Free Press.

Goldman, J., Stein, C. L., & Guerry, S. (1983). *Psychological methods of child assessment.* New York: Brunner/Mazel.

Mash, E. J., & Terdal, L. G. (Eds.). (1997). *Assessment of childhood disorders* (3rd ed.). New York: Guilford Press.

McDowell, I., & Newell, C. (1996). *Measuring health: A guide to rating scales and questionnaires* (2nd ed.). New York: Oxford University Press.

Perrin, E. C., Stein, E., & Drotar, D. (1991). Cautions in using the Child Behavior Checklist: Observations based on research about children with a chronic illness. *Journal of Pediatric Psychology, 16,* 411–421.

Chapter 2

Methods of Evaluation and Psychometric Issues

GARY R. GEFFKEN

There are multiple methods of assessment that are described in this handbook. Many methods focus on the child, though some focus on parents, family, or health care professionals. The assessment techniques rely on norm-referenced tests, observations, interviews, and informal assessment. The majority of measures reviewed in this book are paper-pencil questionnaires. Although some measures have a relatively stronger research base, others have a developing research base. Measures of child health reviewed in this handbook, for the most part, do not have samples stratified on national census data; the area of measurement of child health reviewed in this handbook is at an earlier state of development.

Norm-Referenced Tests

Norm-referenced tests provide a basis from which to evaluate comparatively the functioning and development of children in both physical and social domains, as well as the effects of intervention. In addition, some of the measures evaluate family members or health care professionals. Norm-referenced tests also are referred to as standardized tests. Standardization of a test involves administering the test in an identical fashion to a normative sample of subjects. This allows for the comparison of a respondent to a reference group who share similar characteristics, such as age, gender, and/or race. The respondent's score identifies him/her as performing at a particular level within the normative group. This may also allow for a comparison of the respondent's performance across several occasions of repeated testing. It is important, however, to be aware of the characteristics of the normative group in interpreting scores. For example, the normative groups ideally should be fairly recent, with a close representation of the population demographics, including age, SES, gender, and race. As already stated, this ideal is rarely met with the measures reviewed in this handbook because of the early stage of development of this area of child health measurement. The size of the normative sample should be large enough to ensure stability of the scores as well as to be sufficiently representative of the target population. Finally, the relevance of the normative group must be considered by the examiner, such as when deciding to use a select segment of the population for comparison instead of the national norm group.

Generally, an individual's responses on a test are summed to obtain a raw score. On ability tests (e.g., tests of health-related knowledge), the raw score represents correct responses to test items, whereas on behavior rating scales (e.g., measures of adherence to medical regimens), the raw score is indicative of responses consistent with the construct that the test is measuring. These raw scores do not tell the examiner how the subject performed in reference to other subjects with similar characteristics (e.g., age-related comparison group), thus the informative value of raw scores to the examiner is quite limited. To account for such discrepancies, the raw scores are converted to standardized scores in order to compare an individual's performance to the standardization sample. In so doing, it is possible to examine how each individual has performed in reference to an appropriate comparison group. The examiner can determine if the child performed in an average, below average, or above average way in comparison to their reference group. These scores may include age-appropriate norms, grade-equivalent scores, deviation scores, percentile rankings, *z*-scores and *t*-scores. For the purposes of measures reviewed in this handbook, a description of percentile rankings and *z*-scores should suffice.

Percentile Rankings

Percentile rankings are a form of standardized scores. Percentile ranks range from a fraction of the 1st to the 99th-plus percentile rank. Using percentile rankings, an individual's score may be described in reference to an appropriate comparison group. A percentile rank represents the percentage of the comparison sample that the individual's performance surpassed. Thus, if a child's score were at the 50th percentile on a health-related knowledge test, it would mean that the child scored better than 50% of the children in the reference group. Similarly, if a child obtained a score at the 98th percentile, it would mean the child scored higher than 98% of the children in the appropriate comparison group.

Z-Scores

A *z*-score expresses a score in terms of the number of standard deviations the raw score is above or below the sample mean. It is equal to the difference between the raw score and the mean, divided by the standard deviation. This makes the score more easily interpretable. The interpretation of a *z*-score of one means that the individual scored one standard deviation above the mean, and knowing the area under the normal curve, the reader can deduce that he/she scored higher than 84% of other individuals on the construct assessed by the test.

Psychometric Issues

A good measure will likely have utility in clinical practice and research and prove to be reliable and valid. While we strive to develop measures that maximize reliability and validity, and thereby reduce random and systematic error, we recognize that no instrument is entirely or completely reliable and valid.

Reliability

Reliability refers to the consistency, dependability, or stability of a measure. When a test is administered to a child, family member, or health care professional, the clinician/researcher needs to know to what degree the test is reliable or dependable. A test would be considered reliable if it was administered to the same child, whose characteristics did not change, on separate occasions, and the test yielded the same results on the separate testing occasions. As Cattell (1986) noted, ". . . a test which is not consistent with itself can scarcely hope to predict anything else" (Cattell, 1986, p. 56). However, tests like those reviewed in this handbook are generally not 100% reliable. The score an individual obtains on a test consists of that person's true score and some degree of error.

A reliability coefficient is a measure of reliability for a test and may range from .00 to 1.00. Zero would indicate the test is totally unreliable and a reliability coefficient of 1.00 would indicate the test is perfectly reliable. It is important to note that there are numerous factors that affect the reliability of a test, or factors that may contribute to error in a test score. Sattler (1992) has identified five such factors, including test length, test-retest interval, variability of scores, guessing, and variation in the test situation. Other possible sources of error variance may come from the actual content of the test, and even error in test scoring (Cohen, Montague, Nathanson, & Swerdlick, 1988).

In general, if a test is well constructed, a longer test will be more reliable than a shorter test. Test-retest interval refers to the time that has elapsed between two separate testing occasions; in general, the longer the interval between test-taking occasions, the more likely it is that constructs assessed such as knowledge, adherence, or quality of life would change. Variability of scores in the normative sample refers to instances when the normative sample has a broad range of scores; reliability is likely to be greater when the normative sample is not characterized by a restricted range of scores. Guessing is another factor affecting the reliability of scores, as it introduces error into the scores. The final factor described by Sattler (1992) is variation in the test situation. This refers to a variety of variables that may have an impact on the individual's performance, including errors in administration, distracting noise outside the testing room, hunger, illness, or lack of sleep. In addition, content or item sampling of the test can affect reliability. Although two or more tests may be designed to measure the same construct, there can be differences in the actual questions themselves. Finally, not all tests are scored by computers, and error may be introduced at this stage if there is a subjective judgment involved on the part of the scorer. All of these factors may introduce error into the individual's score.

Test-Retest Reliability

Test-retest reliability refers to the stability of a measure when it is administered between two different testing sessions. It is determined by giving the same test on two occasions to the same sample of individuals. The scores between the two testing sessions are correlated, yielding a correlation coefficient that describes the degree of test-retest reliability. Factors that may influence the test-retest reliability estimate include carry-over effects from the first administration and the length of time between the test administrations. If the interval between the tests is short, the child may remember his/her original answers, thus biasing the second test. Reactivity also may occur as a result of taking the test. For example, if a child was completing a questionnaire assessing their knowledge of disease and looked up some of the answers to questions he/she didn't know on the first test, it would change his/her knowledge base. In sum, the test-retest measure of reliability is appropriate only when the characteristic of interest is one that is fairly stable over time, as opposed to a state-like characteristic that may fluctuate frequently. As a result, test-retest correlations are often considered instead to be stability or dependability coefficients (Cattell, 1986).

Alternate-Form Reliability

Alternate-form reliability refers to the degree of consistency between two different versions of the same instrument. Most, but not all, of the instruments discussed in this handbook will not have alternate-form reliability. In alternate-form reliability, two versions of the same instrument are administered on either one occasion or separate occasions to a large group of individuals, and the degree of association (or correlation) between the two differing forms is calculated. Administering an alternate form of the same instrument holds an advantage over test-retest in that carry-over effects are less of a problem. However, construction of a parallel alternate form of a measure is difficult. The same type of content, form, and number of items as well as the range and difficulty level of items must be equivalent (Anastasi, 1982).

Split-Half Reliability

The simplest way to test split-half reliability is to divide one instrument in half, using each half as an alternate form. Two scores are then calculated for each individual in a sample completing the instrument by dividing the measure into comparable halves. Commonly, the odd-numbered items are compared with the even-numbered items, which gives a measure of consistency within the same content domain. Odd-even splits are preferable to first-half–last-half splits, because an equal number of items from the beginning, middle, and end of the instrument are sampled. The correlation of the two sets of scores derived from the split gives the split-half reliability of the instrument. The split-half method of calculating reliability has a potential vulnerability when one considers that the longer a test, the higher the reliability. One method developed to estimate the effect that lengthening or shortening an instrument will have on reliability is known as the Spearman-Brown Formula.

Internal Consistency

Internal consistency is a form of reliability that assesses the homogeneity of items, or the degree to which the individual items on a scale measure the same construct or characteristic. In order to measure the internal consistency, an instrument only needs to be administered on one occasion. Internal consistency methods involve computing the correlations among all of the items in the measure as well as the average of those intercorrelations. Cronbach (1951) developed an alternative method for estimating internal consistency, termed *coefficient alpha*. Cronbach's alpha represents the average of all possible split-half reliability coefficients. When the dependent variable is a dichotomous item, a different formula is used, known as the *Kuder-Richardson Formula 20* (KR-20; Kuder & Richardson, 1937).

Inter-Rater Reliability

Inter-rater reliability is important to measure when collecting information via behavioral observation when some degree of subjectivity is required to score a measure. Inter-rater reliability is assessed when two or more individuals score the same situation or set of responses, and their ratings are correlated. A high correlation between raters would indicate that scorer reliability is high and not contributing to error variance. For example, an inter-rater reliability coefficient of .95 would mean that 95% of the variance in scores was due to an actual difference in the measure, while 5% is attributable to error variance. Coefficient alpha or kappa may be used to supply the reliability estimate. The kappa statistic may be used for ratings using nominal scales of measurement (Cohen, 1960) as well as for multiple raters (Fliess, 1971).

Validity

Validity is another important psychometric aspect of a test that answers the question: Does this test really measure what it is intended to measure? A test cannot be valid unless it is fairly reliable. While reliability is necessary, it is not a sufficient condition to establish validity. Several types of validity are described below: face validity, content validity, convergent/discriminant validity, construct validity, and criterion-related validity, under which predictive and concurrent validity fall.

Face validity concerns the extent to which a test appears to measure what it purports to measure. *Content validity* refers to the extent to which a measure adequately assesses the domain or construct of interest. More specifically, content validity indicates that the items of a measure adequately sample behavior domains or constructs the instrument is intended to measure. Although there is no statistical measure of content validity, judgments concerning content validity are not arbitrary. Murphy and Davidshofer (1988) list three steps for assessing content validity: (1) describe the content domain, (2) determine the areas of the domain measured by each item, and (3) compare the structure of the instrument with the structure of the content domain. *Convergent validity* can be assessed by examining the correlations between different measurements of the same construct (e.g., child, parental, and observer reports of social behaviors). If the correlations are relatively high, one can be more confident that there is measurement of the proposed construct. *Discriminant validity* can be assessed by examining both high and low correlations between measures of different constructs. The degree to which a test measures a psychological trait or construct is referred to as *construct validity*. Empirical procedures can be used to measure how questionnaire items relate to a theory or model from which a construct is derived. Correlational analyses and factor analyses can be used to demonstrate a relationship between the proposed instrument and other previously validated measures of the same or similar constructs.

Criterion-related validity refers to the extent to which an instrument can be used to predict outcome measures or a criterion. The criterion is the standard against which the instrument is evaluated and can include a certain behavior or a group of behaviors, a test score, an amount of time, a diagnosis, measures of adjustment, an index of school attendance, and so forth (Cohen et al., 1988). Criterion-related validity is normally expressed as a correlation coefficient between the test score and the criterion measure. There is a differentiation between two types of criterion-related validity: predictive and concurrent. Predictive validity is assessed by obtaining test scores at one point in time and the criterion measures at some point in the future. Correlations between the two tests indicate the predictive validity of the instrument; that is, how accurately the instrument predicts the performance on a criterion measure. Concurrent validity is assessed when both the test and the criterion measure are administered at the same point in time. The resulting correlation coefficient measures how accurately a test score indicates the individual's status on the criterion.

Interviews

Clinical assessment interviews often provide valuable information concerning the child, such as health regimen compliance, according to the perspectives of multiple individuals who know the child well. In clinical practice, the interview is an essential method in the assessment of child health. The clinical interview possesses more flexibility in administration than questionnaires do, although there are some important ways the interview is different from everyday conversation (Kadushin, 1983). The assessment interview, for example, has a distinct purpose and is directed by the interviewer in a non-reciprocal, organized manner. Roles are clearly defined, and the clinician attempts to establish rapport as well as trust between him/herself and the client. Particularly distinguishing is the fact that unlike ordinary conversation, potentially disturbing information is possibly targeted for discussion in order to gain a greater understanding of the problem.

Flexibility is a major advantage of the interview as an assessment tool (Edelbrock & Costello, 1988; Sattler, 1992). The interview allows the clinician to clarify vague responses or misunderstandings; become aware of the beliefs, expectations, and value systems of parents; discover the context and chronological development of the problem behavior; and observe the interviewee's verbal and nonverbal actions that aide in evaluating the validity of the problem.

Those factors that give the interview its advantages may also be seen as weaknesses (Korchin, 1976). For example, the flexibility that the interview offers also permits unreliability and bias to appear, as well as making validity difficult to establish. Reliability may be evaluated, however, by comparing information between informants such as a parent and child (interobserver agreement), within the interview (internal consistency), across interviews (test-retest reliability), and between interviewers (method error) (Mash & Terdal, 1997). Validity of the interview (Mash & Terdal, 1997) may be established by evaluating the extent to which the information obtained in the interview agrees with information obtained through other methods (concurrent validity), and the degree to which the interview information is able to predict the treatment plan or treatment outcome (predictive validity).

Observational Assessment of Behavior

Behavioral observation is often used when a health care professional wants an additional, objective view into the spontaneous behavior of a child in a particular setting (e.g., hospital, primary care setting, school, or home). The systematic observation of behavior requires a trained observer who objectively watches and records each behavior as it occurs. It is assumed that the behaviors observed will be a representative sample of the child's behavioral repertoire.

Used in conjunction with other assessment procedures, the observation of behavior provides much personalized information in order to aide in diagnosis and in implementing strategies for intervention. Behavioral observation works most effectively with those behaviors that occur relatively frequently, and those that are unambiguously defined. The observational method may also be used to evaluate a child's progress over time.

Observational assessment is primarily used in an ecological assessment, which focuses on the content of the setting, the operations of the setting, and the opportunities it provides to a child within the setting. For an example of observational methods in child health assessment, the reader is referred to Reynolds, Johnson, and Silverstein's (1990) use of observation at a camp for children with diabetes. Reynolds and colleagues' unobtrusive observation of meals, exercise, glucose testing, and insulin injections allowed an examination of the accuracy of 24-hour recall interviews with children about their diabetes regimen.

Assessment of behaviors is performed by an observational recording method along with a coding method. The recording methods commonly used include narrative recording, event recording, interval recording, and ratings recording. Coding systems may be used to categorize a wide range of behaviors, or simply the presence or absence of a particular behavior. Narrative recordings can include anything that seems important to the observer, or it may simply be a record of behavior as it occurs. Narrative recordings describe events qualitatively with no need for quantitative-data recording. Interval recording involves recording the behavior as it occurs within a certain time frame. Event recording tallies each occurrence of the behavior as it occurs in the sampling period. The rating method is more subjective, involving the rating of a particular behavior on a checklist or scale at the end of observation.

As with any other assessment data, it is imperative to consider the reliability and validity of the observations. Many variables, including the observer, child, setting, measures, or an interaction among these, may introduce sources of error. Sattler (1992) notes several ways in which to reduce sources of error, some of which include having precise definitions of behavior, well-trained observers, recording checks, and being as neutral as possible in the environment.

Informal Assessment

Informal assessment procedures are often used in addition to more formal assessments such as norm-referenced tests with criterion-reference groups. For example, a child health researcher may want to develop new hypotheses about a child health condition and therefore may conduct open-ended interviews about the child health condition with relevant groups of children, parents, nurses, pediatric psychologists, and physicians. In such a case, it could be important to obtain information from all sources in the child's environment that may have an influence upon the child's behavior. With informal assessment procedures, the reliability and validity of such data are not known, so they must be used with consideration and caution.

References

Anastasi, A. (1982). *Psychological testing* (5th ed.). New York: Macmillan.

Cattell, R. B. (1986). The psychometric properties of tests: Consistency, validity, and efficiency. In R. B. Cattell & R. C. Johnson (Eds.), *Functional psychological testing: Principles and instruments* (p. 56). New York: Brunner/Mazel.

Cohen, J. (1960). A coefficient of agreement for nominal scales. *Educational and Psychological Measurement, 20,* 37–46.

Cohen, R. J., Montague, P., Nathanson, L. S., & Swerdlik, M. E. (1988). *Psychological testing: An introduction to tests and measurement.* Mountain View, CA: Mayfield Publishing Co.

Cronbach, L. J. (1951). Coefficient alpha and the internal structure of tests. *Psychometrika, 16,* 297–334.

Edelbrock, C., & Costello, A. J. (1988). Structured psychiatric interview for children. In M. Rutter, A. H. Tuma, & I. Lann (Eds.), *Assessment diagnosis in child psychopathology* (pp. 87–112). New York: Guilford Press.

Fleiss, J. L. (1971). Measuring nominal scale agreement among many raters. *Psychological Bulletin, 76,* 378–382.

Kadushin, A. (1983). *The social work interview* (2nd ed.). New York: Columbia University Press.

Korchin, S. J. (1976). *Modern clinical psychology.* New York: Basic Books.

Kuder, G. F., & Richardson, M. W. (1937). The theory of the estimation of reliability. *Psychometrika, 2,* 151–160.

Mash, E. J., & Terdal, L. G. (1997). Assessment of child and family disturbance: A behavioral-systems approach. In E. J. Mash & L. G. Terdal (Eds.), *Assessment of childhood disorders* (3rd ed.) (pp. 3–68.) New York: Guilford Press.

Murphy, K. R., & Davidshofer, C. O. (1988). *Psychological testing: Principles and applications.* New Jersey: Prentice Hall.

Reynolds, L. A., Johnson, S. B., & Silverstein, J. (1990). Assessing daily diabetes management by 24-hour recall interview: The validity of children reports. *Journal of Pediatric Psychology, 15,* 493–509.

Sattler, J. M. (1992). *Assessment of children* (Rev. and updated ed.). San Diego, CA: Author.

Chapter 3

Selecting and Administering Child Health Instruments

RANDI M. STREISAND

The assessment of children is a complicated enterprise. When children are the focus of the assessment, matters become more complex because it is important to consider as much of the child's environment as possible (e.g., family, school, peers). Assessment is further complicated when aspects such as the child's health must also be considered. In the past, children were often either considered "little adults," or given little voice for their own concerns. More recently, however, children have been included in the assessment process as active participants capable of rendering a perspective regarding their own functioning. Because children vary greatly in their developmental levels, as well as in their contextual surroundings, many considerations are necessary in their assessment. This chapter expands upon information presented in Chapters 1 and 2, and reviews how one finds appropriate child health measurement tools in addition to evaluating their potential utility for both clinical and research purposes.

Clinical Assessment

Referral Question to Be Answered

Clinically, the first consideration in selecting appropriate assessment tools is the referral question. Referrals typically occur as a result of some type of problem exhibited by the child. For example, parents may be dissatisfied with their child's performance, a teacher may be concerned with a student's behavior, or a child may express displeasure about events in his/her life. Just as the referral may have resulted from various sources within the child's life, the referral problem may not be problematic to each of the individuals in the child's environment. For example, the child's view may differ from the view of both the parent and teacher, and the child may not understand why he/she has been brought in for psychological assessment. In consideration of the referral question, one should keep in mind for whom the referral problem is actually problematic.

The problem that is being considered typically represents some disturbance in a developmental transition (e.g., oppositional behavior at home, difficulty in school). Children with chronic illnesses are also likely to be assessed for changes from previous functioning or difficulties adapting and adjusting to their illness and treatment. For example, children with cancer who undergo radiation are often given cognitive assessments pre- and postradiation to examine changes or declines in functioning. This is one of the challenges in working with children and families with illnesses: Is the referral problem related to the child's illness and likely to be transient, or is it more of a developmental consideration?

Consider the question of the referral source. If the assessment question is a diagnostic issue, it would be important to choose an instrument or set of instruments that would enable a health care professional to either make or rule out a diagnosis. Several structured or semistructured interviews, in addition to paper-and-pencil checklists, allow for an examination of several disorders or diagnoses. Similarly, if the question pertains to strategies that may help the child to better adjust to his/her illness, then the use of an assessment tool that focuses on adjustment is warranted.

Types of Measures

Once the referral question has been clarified and prior to selecting specific measures, one should consider the possible types of assessment instruments for answering the referral question. Sattler (1992) described four types of information to be gained in child assessment: (1) personal information about the child and his/her family that can be obtained from interviews and behavioral-checklist reports; (2) information about the child's behavior within different settings (for example, children's behavior may be observed in schools, with other family members, and in peer groups) that comes from observational assessment; (3) information gathered from standardized tests which are useful for comparing a child to his/her comparison group, and allow for the evaluation of changes associated with other aspects of the child's life such as illness; and (4) information related to a child's specialized skills which may otherwise not be measured through using standardized tests obtained from informal assessments. A discussion of each of the uses of these methods is found in more detail in Chapter 2. In addition to choosing the method most relevant to the assessment question, the health care professional must also consider the availability of respondents, the level of training of the person administering the assessment, the length of time allotted for the assessment, and cost in selecting which is the most appropriate method to use.

In considering who would be the most appropriate provider of information, it is important to remember that the problem that brings the child for an assessment may only be problematic for the parents, and not necessarily for the child. The child may even be unaware of his/her behavior. If the child, or possibly the parent, is not experiencing difficulties, his/her responses are likely to indicate the absence of difficulties. Therefore, getting as many respondents as possible increases the breadth of information that may be gathered. Other people in the child's environment who may also provide useful information include siblings, grandparents, nurses/physicians, and teachers. Aside from the clinical interview, few assessment tools are readily used with the perceptions of multiple respondents. Instead, both observational and self-report measures often focus on one particular person's perception of the situation. Some instruments, however, do have multiple versions that vary according to the respondent involved. For example, in the assessment of general child problems, the Child Behavior Checklist (Achenbach, 1991), Eyberg Child Behavior Inventory (Eyberg & Ross, 1978; Sutter & Eyberg, 1984), and Conners Ratings Scales (Goyette, Conners, & Ulrich, 1978) each have three forms: youth, parent, and teacher. Within the child health arena, some of the measures described in this handbook have also been designed for use with multiple respondents (e.g., Attitudes Toward Children with Handicaps, Perceived Illness Experience). These types of assessment tools can only enrich the clinical assessment. After the type of assessment tool has been discerned, it is time to search for measures that will provide information to help answer the referral question. Assessment resource books, journal articles, and testing brochures supply information about the different assessment tools available for the particular content that is to be explored. Many behaviors are actually multidimensional, requiring the use of multiple assessment tools. Throughout this chapter, however, the selection of one appropriate measure for each individual construct is discussed. The author believes that the reader will apply recommended procedures for each additional measure that is to be selected.

Reliability and Validity

Psychometric properties of measures in clinical assessment are crucial because the results of the assessment may lead to certain interventions or even "labeling" of the child. Therefore it is very important to have a good understanding of the psychometric properties of all instruments used. A measure that has been standardized, however, has not necessarily been proven to be psychometrically sound. Kenny, Holden, and Santilli (1991) suggest the importance of recognizing that standardization refers to a uniform set of procedures for administration and scoring and does not indicate that a measure is either reliable or valid.

As described in Chapter 2, reliability refers to the consistency of the measure. Do results and interpretations look similar when similar responses are given? Will the same diagnosis or recommendation for treatment be given for the reporting of similar symptoms? If the reliability of an instrument is unknown, and it is still chosen as a clinical assessment tool, much caution must be taken in interpreting findings.

Measures can be reliable without being valid. Validity refers to the accuracy of a measure, what the test actually measures, and the generalizations that can be made from the measure's findings. Is the construct that is supposedly being measured actually what is measured by the assessment tool? Content validity refers to the measure representing what it is designed to assess. When relying on measures of uncertain validity, it is impossible to accurately evaluate the referral problem.

Appropriateness of the Measure

Although the content of the referral question and the number of respondents available may have helped to determine possible assessment tools, not all tools will be equally appropriate for each clinical assessment. There are several more points to consider. Specifically, one should take into account the standardization sample of the measure, the child's developmental level, and the child's environment. Kenny and colleagues (1991) cite the importance of paying attention to the composition of the standardization sample from which normative data for the measure were derived. The standardization sample of the measure should include children with demographic backgrounds similar to that of the child who is being assessed. Using a scoring system designed for use with a population that is very different from the population that the individual child fits into means that conclusions should be drawn with caution. In these circumstances it is difficult to discern if differences are due to distinctions between the particular child and the average child represented from the standardization sample or due to differences between the children's demographic backgrounds.

For first time or baseline assessments, a measure that compares particular responses to other children of a similar background is important given that no previous data on a child undergoing such an assessment exists. This becomes less important at later assessments where the child's original data can serve as a comparison for future assessments.

In terms of developmental status, if a child is going to give information via self-report, the developmental level of both the child and the instrument must be considered. Has the child demonstrated an ability to read and understand questions posed to him/her? Has the measure been found to have a reading level appropriate for this particular child? Most word processing programs include tools for determining the reading level of a document, and therefore a measure's reading level should be reported by its authors.

Is the measure appropriate for the constraints of the clinical assessment? One must consider the realms of the child's environment that are available for assessment (i.e., school, home, peer group). Also, expectations regarding turnaround time for the referral question should be considered. Does the physician need recommendations for current treatment, is the parent hoping to begin an intervention next week, or does the school system need results only by the start of the next school term? These are important questions to consider if an assessment physically outside of the psychological evaluation is going to take place. For example, one must have adequate time to properly plan for and conduct a behavioral assessment at the child's school. Similarly, if self-report or interview measures are going to be used, is there adequate time for their accurate completion during the time allotted?

Scores Obtained

After the content and general appropriateness of the measure have been considered, it is time to revisit the concept of the referral question. The list of measures to choose from for a particular clinical assessment has likely been narrowed down, and it is time to contemplate which of the possible measures will yield scores and other information that will be the most useful. Many measures have multiple domains. If one particular domain is of interest to the referral question, yet only one total score for the measure can be obtained, this measure may not be the best choice. Relatedly, the type of information that the score(s) gives is important. Some measures, such as those designed for diagnostic purposes, have cut-off scores. Others utilize t-scores or some other means of comparison to a standardization group. Still others provide data related to clinical and subclinical levels. One should evaluate the definition of clinical and subclinical levels, and how the distinctions were made. For example, if a measure has a specified cut-off score of above 20 indicating maladjustment to illness, and below 18 indicating relative adjustment, it is important to understand whether the scores were rationally or empirically set at 20 and 18. Have clinically diagnosed children been correctly classified by using this scale?

Although a measure may have an extensive scoring system, one may be uncertain how to interpret these scores. Measures that have been used with similar clinical populations would be most helpful in providing rich clinical data. These measures are more likely to have larger standardization samples, and they are also likely to have more information available regarding interpretation. Similarly, while many copyrighted measures offer scoring instructions and some basis for their interpretation, many measures do not have such information readily accessible. However, many authors provide scoring and interpretive guidelines upon request.

Other Considerations

As previously described, time available for the assessment is one factor in choosing a measure. Another concern might be the actual financial cost of the measure. This cost includes the cost to both the evaluator and the child and his/her family. Many measures are copyrighted, and these instruments vary in cost between authors giving their permission for the measure's use free of charge, and paying the author or publishing company a predetermined fee for use of the instrument. During the course of a clinical assessment, it may not be financially possible to incorporate the use of a particular instrument because the evaluator simply does not have adequate resources.

Of equal concern is the cost to the child and his/her family. While clinics or practitioners vary in terms of their means of charging families, many assessments are charged on either an hourly or per test/instrument-given basis. Either way, using more assessment tools requires more time, resulting in more money required of the child and the family. Therefore, length of the assessment tool, in addition to the practicality of its findings, are of much importance.

Summary and Clinical Case Example

After paying careful attention to the referral question, different types of measures should be considered, each measure's reliability and validity evaluated, the appropriateness of the measure to the child's developmental level and environment assessed, and the relevance of the measure's scoring system to the referral question addressed. Finally, one should also keep in mind the costs in time and money to both the child and family, and the assessors.

For further illustration, assume that a young girl, "Nikki," with a history of asthma has been referred for psychological assessment. Nikki's pediatrician referred her because the family, and Nikki in particular, appeared to be under a great deal of stress. The physician indicated that Nikki seemed to have trouble coping with the demands of her asthma, and in general, appeared to be "stressed-out." Furthermore, the physician noted that he needs feedback about the family right away as he is meeting with them later in the week. The first step in selecting instruments for Nikki's assessment is to clarify the interest of the referring physician. Does Nikki's physician want to know if she is clinically stressed, has been nonadherent to her regimen, or if the family is having difficulty adjusting to changes in Nikki's medical condition and treatment? All of these questions are reasonable ones given the nature of the referral.

In determining the type of measure most appropriate for Nikki's assessment, assume that upon conferring with the referring physician and the family, the primary question is related to Nikki's level of stress. Since it is Nikki's stress level that is of most concern, hers is likely the point of view we are most interested in. Self-report measures that ask Nikki to indicate her own feelings of stress may be appropriate. In addition, it might be useful to gather information from her parents on behavioral-checklist types of questionnaires. Again, we would want to search for measures that include domains or components on child stress. Although watching Nikki carry out her regimen, or observing family interactions surrounding Nikki's asthma would provide useful information, these types of assessments could not be carried out and completed within the time allotted for answering the specific referral question.

At this point, we have decided to select self-report measures for Nikki to complete, in addition to measures to which her parents can give additional information. Several measures are likely to be available to us. Considering each of the measure's reliability and validity is the next step in selecting which one(s) to use. At the same time, we can assess each measure for its appropriateness for Nikki and her parents. Does the measure include children of Nikki's age and demographic background in the standardization sample? Is its reading level appropriate for Nikki?

After considering the measure's appropriateness and psychometric properties, we will narrow down our selection by assessing the information, or scores, that each measure provides. If we are interested in Nikki's level of stress, does the measure have a domain of general or specific type of stressors, and what does such information indicate? Finally, consider the cost of each of the measures. Although self-report instruments often require the least amount of time to complete, is there sufficient time for Nikki and her parents to finish them during the assessment day? Also, how much will Nikki's family or insurance company be charged for each of the measures that she may be given?

Assessment in Research

Research Question

Similar to the referral question in clinical assessment, the research question is the most important consideration in determining the use of instruments in a research-based assessment. For example, in evaluating a child's adherence related to his/her illness, it might be important to explore the construct of knowledge in the research question. Does this construct of knowledge represent the main concern and therefore the construct to be measured? Or, perhaps it is only one of many constructs that would be of interest.

Sample Population

Now that the construct of interest, or research question, has been determined, one must contemplate the type of population to be examined. Using the hypothesis of examining pain in children with chronic illness, the researcher must consider the specific population of children that will be investigated. For example, does the study include only children with chronic illnesses, or does it also include acute illnesses? Or, perhaps the study is a comparison of chronic versus acute children.

For the purpose of illustration, suppose that the researchers decided to examine differences in pain experiences between children with JRA and SCD. The next consideration is that of the sample or the population of the respondent. Who's perspective is of interest? If one is interested in obtaining the child's perception of pain, as opposed to that of either the parent, nurse, or physician, a very different measure will be chosen. Relatedly, one must consider the chosen target group in determining who will be the respondent. For example, if young children or infants were the group of interest, it would probably be necessary to include a parent or health care professional in the group of respondents. Some measures, however, have been designed for use with younger children.

Appropriateness of the Measure

In addition to the measure being appropriate for the construct of interest, it must also be appropriate for the sample or population to be studied. The age of the children to be included in the study will guide measurement selection. Are infants, young children, or adolescents the primary target group? If paper-and-pencil measures are inappropriate, other types such as observation or an interview might be more appropriate for the younger age group. Or, a different assessment tool with a more child-friendly format may be useful. Consideration of the child's developmental level must therefore be a factor in the decision making relative to the type of assessment tool that will be used.

Reliability, Validity, and Sensitivity

While there is less risk of diagnostic error in a research assessment versus a clinical assessment, the psychometric properties of the instrument continue to be of great importance. Although research findings do not indicate appropriate interventions or diagnostic categories for individual children, generalization of results of psychological research typically lead to clinical implications. In terms of reliability, the measure must reliably indicate similar results for respondents in other situations who provide similar responses.

If an observational measure is utilized, inter-rater reliability should be examined. Inter-rater reliability ensures the likelihood that trained observers will agree on the occurrence (or absence) of a behavior. Consider the example of comparing the pain of young children with SCD versus young children with JRA. If an observational measure was used and different raters observed the SCD versus JRA children, it would be unclear if standard measures of the child's pain were being recorded. Inter-rater reliability would allow researchers to examine the consistency between raters.

Validity of a research measure is paramount to the research question. Once a researcher has chosen the construct of interest, only a valid instrument focused on such a construct would accurately provide a measure of the research question. The assessment tool must be valid in that it truly measures what it purports to measure, yet its external validity is also worth consideration. Assuming that one motivation of the research question is to provide information for children not included in the study sample, one should use a measure that lends itself to generalizability of its findings.

In research examining changes over time, sensitivity of the measure must be examined. Johnson (1991) defines sensitivity as "... the degree to which a measure is able to detect small variations in levels of the construct the instrument was designed to measure." If an assessment tool yields scores in a restricted range, and is therefore less sensitive to changes, it may be difficult for the researcher to discern changes in the construct that is of interest. Returning to the example of examining children's pain, if one were interested in observing differences in reported pain between pre- and post-pain management intervention, it would be important to use a sensitive measure of the child's pain that is likely to illustrate changes when they exist.

As noted earlier, it is important to pay attention to the composition of the standardization sample from which normative data for the measure were derived (Kenny et al., 1991). The sample chosen for examination in a particular study should be well represented by the measure's original standardization sample. For example, in conducting research with predominately middle- to upper-class Caucasian males with cancer, it would be important to find a standardization sample that was not based solely on either minority children, children from low socioeconomic status families, or healthy children. If a measure with such a standardization sample was utilized, caution must be taken in comparing children using scores obtained from standardization procedures.

Due to the relative infancy of the field of child health assessment, relatively few standardized and psychometrically sound measures exist. As a result, many researchers choose to create their own assessment tools for use in investigations. Because the development of reliable and valid measures takes much time, many measures are created and used in investigations prior to their complete psychometric evaluation. In such circumstances, findings are limited.

Interpretations

Just as scoring is important in the clinical assessment, results and interpretations are important in the research assessment. As is the case with the other steps in choosing an instrument, considering possible interpretations is related to the original research question. By choosing measures that have standardized scoring systems, or clinical and subclinical levels for a variety of domains, one can more easily make interpretations regarding findings. Returning again to the example of pain in young children with SCD and JRA, consider the use of a 7-point Likert scale on which the child rates his/her pain. If higher numbers represent increased feelings of pain, and the average rating of pain in the sample is on the high end, a reasonable finding would be that children in the sample, on average, indicated feeling high levels of pain. However, without a standardization group, or an available comparison or cut-off score for the scale, it would not be possible to make interpretations related to how much pain children in the sample report experiencing compared to other children.

Other Considerations

Time is often limited in a research environment. Unlike a clinical setting in which children or their families are likely motivated to complete assessments for an answer to the referral question, research assessments are voluntary, and many participants are concerned with the amount of time that may be spent as a participant. However, research settings vary, and one study may have a greater amount of time to spend with the child and his/her family than does another study. For example, considering pain in children with SCD and JRA, time allotted for completion of research measures would be dependent on the setting in which the research was conducted. If the research question was related to inpatient hospital stays, parents may be available for longer assessments than they would be during short outpatient visits.

Measures must be administered (and scored) in a standardized way in order for normative data to be used. Research projects must therefore be planned accordingly, allowing for standard practices to be completed in the allotted time. In their clinic visit, many families may be unwilling to remain once the physician has allowed them to go, simply so that the research assessment can be completed. To ensure that data are accurate and complete, it is essential that the number of questionnaires or other assessment tools given be reasonable. Again, the population and setting will help to determine how much of a constraint time might be in the research assessment.

Related to the constraint of time is the financial cost of the research assessment. As participants do not pay to be in a research study, the cost of measurement is entirely that of the researcher. Studies that are supported by grants typically have cost of measurement included in their budgets. Other research that is not supported by grant funds can range from having little to having considerable support for measures used in the study. If measures are too costly, it is possible that funds will be depleted while the study is still underway. As such, financial costs of measures, in addition to their cost in terms of time, are an important consideration in choosing measures in research assessments. However, many copyrighted measures offer discounts to students whose research is unlikely to be financially supported.

Conclusions

Clearly, there are many considerations in the selection of assessment tools for research projects. After determining the research question to be examined, participants to be included in the study need to be decided upon. Following their selection, measures that are appropriate in terms of their developmental level and respondent can be considered. Psychometric properties of the measures need to be investigated before their selection, and scoring and interpretation of scores should also be examined. Finally, there are time and monetary considerations for each particular research setting.

References

Achenbach, T. M. (1991). *Manual for the Child Behavior Checklist/4–18 and 1991 Profile.* Burlington, VT: University of Vermont Department of Psychiatry.

Eyberg, S. M., & Ross, A. W. (1978). Assessment of child behavior problems: The validation of a new inventory. *Journal of Clinical Child Psychology, 7,* 113–116.

Goyette, C. H., Conners, C. K., & Ulrich, R. F. (1978). Normative data on the revised Conners Parent and Teacher Rating Scales. *Journal of Abnormal Child Psychology, 6,* 221–236.

Johnson, S. B. (1991). Methodological considerations in pediatric behavioral research: Measurement. *Journal of Developmental and Behavioral Pediatrics, 12,* 361–369.

Kenny, T. J., Holden, E. W., & Santilli, L. (1991). The meaning of measures: Pitfalls in behavioral and developmental research. *Journal of Developmental and Behavioral Pediatrics, 12,* 355–360.

Sattler, J. M. (1992). *Assessment of children* (Rev. and updated ed.). San Diego, CA: Author.

Sutter, J., & Eyberg, S. (1984). *Sutter-Eyberg Student Behavior Inventory.* Unpublished manuscript, University of Florida, Gainesville.

Chapter 4

General and Illness-Specific Adjustment

GARY R. GEFFKEN
RANDI M. STREISAND

The increasing effectiveness of medical interventions has led to improved survival rates and decreased morbidity for many children with chronic health conditions. Consequently, there are many more children living with a chronic health condition today than in years past. Indeed, it has been estimated that as many as 10 to 20% of the general population has a chronic physical health condition (Cadman, Boyle, Szatmari, & Offord, 1987). With a larger number of children living with chronic health conditions, researchers have increasingly focused on the psychosocial adjustment of these children. Lavigne and Faier-Routman (1992), for instance, noted that several hundred studies have provided data on children's adjustment to chronic health conditions, and this number has likely increased substantially since the publication of their comprehensive review.

Are children with chronic health conditions at increased risk for adjustment problems? In their review of epidemiological studies, clinical studies, and meta-analytic findings, Wallander and Thompson (1995) concluded that there is no direct relationship between chronic health conditions and psychosocial adjustment, although these children are more likely to experience difficulties that fall short of major psychiatric disturbance. This general conclusion also has been reached by other child health professionals (Eiser, 1990; Garrison & McQuiston, 1989; Lavigne & Faier-Routman, 1992) and has subsequently guided research aimed at delineating the correlates of psychosocial adjustment in children with chronic health conditions.

General and illness-specific adjustment is measured by child health clinicians and researchers to assess behavioral and psychosocial problems that arise in the context of a physical health condition. Indeed, the assessment of children's affective and behavioral functioning is basic to the measurement of adjustment. Because chronic physical conditions can affect the lives of children in areas such as development, social functioning, peer and familial relations, and negative emotions, this chapter reviews instruments that have been developed to assess various aspects of general and illness-specific adjustment. Instruments included for review in this chapter involve measuring children's acceptance of illness, behavior in relation to illness and hospitalization, physical self-concept, physical symptoms, and peer and parent relations, among others.

Instruments used to measure adjustment to physical health conditions in children have varying methodologies, structure, and assessment content. In the research literature, adjustment has been measured using self-report, parent/teacher report, interviewer-administered, and observational methods, or some combination of these approaches. In many cases assessment methodology can be modified with little difficulty to meet the needs of the clinician and/or child at hand. A number of proposed conceptual models examine the behavioral aspects of illness-related adjustment in general (e.g., Behavioral Profile Rating Scale, Deasy-Spinetta School Behavior Questionnaire) and in hospitalization settings (e.g., Children's Eating Behavior Inventory, Hospitalization Self-Report Instrument, Memories of Hospitalization Questionnaire). Other instruments include the measurement of social functioning (e.g., Diabetes Adjustment Scale, Perceived Illness Experience Scale) in relation to chronic health conditions.

Adjustment measures used in assessing children with chronic health conditions are based on general and illness-specific constructs, which allow for comparison of behavior and psychosocial functioning across a diverse range of children. General measures include those that examine behavioral aspects of children in clinical settings (e.g., Pediatric Inpatient Scale) and those that can be used in the school setting (e.g., Deasy-Spinetta School Behavioral Questionnaire). Other instruments (e.g., Diabetes Adjustment Scale) are useful in clinical settings to assess adjustment in order to better meet the needs of patients with specific types of conditions. Illness-specific conditions covered in this chapter include such chronic conditions as diabetes, cystic fibrosis, and cancer. Although validity and reliability are generally good in many measures, there is still a need for further research with larger samples and more with diverse groups for the measurement of cultural variation, ethnicity, and socioeconomic status for standardization and generalizability of most assessments.

In this chapter we review general and illness-specific adjustment measures that are available to child health professionals. Some measures were originally developed for adults and have been revised for use with children (e.g., Acceptance of Illness Scale, Perceived Illness Experience Scale), but most were designed to assess the adjustment of children specifically. There is a need to monitor continuously the adjustment of children with chronic health conditions as we develop and implement innovative treatment approaches designed to enhance the quality of living of our youth. The following collection of instruments provides a useful starting point for identifying and evaluating those measurement tools that may be especially helpful in this regard.

REVIEWS

Acceptance of Illness Scale (AIS)

B. J. Felton, 1984

Manual and Address Information

No manual. Direct inquiries to: Barbara Felton, Six Washington Place, 2nd Floor, New York, NY 10003-6634, (212) 673-3556, barbara@xp.psych.nyu.edu.

Purpose

The AIS was designed to measure adjustment to or acceptance of illness. The AIS focuses specifically on the degree to which respondents are able to accept their illness without expressing negative feelings.

Format, Administration, and Scoring

The AIS is a self-report measure in which respondents use a 5-point Likert scale (1 = strongly agree to 5 = strongly disagree) to rate their degree of agreement with eight statements about their attitudes toward their health and its effect on their life. Total score can range from 8 (extremely low acceptance/adjustment) to 40 (extremely high acceptance/adjustment). The AIS was designed originally as an illness-specific measure of adjustment, in the context of long-term illness, for middle-age and older adults, but it subsequently has been adapted for use with children. Sample items include:

> "I have a hard time adjusting to the limitations of my illness."
>
> "I think people are often uncomfortable being around me because of my illness."

Psychometric Information

Internal consistency (Cronbach's alpha) estimates have ranged from .81 to .83, and test-retest reliability (Spearman's rho) over a 7-month period in one study was .69. There is evidence that the AIS has construct validity. Significant negative correlations between the AIS and the use of wish-fulfilling fantasy as a coping strategy are consistent with the authors' hypotheses about the measure. Research also suggests that sibling conflict is predictive of negative acceptance of illness.

Comment

The AIS appears to be a straightforward measure of adjustment and ability to accept the illness. Findings offer some support for the construct validity of the measure, however, more validity information is needed. Due to the fact that most of the psychometric information on this measure emanates from studies of adults, the usefulness of the AIS in assessing the adjustment/acceptance of illness of children remains uncertain. It is brief, easy to administer, and can be used with children as young as 9 or 10 years old.

Relevant References

Felton, B. J., & Revenson, T. A. (1984). Coping with chronic illness: A study of illness controllability and the influence of coping strategies on psychological adjustment. *Journal of Consulting and Clinical Psychology, 53,* 343–353.

Hanson, C. L., Henggeler, S., Harris, M. A., Cigrang, J. A., Schinkel, A. M., Rodrigue, J. R., & Klesges, R. C. (1992). Contributions of sibling relations to the adaptation of youths with insulin-dependent diabetes mellitus. *Journal of Consulting and Clinical Psychology, 60,* 104–112.

Behavioral Profile Rating Scale (BPRS)

B. G. Melamed, 1975

Manual and Address Information

No manual. Direct inquiries to: Barbara G. Melamed, 1300 Morris Park Avenue, Albert Einstein College of Medicine, Bronx, NY 10461, (718) 430-3968.

Purpose

The BPRS is an observational rating scale that was designed to provide an objective measure of children's disruptive behavior during dental procedures.

Format, Administration, and Scoring

The BPRS consists of 27 categories across two dimensions: separation from mother and office behavior. The 27 categories were rationally chosen in that they are supposedly common fear-induced reactions to dental procedures. Examples of categories include: Refuses to Leave Mother, Crying, and Leaves Chair. Each category or behavior has a weighted factor indicating degree of disruption as determined by dentists' ratings. Factor weightings range from 1 ("inappropriate mouth closing") to 5 ("dislodges instruments").

Trained observers, including dentists, can assess the child's behavior using the BPRS. Children are observed during dental procedures for successive 3-minute observation periods. The scale allows for the coding of behavior frequency during each of the 3-minute assessment periods. A total score is obtained by multiplying the frequency of each behavior by its weighted factor. Each category is then summed for one total score. The total score can be divided by the number of 3-minute observation periods in order to reflect the frequency of disruptive behaviors per 3-minute interval.

Psychometric Information

The BPRS was developed for use in a small study ($n = 14$) and has subsequently been used with larger samples across multiple investigations. In its initial use, multiple observers assessed children's (ages 5 to 9) behaviors during dental visits. Interrater reliability was initially reported at .98, and subsequent studies have yielded similar levels of agreement. Significant correlations between the BPRS and various observational and self-report measures of fear and anxiety have been provided by the developers as evidence of concurrent validity. Furthermore, BPRS ratings have differentiated groups of children receiving from groups not receiving interventions to modify dental visit behaviors.

Comment

The BPRS is objective, has high inter-rater reliability, and has been used successfully in both descriptive and treatment outcome studies. However, the intensity of training necessary in order to reach the high levels of reported inter-rater reliability is undescribed but likely quite high. The 27 categories allow observers to quantify a broad range of reactions that children may have to dental procedures. Although it has been used with children (ages 3 to 11), its utility with older children has not been examined. Satisfactory concurrent validity has been established, yet sufficient normative data have not been provided. Overall, the BPRS appears to be a reliable and valid instrument in investigating children's disruptive behaviors during dental visits and procedures, and it shows promise as a tool to assess the effectiveness of interventions designed to decrease disruptive behaviors.

Relevant References

Melamed, B. G., Weinstein, D., Hawes, R., & Katin-Borland, M. (1975). Reduction of fear-related dental management problems with use of filmed modeling. *Journal of the American Dental Association, 90,* 822–826.

Melamed, B. G., Yurcheson, R., Fleece, E. L., Hutcherson, S., & Hawes, R. (1978). Effects of film modeling on the reduction of anxiety-related behaviors in individuals varying in level of previous experience in the stress situation. *Journal of Consulting and Clinical Psychology, 46,* 1357–1367.

Siegel, L. J., & Peterson, L. (1980). Stress reduction in young dental patients through coping skills and sensory information. *Journal of Consulting and Clinical Psychology, 46,* 785–787.

Siegel, L. J., & Peterson, L. (1981). Maintenance effects of coping skills and sensory information on young children's response to repeated dental procedures. *Behavior Therapy, 12,* 530–535.

Behavioral Upset in Medical Patients-Revised (BUMP-R)

C. F. Saylor, 1987; C. M. Rodriguez, 1994

Manual and Address Information

No manual. Items are published in a table in Rodriguez and Boggs (1994). The most recent version of this measure can be obtained from: Stephen R. Boggs, Department of Clinical and Health Psychology, P.O. Box 100165, University of Florida Health Science Center, Gainesville, FL 32610, (352) 395-0490, sboggs@hp.ufl.edu.

Purpose

The BUMP-R is a downward extension of a questionnaire originally designed to measure emotional distress in adult medical patients. Saylor and colleagues revised it for use with hospitalized children; and Rodriguez and Boggs further evaluated its use with hospitalized children 4 to 12 years old.

Format, Administration, and Scoring

The BUMP-R is a parent rating scale comprised of 56 items designed to measure a child's emotional distress both in the hospital and at home. Using a 5-point Likert-type scale (0 = never to 4 = always), parents respond to 28 items by indicating the frequency with which the behavior has occurred during the child's current hospitalization. Parents then rate the same 28 items in reference to the child's behavior at home immediately preceding hospitalization. The BUMP-R is most appropriate for children 4 to 12 years old, and it takes approximately 10 to 15 minutes for parents to complete. Scores are obtained for the Hospital total, the Home total, and the four BUMP-R Hospital subscales by summing item responses within the respective domains. The four empirically derived factors for the BUMP-R Hospital version include: Negativity/Agitation (11 items), Amiability (8 items), Dysphoria (4 items), and Noncompliance (4 items). One item loaded on two factors, and two items did not load on any factor. Sample items include:

> Is irritable or grouchy. (Negativity/Agitation)
> Shows interest in recovery (takes initiative). (Amiability)
> Looks depressed or sad. (Dysphoria)
> Has to be told to follow hospital routine. (Noncompliance)

Psychometric Information

The BUMP-R originally was developed by Zeldow and Braun (1985) for nurses to use in rating distress in hospitalized adult medical patients. It had 32 items, four factors (behavioral regression, poor patient-staff relationship, depression and anxiety, and passivity and withdrawal), and high internal consistency (alpha = .93).

Saylor and colleagues (1987) revised it by deleting items found to be developmentally inappropriate for children and by having parents complete it in reference to their child's behavior both during hospitalization and at home before hospitalization.

Rodriguez and Boggs (1994) examined its reliability and utility in a sample of 151 hospitalized children (ages 4–12; 70% White, 27% Black; 92% lower to middle socioeconomic status). Medical diagnoses included both acute (e.g., appendicitis, 32%) and chronic (e.g., nephrotic syndrome, cystic fibrosis, 68%) health conditions. BUMP-R scores were not significantly correlated with demographic or medical factors, although there was a slight trend for younger children to have higher BUMP-R Hospital scores ($r = -.17$). BUMP-R Hospital scores were significantly higher than BUMP-R Home scores, and these two scores were significantly correlated ($r = .50$).

Internal consistency reliability coefficients (Cronbach's alpha) were .87 for the BUMP-R Hospital total, .86 for Negativity/Agitation, .79 for Amiability, .68 for Dysphoria, and .68 for Noncompliance. No internal consistency data were reported for the BUMP-R Home total.

Comment

The BUMP-R is one of the few measures of child distress that has been developed for use in a pediatric inpatient setting. It assesses a range of behaviors and can be easily and quickly completed by parents. The internal consistency estimates and factor structure of the BUMP-R Hospital version are adequate and provide preliminary psychometric support. The strong association between BUMP-R Home and BUMP-R Hospital scores in both the Saylor and collegues and Rodriguez and Boggs studies suggest that children displaying behavioral difficulties at home may be especially at risk for emotional distress during hospitalization. Although this measure may prove to be clinically useful in identifying children who may benefit from psychological services during hospitalization, more research is clearly needed before its true clinical utility can be determined. In particular, additional information is needed about the instrument's internal consistency (e.g., BUMP-R Home), test-retest reliability, inter-rater reliability, stability of the factor structure, and discriminant and predictive validity.

Relevant References

Rodriguez, C. M., & Boggs, S. R. (1994). Behavioral Upset in Medical Patients-Revised: Evaluation of a parent report measure of distress for pediatric populations. *Journal of Pediatric Psychology, 19,* 319–324.

Saylor, C. F., Pallmeyer, T. P., Finch, A. J., Jr., Eason, L., Trieber, F., & Folger, C. (1987). Predictors of psychological distress in hospitalized pediatric patients. *Journal of the American Academy of Child and Adolescent Psychiatry, 26,* 232–236.

Zeldow, P. B., & Braun, L. (1985). Measuring regression in hospitalized medical patients: The BUMP scale. *General Hospital Psychiatry, 7,* 49–53.

Children's Eating Behavior Inventory (CEBI)

L. A. Archer, 1991

Manual and Address Information

No manual. Direct inquiries to: Lynda A. Archer, 1 Young Street, Suite 414, Hamilton, Ontario, Canada L8N 1T8.

Purpose

The CEBI is a conceptually derived instrument intended to assess parent, child, and familial interactions relating to functional eating and mealtime (E/M) problems across a wide age span of children (ages 2–12) and in a variety of medical and developmental disorders.

Format, Administration, and Scoring

The CEBI is a 40-item parent report instrument developed to assess how often a particular type of behavior occurs during eating and mealtime situations. The scale consists of two domains of items: those pertaining to the child and those pertaining to the parent and family system. The child domain includes 28 items, which assess food preferences, motor skills, and behavioral compliance. The parent domain contains 12 items and examines parental child behavior controls, thoughts and feelings about feeding one's child, and interactions between family members. In order that single-parent families and families with only one child be included in the assessment, two skip patterns were developed. Single parents skip four items, and two-parent families with only one child skip one item. A weighting system was devised to compensate for the omitted items. The questionnaire takes approximately 15 minutes to complete. A Spanish translation of the CEBI is available.

Parents use a 5-point Likert scale (never, seldom, sometimes, often, or always) to rate how often a particular behavior occurs. Twenty-eight of the items receive a positive scoring; the remaining items are reverse scored. In addition, respondents indicate whether or not the behavior is a problem for them. The summation of the rating scores provides a total eating problems score, whereas the total number of items perceived to be a problem is obtained by adding the total number of "Yes" responses to the question "Is this a problem for you?" Sample items include:

> My child takes more than half an hour to eat his/her meals.
> I find our meals stressful.
> My child enjoys eating.
> My child feeds him/her self as expected for his/her age.

Psychometric Information

This measure was initially standardized using children with identified eating problems from outpatient pediatric and mental health clinics ($n = 110$) and normally developing children ($N = 206$) recruited from 11 community family physicians' offices. Test-retest reliability (4–6 weeks) for 38 cases (28 clinic and 10 nonclinic) was .87 for the total eating problem score and .84 for the percentage of items perceived to be a problem.

Regarding construct validity, mothers of children seen in the clinic reported significantly higher eating problem scores and reported a significantly higher proportion of the behaviors to be a problem. Additional studies are ongoing in which direct observational data are being used to examine construct and concurrent validity. However, no data are currently available to permit the assessment of concurrent validity.

Comment

The CEBI needs a substantial amount of additional research with more diverse groups of children; however, it has begun the process of establishing itself as a useful screening tool for detecting eating problems in children. Of particular note is its utility with children who have developmental and/or physical disabilities. The authors have developed a shorter revised version of the CEBI (published as an appendix in Babbitt, Edlen-Nezin, Manikam, Summers & Murphy, 1995), although its psychometric properties await evaluation.

Relevant References

Archer, L. A., Rosenbaum, P. L., & Streiner, D. L. (1991). The children's eating behavior inventory: reliability and validity results. *Journal of Pediatric Psychology, 16,* 629–642.

Babbitt, R. L., Edlen-Nezin, L., Manikam, R., Summers, J. A., & Murphy, C. M. (1995). Assessment of eating and weight-related problems in children and special populations. In D. B. Allison (Ed.), *Methods for the assessment of eating behaviors and weight related problems.* Newbury Park, CA: Sage.

Children's Physical Self-Concept Scale (CPSS)

R. J. Stein, 1998

Manual and Address Information

A manual is available. Direct inquiries to: Risa J. Stein, Department of Psychology, Rockhurst College, 1100 Rockhurst Road., Kansas City, MO 64110-2561.

Purpose

The CPSS was developed to provide a comprehensive assessment of young children's physical self-concept.

Format, Administration, and Scoring

This 27-item interviewer-administered measure is appropriate for use with children in first through sixth grades and who have minimal or no reading skills. The CPSS can be administered one-on-one or in small groups (e.g., classrooms). Children are provided with a response booklet on which they mark their responses to item stems that are read aloud by the test administrator. Practice items are provided to the children to familiarize them with the task demand. Children indicate their level of agreement with each item stem by referring to four drinking glasses with increasing water levels, each corresponding to a numerical value (1 through 4).

The CPSS contains three scales, each with nine items. The Physical Performance scale examines the child's self-perception of stamina, strength, and agility. The Physical Appearance scale measures perceived attractiveness (e.g., facial features) and other physical attributes that are not affected by lifestyle changes. The Weight Control scale taps body weight concerns as well as eating and exercise activities. Scores range from 27 to 108 for the entire measure and 9 to 36 for the three scales. Sample items include:

> I am bad at sports. (Physical Performance)
> I can run fast. (Physical Performance)
> My hair looks nice. (Physical Appearance)
> I am ugly. (Physical Appearance)
> I worry about how much I weigh. (Weight Control)
> I skip meals. (Weight Control)

Psychometric Information

Fifty-three items were first generated through a literature search and adaptation of existing self-report measures, and these items were then classified into three broad conceptual domains. A field sample of 30 first and fifth graders completed the initial CPSS and refinements were made on the basis of psychometric evaluation and problems in administration. Subsequently, the 27-item CPSS was given to a standardization sample of 316 first, second, fourth, and fifth graders (35% female, 84% White, 40% overweight). Alpha coefficients for the entire sample were .77 for the Global Score, .67 for Physical Performance, .81 for Physical Appearance, and .60 for Weight Control. Alpha coefficients were consistently higher for 4th and 5th graders (Global Score = .82, Physical Performance = .68, Physical Appearance = .81, Weight Control = .68) than for 1st and 2nd graders (Global Score = .70, Physical Performance = .67, Physical Appearance = .78, Weight Control = .55). Test-retest correlations for the sample yielded correlations greater than or equal to .80.

Correlational analyses showed that the three scales were relatively unique (range = .08–.26). Also, normal weight children and boys scored significantly higher on the CPSS compared to overweight children and girls. As an additional validity indication, the CPSS Global Score and Physical Appearance scale distinguished children with normal weight and diabetes (higher scores) from children who were overweight (lower scores).

Comment

The CPSS is the first known measure of physical self-concept available for use with children as young as 6 years old. It appears to be quite easy to administer and, giving it in small group situations makes it a cost-effective assessment tool. Internal consistency reliability is generally good, although the Weight Control scale may need additional items and further evaluation. The authors also provided good evidence for its construct validity. The CPSS standardization sample was relatively large, but it was not very diverse (e.g., all children attended Catholic schools and wore uniforms). Therefore, more research should examine its psychometric stability and applicability with other children, especially given the ethnic differences reported in the self-concept literature. Though the authors' focus was on using the CPSS to examine children with weight problems, it may prove to be a very useful tool in research with other pediatric populations in which physical appearance, activity, and weight are affected by disease and/or medical treatments.

Relevant References

Stein, R. J., Bracken, B. A., Haddock, C. K., & Shaddish, W. R. (1998). Preliminary development of the Children's Physical Self-Concept Scale. *Journal of Developmental and Behavioral Pediatrics, 19*, 1–8.

Children's Somatization Inventory (CSI)

L. S. Walker, 1989

Manual and Address Information

A preliminary manual is available. Direct inquiries to: Lynn S. Walker, Adolescent Medicine, Vanderbilt University Medical Center, Nashville, TN 37232-3571, walkerls@ctrvax.vanderbilt.edu.

Purpose

The CSI was designed to assess the degree of somatization symptoms in pediatric patients with recurrent abdominal pain.

Format, Administration, and Scoring

The CSI consists of 35 psychophysiological symptoms for which the parent or the child is asked to rate how often each symptom has been troublesome in the past 2 weeks using a 5-point scale (0 = not at all, 5 = a whole lot). The 2-week time frame may be altered for the purposes of a particular study or clinical situation. The CSI includes 12 symptoms drawn from the Hopkins Symptom Checklist (HSCL) that have a primary factor loading on the somatization subscale of the instrument, as well as an additional somatic symptom (constipation) from the HSCL. The CSI also includes 26 symptoms from the DSM-III-R criteria for somatization disorder. DSM-III-R symptoms associated with psychosexual functioning and female reproductive symptoms were not included because they are not applicable to most children. Symptoms from the following four of the six DSM-III-R criteria categories are included: (a) conversion of pseudoneurological (e.g., fainting, difficulty swallowing), (b) gastrointestinal (e.g., abdominal pain, nausea), (c) pain (e.g., back pain), and (d) cardiopulmonary (e.g., dizziness, shortness of breath). A total symptom intensity score is tabulated by summing item responses. Higher intensity scores are indicative of greater symptomatology. Examples of symptoms include: headaches, difficulty urinating, vomiting, nausea or upset stomach, heavy feelings in your arms or legs, sore muscles, pain in your heart or chest, losing your voice, and deafness.

Both parent-report and child-report versions of the CSI exist, and it is currently available in both English and Spanish. The parent version of the CSI is self-report, asking the parent to comment on how much their child was bothered by each symptom over the past 2 weeks. For children younger than 12, the CSI is intended to be verbally administered, with children being provided with an index card containing printed response options.

Psychometric Information

Normative information and validation of the CSI was examined using a community-based sample of 540 children and adolescents in grades 2 through 12 attending public and private schools in a moderately sized southern community (57% female). The CSI was found to have high internal consistency (.92). A factor analysis resulted in four factors: conversion symptoms, cardiovascular symptoms, gastrointestinal symptoms, and pain and weakness (authors note that these four categories correspond to the first four categories defining somatization disorder in the DSM-III-R). The average number of symptoms reported by children in the sample was less than two, with adolescent girls most likely to endorse somatic complaints. Children from lower SES levels also were more likely to exhibit somatic complaints.

Concurrent validity was examined by correlating the CSI with the parents' report of their child's somatic complaints, as well as with another measure of somatic complaints (Pennebaker Inventory of Limbic Languidness, or PILL). The CSI and PILL were highly correlated (.76), and the correlation between the CSI and the parent rating (P = CSI) of their child's somatic symptoms was small but significant (.20).

Construct validity has been suggested, given significant correlations with various other constructs hypothesized to be associated with somatic complaints (i.e., anxiety, depression). Discriminant validity has also been suggested, given that the CSI did not correlate significantly with a measure of externalizing behavior problems.

Test-retest reliability (3 months) was reported to be .50 for healthy patients and .66 for patients with recurrent abdominal pain. Also, the CSI differentiated between those patients who had recurrent abdominal pain with and without an organic basis. The test-retest reliability coefficient was not significant for a group of patients with organically based abdominal pain (.13), although the majority had received medical treatment for their condition between test administrations.

Comment

The CSI is an easily administered, psychometrically sound measure that may be used to obtain information regarding the level of a child's somatic distress either in a clinical or in a community sample. The CSI differentiates itself from other tests assessing somatic symptomatology by using the child as an informant of his/her physical problems, thereby providing insight into the child's perception of symptoms rather than relying solely on observable evidence of their presence. Although the parent/child concordance rate is low, this is what the literature often reports to be the case; parents may be unaware of their child's emotions or subjective perceptions of pain. The CSI contains four factors that are consistent with the first four categories defining somatization disorder in the DSM-III-R. Note that because the CSI does not assess information as to a possible organic basis for symptoms, the duration of symptoms, or the degree of dysfunction associated with the symptoms, it cannot be used as a diagnostic tool for somatization disorder in children. However, the CSI does provide very useful information in the context of a more comprehensive assessment of somatization disorder. Future research must now move toward examining the utility of the CSI with children from diverse ethnic and socioeconomic backgrounds, although it is noteworthy that the instrument has been translated into Spanish.

Relevant References

Garber, J., Walker, L. S., & Zeman, J. (1991). Somatization symptoms in a community sample of children and adolescents: Further validation of the Children's Somatization Inventory. *Psychological Assessment: A Journal of Consulting and Clinical Psychology, 3,* 588–595.

Walker, L. S., & Garber, J. (1993). *Children's Somatization Inventory: Preliminary manual.* Nashville, TN: Vanderbilt University Medical Center.

Walker, L. S., Garber, J., & Greene, J. W. (1993). Psychosocial correlates of recurrent childhood pain: A comparison of pediatric patients with recurrent abdominal pain, organic illness, and psychiatric disorders. *Journal of Abnormal Psychology, 102,* 248–258.

Walker, L. S., Garber, J., Van Slyke, D. A., & Greene, J. W. (1995). Long-term health outcomes in patients with recurrent abdominal pain. *Journal of Pediatric Psychology, 20,* 233–245.

Deasy-Spinetta School Behavior Questionnaire (DSBQ)

P. Deasy-Spinetta, 1980

Manual and Address Information

No manual. Direct inquiries to: Patricia Deasy-Spinetta, Department of Psychology, San Diego State University, San Diego, CA 92182.

Purpose

The DSBQ was developed to assess the school behaviors of children with cancer.

Format, Administration, and Scoring

The DSBQ is a 44-item forced-choice (yes/no) teacher-report questionnaire. Items were assessed by school teachers to determine their appropriateness and difficulty of response. Teachers are asked to indicate whether or not a statement describes a child's attitudes or behaviors. The items cover a variety of behaviors, including open expression of certain emotions as well as play and classroom behaviors. Items are scored so that the higher the score, the more the item corresponds to normal student behavior patterns. A score of 44 would indicate behavior typical of a child of that age.

Psychometric Information

There is very limited information on the standardization or validity of the DSBQ. Furthermore, although no explicit description of its reliability has been reported, the DSBQ has been used in several studies to compare children with chronic illness (e.g., cancer, heart disease) to healthy children. In each of these studies, differences in certain aspects of the functioning of chronically ill children were assessed.

Comment

Though initial investigations using this measure may support its utility, specific information about its reliability and validity is needed. It is one of the few instruments that have been developed specifically to gather teachers' perceptions of children's adjustment. In light of the importance of obtaining information from multiple sources and in multiple contexts, the DSBQ may hold promise as a school-based assessment tool.

Relevant References

Campbell, L. A., Kirkpatrick, S. E., Berry, C. C., & Lamberti, J. J. (1995). Preparing children with congenital heart disease for cardiac surgery. *Journal of Pediatric Psychology, 20,* 313–328.

Deasy-Spinetta, P. (1981). The school and the child with cancer. In J. J. Spinetta & P. Deasy-Spinetta (Eds.), *Living with childhood cancer* (pp. 153–168). St. Louis, MO: C. V. Mosby Company.

Deasy-Spinetta, P., & Spinetta, J. J. (1980). The child with cancer in school. *American Journal of Pediatric Hematology/Oncology, 2,* 89–94.

Fowler, M. G., Johnson, M. P., Welshimer, K. J., Atkinson, S. S., & Loda, F. A. (1987). Factors relating to school absence among children with cardiac conditions. *American Journal of Diseases of Children, 141,* 1317–1320.

Diabetes Adjustment Scale (DAS)

B. Sullivan, 1978

Manual and Address Information

No manual. Address inquiries to: Barbara-Jean Sullivan, Yale University School of Nursing, 855 Howard Avenue, New Haven, CT 06512.

Purpose

The DAS was developed to examine adolescents' feelings about their diabetes.

Format, Administration, and Scoring

The DAS consists of 37 true or false items to which the adolescent responds. The measure is scored with responses indicative of positive adjustment receiving a score of 1, and negative adjustment receiving a score of 2. Determination of which responses were considered positive or negative were based on clinical experiences of a team of specialists in pediatrics and psychiatry. Sample items include:

Sometimes I fake insulin reactions.
I feel it is necessary to cover up the bumpy areas of my body with clothes.
I feel that it is harder to make friends when you have diabetes.

Psychometric Information

DAS items were selected from a list of 86 items generated from interviews with adolescents with diabetes, their parents, their clinicians, and individuals who live with adolescents who have diabetes, as well as literature on developmental issues and the psychological impact of diabetes. Final decisions on which items would be included were based on clinicians' impressions of which items related to how diabetes influences lifestyles.

Factor analysis of the DAS using a sample of 105 adolescent girls (ages 12–16) with diabetes yielded six domains of adjustment: dependence/independence issues, peer relationships, family relationships, attitudes toward health and diabetes, and school adjustment. Although no specific reliability data have been reported, the DAS has been found to be correlated in the expected direction with measures of self-esteem and depression.

Comment

Though there are some preliminary data to support the utility of the DAS, psychometric data are very limited and indicate the need for further evaluation. Additionally, the gathering of more information related to scoring of the ambiguous items is warranted. For example, on the item, "I feel it is necessary to cover up the bumpy areas of my body with clothing," a "True" response might be considered either as a positive adjustment or as a failure to accept the reality of diabetes. Finally, appropriateness of this measure for various age groups should be explored, as should its use with culturally diverse patient groups.

Relevant References

Sullivan, B.(1979a). Adjustment in diabetic adolescent girls: I. Development of the diabetic adjustment scale. *Psychosomatic Medicine, 41,* 119–126.

Sullivan, B. (1979b). Adjustment in diabetic adolescent girls: II. Adjustment, self-esteem, and depression in diabetic adolescent girls. *Psychosomatic Medicine, 41,* 127–138.

Hospitalization Self Report Instrument (HSRI)
Memories of Hospitalization Questionnaire (MHQ)

C. Denholm, 1986

Manual and Address Information

No manual. Direct inquiries to: Carey Denholm, School of Child and Youth Care, The University of Victoria, P.O. Box 1700, Victoria, British Columbia, Canada V8W 2Y2.

Purpose

The HSRI was designed to record the positive and negative events experienced by adolescents during hospitalization, whereas the MHQ was developed to assess the specific positive and negative memories of the hospitalization.

Format, Administration, and Scoring

The HRSI asks adolescents to write about both positive and negative experiences and reactions they had while in the hospital. The instrument is typically completed by the adolescent within the first few days after discharge. Statements provided by the adolescents are coded as either positive or negative experiences. The four categories of positive experiences include: nursing care and preparation (e.g., "The nurses were really nice and helpful"), personal reflections (e.g., "I think I matured through the whole experience"), visitation and patient interaction (e.g., "I enjoyed having my roommates to talk to"), and activities and routine events (e.g., "The meals were good"). The six categories of negative experiences include: reactions following medical/surgical events (e.g., "I was in a lot of pain"), activities and routine events, personal reflections, specific procedures (e.g., "The nasogastric tube was horrible"), nursing care and preparation, and visitation and patient interaction.

The MHQ was designed using the same format as the HRSI, including three additional aspects. The five categories of positive experiences include: nursing care and preparation, visitation/patient interaction, activities and routine events, environment and atmosphere, and personal reflections. The six categories of negative experiences are the same as those used in the HSRI. The three additional aspects of the MHQ include asking adolescents to describe any significant learning they could attribute to hospitalization, to indicate how often during the past 4 years this experience had come to mind, and to suggest three things (if any) they would change at the hospital.

Psychometric Information

The HSRI was initially developed with 42 female and 43 male adolescents (ages 14–16) hospitalized as a result of either an emergency or an acute condition within the prior 36 hours, in one of two general hospitals in Victoria, British Columbia. Patients undergoing treatment for serious physical injury were excluded from the study, as were patients admitted to gynecology or psychiatric units and patients that had been hospitalized within the previous 2 years. The questionnaire was also given to a control group of 63 nonhospitalized adolescents. Basic demographic information concerning the groups was not reported, although no significant differences emerged in terms of these variables.

Inter-rater reliability by three independent judges was reported to be 90% for positive statements and 74% for negative statements. Responses and impressions of the adolescents who completed the MHQ were found to be stable over the 4-year interim, with the exception that 32% of the participants stated that they had no negative memories, although they had previously reported such experiences on the HSRI. Because both instruments are open-ended questionnaires, it is important for their reliability to be routinely assessed with each investigation.

Comment

Though they lack psychometric data, the HSRI and MHQ can provide useful information regarding the experiences and personal outcomes of hospitalized adolescents, an area that has not received much attention in the literature to date. Information regarding which factors in the delivery of health care are more or less influential in producing positive perceptions for hospitalized adolescents is highly valuable in the implementation and evaluation of specialized adolescent health programs. These factors include the positive skills and characteristics of health care providers, as well as the type and amount of education and personal attention desired.

Relevant References

Denholm, C. (1990). Memories of adolescent hospitalization: Results from a 4-year follow-up study. *Children's Health Care, 19,* 101–105.

Denholm, C. (1989). Reactions of adolescents following hospitalization for acute conditions. *Children's Health Care, 18,* 210–217.

Denholm, C. (1988). Positive and negative experiences of hospitalized adolescents. *Adolescence, 23,* 115–126.

Living with a Chronic Illness (LCI)

C. D. Adams, 1998

Manual and Address Information

No manual. Direct inquiries to: Christina D. Adams, Department of Psychology, West Virginia University, P.O. Box 6040, Morgantown, WV 26506, cadams4@wvu.edu.

Purpose

The LCI was developed to assess children's health-related social functioning. It was designed to be a pediatric-specific tool for the measurement of children's social activities and interactions.

Format, Administration, and Scoring

The LCI scale is a 29-item self-report measure. Younger children are assisted in completing the measure, and older children complete the measure themselves. The LCI has an estimated Flesch-Kincaid reading grade level of 4.6. Completion of the measure takes approximately 10 to 15 minutes. Children are asked to indicate whether the problem (item) has occurred in the past 6 months by circling true or false. For each "true" response, children indicate whether they feel that the problem is a result of their illness ("yes" or "no") and how upset they are by the problem (4-point Likert scale: not at all to very much). Items to which children answer affirmatively are summed, yielding two scores: illness-related difficulties and non–illness-related difficulties. Sample items include:

> Other kids tease me about the way I look.
> I do not play team sports (e.g., soccer, football, softball).
> Other children do not invite me to play or take part in activities.

Psychometric Information

Items on the LCI scale were largely compiled from existing non–pediatric-specific social functioning measures and from the authors' clinical experiences. Face validity of items was examined by a group of clinical child psychologists and pediatricians. The LCI scale was standardized on 135 families of chronically ill children. Children were 8 to 18 years old, with the majority of children having one of the following chronic illnesses: epilepsy, cancer, asthma, arthritis/lupus, sickle-cell anemia, and cystic fibrosis. Data were also collected on healthy children seen during an acute-care physician visit. The sample was comprised of 69% Caucasian, 28% African American, and 3% other ethnic minority children. Children were from predominately lower to middle-class families.

Psychometric data are preliminary and indicate concurrent validity with such standardized measures of social competence as the Child Behavior Checklist, Youth Self-Report, and Teacher Report Form. Similarly, on the parent version of the LCI, the number of parent-reported clinic visits significantly predicted illness-related social difficulties as reported by the child. Internal consistency for the child version of the LCI was .83. Descriptive data for the measure across a number of chronic illnesses have been reported.

Comment

The LCI scale is one of the few attempts at measuring social functioning specific to pediatric conditions. It is relatively straightforward to administer, has both child/adolescent and parent versions, and can be used across multiple medical conditions. Its reading level makes it appropriate for most children in the fourth grade or higher. The LCI has the potential of providing meaningful clinical data about a child's day-to-day functioning. Aside from its reported concurrent validity with other self-report measures, and aside from its satisfactory internal consistency, little is known about its psychometric properties. Additional estimates of reliability and validity are therefore needed before its true clinical utility can be determined.

Relevant References

Adams, C. D., Streisand, R., Zawacki, T., & Rodrigue, J. R. (1997, November). *Living with a chronic illness: A measure of social activities and competence for children and adolescents.* Poster presented at the 31st annual meeting of the Association for the Advancement of Behavior Therapy, Miami, Florida.

Negative Behavioral Changes (NBC)

H. M. Y. Koomen, 1993

Manual and Address Information

No manual. Direct inquiries to: Helma Koomen, Department of Developmental Psychology, Free University, Van der Beechorststraat 1, 1081 BT, Amsterdam, The Netherlands, HMY.Koomen@psy.vu.nl.

Purpose

The NBC scale is intended to measure the increase or decrease in negative behaviors (crying, fearfulness) displayed by children after hospitalization.

Format, Administration, and Scoring

The NBC is a revised and extended version of the Negative Behavioral Changes Scale. Identical sets of yes/no items are used to measure behavioral changes during and after hospital admission. The mother is asked whether her child, compared to the period before admission, behaved differently during hospitalization and in the first few days after hospitalization. Sample items include:

He/She did cry more often than he/she used to.
He/She clung to me more than before.

Negative behavioral changes "yes" are coded as 1 and "no" receives a code of 0. The scale assesses major changes in three domains: intensified attachment/

affectionate behavior, protest against being left alone by the mother, and seeking contact with the mother.

Psychometric Information

The initial standardization sample included 107 infants (53 with cleft lip/palate, 54 healthy) ages 4 to 22 months and their mothers. Internal consistency estimates were .83 for measuring behavioral changes during hospitalization and .86 for after hospitalization. The NBC scale correlated .81 with a parent report measure of attachment behavior. Also, for children with cleft lip/palate, the negative changes after hospitalization were found to contribute significantly to the prediction and intensity of attachment behavior as perceived by parents.

Comment

The NBC scale appears to be a relatively quick means for assessing change in young children resulting from hospitalization. It adds to the literature in that few measures are hospital-specific, with even fewer allowing for assessment of changes over time. While the internal consistency of this measure appears sufficient, further reliability estimates (i.e., test-retest) and further data on its validity are needed. In addition, preliminary data has relied on mothers' report, and data on fathers or other caregivers would be beneficial.

Relevant References

Koomen, H. M. Y., & Hoeksma, J. B. (1993). Early hospitalization and disturbances of infant behavioral and the mother-infant relationship. *Journal of Child Psychology and Psychiatry, 34*, 917–934.

Negative Events Related to Short Stature (NERSS)

G. D. Zimet, 1995

Manual and Address Information

No manual. Direct inquiries to: Gregory D. Zimet, Section of Adolescent Medicine, 702 Barnhill Drive, Indianapolis, IN 46202-5225, gzimet@iupui.edu.

Purpose

The NERSS is part of a semistructured interview designed to assess children's and parents' attitudes and perceptions related to short stature.

Format, Administration, and Scoring

The NERSS is a 12- and 13-item (parent and child versions, respectively) scale that is administered as part of a structured interview. Parents and children ages 9 and older respond to items on a 5-point Likert scale (0 = never to 4 = all the time). Content areas were rationally derived and include teasing, exclusion from sports, overprotection from parents, difficulty finding clothing, and difficulty reaching things. A total NERSS score is computed by summing items and dividing by the number of responses.

Psychometric Information

The initial standardization sample included 41 boys and girls ages 9 to 16 years from mostly middle-class families. Medical diagnoses varied, and the majority of children had heights below the fifth percentile. Internal consistency of the NERSS was .76 for the parent version and .80 for the child version. Parent and child responses on the NERSS were not significantly different from one another. The NERSS provided different findings than other standardized measures of psychosocial adjustment, which the authors interpreted as support for its discriminant validity. Additional reliability and descriptive data have not been reported.

Comment

The NERSS is a short-interview format assessment tool used specifically with children of short stature and their parents. It has been used with an adequate sample of parents of children with varying degrees of medical diagnoses. Acceptable internal consistency has been reported, and discriminant validity has been suggested. Unfortunately, there have been no reports of its reliability. Furthermore, generalizability of findings from the initial sample demographic characteristics is limited, given that the standardization sample included predominantly middle class families. Overall, the NERSS is a promising assessment tool for both clinicians and researchers interested in specifically evaluating attitudes related to a child's short stature. Further examination of its psychometric properties is warranted prior to its use in clinical practice.

Relevant References

Zimet, G. D., Cutler, M., Litvene, M., Dahms, W., Owens, R., & Cuttler, L. (1995). Psychological adjustment of children evaluated for short stature: A preliminary report. *Journal of Developmental and Behavioral Pediatrics, 16,* 264–270.

Nurse's Rating Form (NRF)

F. F. Worchel, 1987

Manual and Address Information

No manual. Direct inquiries to: Frances Worchel, Department of Educational Psychology, Texas A & M University, College Station, TX 77843-4225, (409) 845-1898, fworchel@tamu.edu.

Purpose

The NRF was developed to measure the behavioral adjustment of children with cancer.

Format, Administration, and Scoring

Using the NRF, children with cancer are rated by hospital caregivers along the dimensions of anxiety, dependency, withdrawal, and compliance. The NRF consists of a 12-item rating scale intended to be completed by nursing personnel. No further information is known regarding the format and scoring of the instrument. Nine of the items come directly from the Child Behavior Checklist, and the remaining three items make inquiries about positive behavior (seeks information, is easygoing, assumes responsibility).

Psychometric Information

The NRF was developed for a study examining control-related coping strategies in 52 children with cancer. Orthogonal factor analysis revealed a two-factor solution, measuring overall adjustment and passive noncompliance. Internal consistency reliability estimates were reported to be .89 for the overall adjustment scale, .70 for the passive noncompliance scale, and .88 for total score. The scale demonstrated concurrent validity with the CBCL; association between the two factors on the NRF and the overall mean for behavior problems on the CBCL were .31 and .37.

Comment

Initial results suggest that the NRF has acceptable psychometric properties, and evidence for both the reliability and validity is presented. Because the NRF has not been used in subsequent investigations, more research is needed on this brief assessment instrument in order to determine its utility and psychometric status. A culturally and geographically diverse standardization sample would be useful in determining the utility of this measure in various cultural groups.

Relevant References

Worchel, F. F., Copeland, D. R., & Barker, D. G. (1987). Control-related coping strategies in pediatric oncology patients. *Journal of Pediatric Psychology, 12,* 25–39.

Pediatric Behavior Scale (PBS)

S. D. Lindgren, 1987

Manual and Address Information

No manual. Items are published in Lindgren and Koeppl (1987). Direct inquiries to: Scott D. Lindgren, Department of Pediatrics, 345 HS, University of Iowa, Iowa City, IA 52242, (319) 353-6142.

Purpose

The PBS was developed to measure child behavior problems in medical settings.

Format, Administration, and Scoring

As a parent-completed questionnaire, the PBS contains 165 items and assesses problem behaviors in six general domains. These general domains include: Conduct (18 items), Attention Deficit (15 items), Depression–Anxiety (29 items), Deviation (28 items), Health (57 items), and Cognition (18 items). Twenty-four behavior dimensions are represented across the six rationally derived general factors. Parents respond to each item using a 4-point rating scale (0 = almost never or not at all to 3 = very often or very much), and mean item scores are derived for each of the six general factors and 24 behavior scales. Scoring profile forms are available for converting raw scores to t-scores separately for boys and girls for each PBS scale. The PBS also contains several questions that are not scored but that provide useful information about family socioeconomic status, the child's academic performance, and any medications prescribed for the child. The PBS is intended for use with parents of children ages 6 to 16. Approximate administration time is 15 to 20 minutes. A teacher-rated version is available, and a preschool checklist for ages 3 to 5 is under development.

The PBS general factors and specific scales include the following:

Factor	Scale	Description
Conduct	Oppositional behavior	disobedient, arguing, defiant, uncooperative
	Aggression	fighting, cruelty, destructive, stealing, lying
	Explosiveness	temper tantrums, irritability, poor emotional control
Attention Deficit	Attention	short attention span, distractibility
	Impulsivity	acts or talks without thinking
	Hyperactivity	restless, fidgety, overactive
Depression–Anxiety	Tension	nervous tension
	Anxiety	fears, worries, dependencies
	Self-Esteem	doubts about self-worth
	Depression	sadness, decreased pleasure, death preoccupation
	Social isolation	withdrawal, rejection, lack of social ties
Deviation	Inappropriate social behavior	immaturity, poor judgment, self-injury
	Perseveration	repetitive, inflexible behavior patterns
	Variability	emotional lability (neurologically impaired children)
	Thought disorder	hallucinations, paranoid ideation, bizarre behavior
Health	Arousal	specific components of seizure-like behavior
	Coordination	problems in coordinated motor movements
	Eating	problems in eating behavior
	Sleeping	sleeping too much or too little, insomnia, nightmares

(continues)

Factor	Scale	Description
Health (*cont.*)	Physical problems	headaches, abdominal pain, seizures, illnesses
Cognition	Expression	problems in expression or language develment
	Comprehension	problems in understanding or memory
	School problems	learning difficulties, poor grades

Psychometric Information

Using a rational approach to scale development, pilot testing was conducted on over 400 items. The final version of the PBS included those 165 items that were most clear and unambiguous to parents and the psychologist panel. The initial normative sample included parents of 106 children (ages 6–16) with mostly neurological disorders, specific developmental/learning disorders, or attention deficit disorders and attending University of Iowa clinics. Medical diagnoses ranged from obesity and migraines to asthma and AIDS.

Median internal consistency reliability coefficients for this sample were .91 for the general factors and .83 for the specific scales. Alpha coefficients for the general factors ranged from .86 to .95. Alpha coefficients for the specific scales ranged from .45 (Eating) to .95 (Hyperactivity), with 15 of the 24 scales having alpha coefficients at or above .80. Inter-rater reliability between mother and father ratings of 33 children ranged from .51 (Health) to .79 (Conduct). Though the authors reported some preliminary data on the discriminant validity of the PBS, they urged caution in interpreting group differences due to the small and nonrepresentative sample in the initial study.

Normative data, used for determination of *t*-scores, were based on parent ratings of 600 children (300 boys, 300 girls, ages 6–12) from both urban and rural areas in the Midwest. Approximately 15% of the children were from minority families, primarily of Hispanic background.

Comment

The PBS is a rationally derived measure intended for use by child health professionals in both outpatient and inpatient medical settings. It is modeled after more widely used behavior checklists (e.g., Child Behavior Checklist, Connors' Parent Rating Scale) yet includes items that are more relevant to children with certain medical problems (e.g., items related to seizures, brain injury, medical noncompliance, etc.). It is easy for parents to complete and the scoring instructions are very clear. Normative data are available, although not on a nationally representative sample. Preliminary reliability data are promising but inconclusive, and further studies are needed to examine more closely the measure's validity and clinical utility. Further development of the PBS should include an examination of cultural and ethnic differences.

Relevant References

Lindgren, S. D., & Koeppl, G. K. (1987). Assessing child behavior problems in a medical setting: Development of the Pediatric Behavior Scale. In Prinz, R. J. (Ed.), *Advances in behavioral assessment of children and families,* Vol. 3 (pp. 57–90). Greenwich, CT: JAI Press.

Max, J. E., Castillo, C. S., Lindgren, S. D., & Arndt, S. (1988). The Neuropsychiatric Rating Schedule: Reliability and validity. *Journal of American Academy of Child and Adolescent Psychiatry, 37,* 297–304.

Stancin, T., & Palermo, T. M. (1997). A review of behavioral screening practices in pediatric settings: Do they pass the test? *Journal of Developmental and Behavioral Pediatrics, 18,* 183–194.

Pediatric Inpatient Behavior Scale (PIBS)

W. G. Kronenberger, 1997

Manual and Address Information

No manual. Direct inquiries to: William G. Kronenberger, Riley Child Psychiatry Clinic, 702 Barnhill Drive, Indianapolis, IN 46202-5200, (317) 274-8162, wkronenb @iupui.edu.

Purpose

The PIBS was designed to assess the behavior of hospitalized children ages 6 to 18. It is intended for use by nurses who have more extensive contact with children during hospitalization.

Format, Administration, and Scoring

This nurse-report rating scale contains 47 items describing behaviors commonly observed in hospitalized children. Using a 3-point rating scale (0 = never, 1 = sometimes, 2 = often), nurses indicate the degree to which they have observed the different behaviors while the child has been in the hospital under their care. In addition to the 47 items, the PIBS includes three additional questions that provide useful information about the nurse's perceptions of the child's need for a psychological or psychiatric consultation, the degree to which the child has been a behavior problem, and the degree of familiarity with the child's behavior. These three questions are answered using 10-point rating scales.

Scores are obtained for 10-factor analytically derived subscales: Oppositional-Noncompliant (8 items), Positive-Sociability (8 items), Withdrawal (6 items), Conduct Problem (4 items), Distress (5 items), Anxiety (6 items), Elimination Problems (3 items), Overactive (2 items), Self-Stim (2 items), and Self-Harm (1 item). Two items (runs around hall/unit and frowns) did not load on any factor but have been retained in the measure. Thirty-nine of the 47 items describe negative or problematic behaviors. Factor scores are obtained by averaging the item scores within each factor. Some of the behaviors included on the PIBS are as follows:

Refuses to take medication (Oppositional-Noncompliant)
Helps others (Positive-Sociability)
Refuses to speak (Withdrawal)
Throws things (Conduct Problem)
Moans and groans about illness/pain (Distress)
Complains of nausea; vomits in anticipation of procedures (Anxiety)
Soils pants; encopretic (Elimination Problem)
Talks excessively; interrupts others (Overactive)
Sucks thumb (Self-Stim)
Talks about harming or killing self (Self-Harm)

Psychometric Information

In developing the PIBS, 15 nurses, social workers, psychologists, and child life specialists first generated a list of 275 positive and negative behaviors they had observed in hospitalized children. After they narrowed the list of behaviors to 47, items were rationally grouped into 13 categories. Subsequent factor analyses using 221 PIBS protocols taken from a general hospitalized, tertiary-care pediatrics sample (i.e., not referred for behavior problems) yielded a 10-factor solution, which is described above. Twenty-two student nurses provided PIBS ratings for 11 children, and inter-rater reliability was reported as follows: Oppositional-Noncompliant (.74), Positive-Sociable (.70), Withdrawal (.43), Conduct Problem (91% agreement), Distress (.79), Anxiety (–.07), Elimination Problem (91% agreement), Overactive (.78), Self-Stim (100% agreement), and Self-Harm (100% agreement).

As a test of criterion validity, the developers reported that PIBS scores discriminated between children in the general pediatric sample with "high intervention need" and those with "midrange to low intervention need" as rated by the nurses. Children in the "high intervention need" group obtained significantly higher scores on 7 of the 10 PIBS subscales. Scores on the Oppositional-Noncompliant and Conduct Problem subscales also were found to discriminate between a clinically referred sample of children ($n = 45$) and a general pediatric sample matched on age, gender, and medical diagnosis, with scores significantly higher for the referred sample. Another study incorporating the PIBS with children undergoing bone marrow transplantation found that prehospitalization scores on the CBCL and measures of stress and family environment were predictive of PIBS scores during hospitalization. Further validity of the PIBS is also illustrated by its use in a psychiatric population with PIBS subscales sensitive to reason for admission, DSM-IV diagnosis, and self-reported child depressive symptomatology.

Comment

The PIBS is an excellent example of a tool that uses the positive methodological and structural elements of more traditional behavior checklists in the measurement of hospitalized children's behavior. The PIBS has several strengths, including its content and discriminant validity, its brevity and cost-effectiveness, a unique focus on the hospitalized child, and its incorporating of the nurse into the assessment process. Because nurses complete this instrument, clinicians are provided with an additional perspective beyond that of the child and parent and they are more likely to obtain nurse cooperation in the implementation of any subsequent treatment plans. Clinicians and researchers will benefit from further evaluation of its internal consistency, inter-rater and test-retest reliability, predictive and concurrent validity, and development of separate norms for children on the basis of age, ethnicity, and medical diagnosis, especially considering that some differences were found on these demographic variables. The developers noted their intention to examine the measure's use with other health professionals, which would likely enhance its clinical utility in the hospital setting. Overall, this measure holds considerable promise as a standard assessment tool for the behavioral health consultation-liaison specialist.

Relevant References

Carter, B. D., Kronenberger, W. G., Edwards, J., Keough, L. Gowan, D., Bodine, K., Kline, R., & Sender, L. (1996, August). Prediction of in-hospital adjustment of children undergoing bone marrow transplantation: The role of pre-BMT child/parent adjustment and family environment. Poster presented at the American Psychological Association, Toronto, Ontario, Canada.

Kronenberger, W. G., Carter, B. D., & Thomas, D. (1997). Assessment of behavior problems in pediatric inpatient settings: Development of the Pediatric Inpatient Behavior Scale. Children's Health Care, 26, 211–232.

Pediatric Symptom Checklist (PSC)

R. C. Wimberger, 1968

Manual and Address Information

No manual. Direct inquiries to: Michael Jellinek, Child Psychiatry Service, BF351, Massachusetts General Hospital, 15 Parkman Street, Boston, MA 02214.

Purpose

The PSC was intended to assist busy pediatricians in outpatient practice as a screening tool for identifying school-age children who may require a more extensive psychosocial evaluation.

Format, Administration, and Scoring

The PSC is a 35-item questionnaire designed to be completed in the pediatric waiting room by the parents of 6- to 12-year-old children in approximately 3 to 5 minutes. Questions assess areas of the child's daily functioning, such as school, friends, play, family, and mood in general. Sample items include:

> Acts as if driven by a motor.
> Fights with other children.
> Has trouble sleeping.

Using a 3-point scale (0 = never, 1 = sometimes, 2 = often), parents rate the frequency of symptoms and behaviors, and an overall PSC score ranging from 0 to 70 is derived by summing the items. Cut-off scores for children in need of attention have been empirically defined as 28 or higher (indicating a "positive" screening) for children ages 6 to 12 as well as 13- to 16-year-olds included in one initial study. For 4- to 5-year-old children, scores up to 24 are indicative of a normal, or "negative," screening, with scores of 25 or more suggestive of the need for further evaluation. These cut-off scores were selected on the basis of their ability to classify at-risk individuals as identified by the CBCL and patients referred for mental health evaluation, while keeping the percentage within the epidemiologic estimates for serious psychosocial problems (~12%). Some practitioners may choose to disregard the cut-off scores and instead use the measure to inquire further about specific problem areas. In order to discourage rash diagnostic labeling based on only a screening measure no subscales are defined.

Psychometric Information

The PSC began as an altered form of the Washington Symptom Checklist and was further revised based on the symptoms of children's disorders presented in the DSM-III, on a review of items from other relevant children's questionnaires, and on the clinical impressions of a group of psychologists, pediatricians, and child psychiatrists. The PSC has been studied extensively with various groups. The PSC has been found to be reliable with numerous types of samples, including economically disadvantaged and minority-group children, and it has been examined in a variety of settings, including the pediatric clinic as well as other outpatient subspecialty clinics.

PSC scores have been compared with child assessments based on in-depth interviews, clinician ratings of functioning, and other validated questionnaires such as the CBCL, and documentation of daily living activities including school functioning. One study reported 79% agreement (kappa = .60) between PSC scores and a clinician's ratings of psychosocial dysfunction, with a sensitivity of .95 and a specificity of .68. In addition, the overall agreement between findings of a "positive" PSC and the presence of a serious psychiatric diagnosis was 87% (kappa = .74, sensitivity = .87, specificity = .89). Test-retest (4 weeks) reliability was .86. The PSC has correlated highly with the Child Behavior Checklist, and one study reported an agreement of 89% between the two instruments. These findings have been replicated using children from diverse ethnic and socioeconomic backgrounds.

Comment

The PSC has several advantages over many other child behavior checklists due to its short administration time and ease in scoring and interpretation. In addition, it shows high agreement with an extensively validated screening instrument, the CBCL. Pediatricians are likely to be the first and only consult for a large percentage of parents concerned about their child's psychosocial functioning. However, primary care physicians have been found to have a relatively low sensitivity when it comes to recognizing psychosocial problems in their practice, with over half of children having problems going unrecognized or nonreferred. With the use of the PSC in a pediatric outpatient setting, children having difficulties in functioning who otherwise may have been overlooked have a larger chance of being identified by this brief measure and their problem areas subsequently evaluated. For those children functioning well, the time need not be spent on unnecessary interrogation.

Relevant References

Jellinek, M. S., & Murphy, J. M. (1990). The recognition of psychosocial disorders in pediatric practice: The current status of the Pediatric Symptom Checklist. *Journal of Developmental and Behavioral Pediatrics, 11,* 272–278.

Jellinek, M. S., Murphy, J. M., Robinson, J., Feins, A., Lamb, S., & Fenton, T. (1988). Pediatric Symptom Checklist: Screening school-age children for psychological dysfunction. *Journal of Pediatrics, 111,* 201–209.

Murphy, J. M., & Jellinek, M. S. (1988). Screening for psychosocial dysfunction in economically disadvantaged and minority group children: Further validation of the Pediatric Symptom Checklist. *American Journal of Orthopsychiatry, 58,* 450–456.

Murphy, J. M., Jellinek, M. S., Reede, J., & Bishop, S. J. (1992). Screening for psychological dysfunction in inner-city children: Further validation of the Pediatric Symptom Checklist. *Journal of the American Academy of Child and Adolescent Psychiatry, 31,* 221–232.

Wimberger, R. C., & Gregory, R. J. (1968). A behavior checklist for use in child psychiatry clinics. *Journal of the American Academy of Child Psychiatry, 7,* 677–681.

Perceived Illness Experience Scale (PIE)-Child Version

C. Eiser, 1995

Manual and Address Information

No manual. Direct inquiries to: Christine Eiser, Department of Psychology, University of Exeter, Exeter Devon, UK EX4 4GQ, ceiser@exeter.ac.uk.

Purpose

The PIE was designed to measure the quality of life, or perceived illness experience, of adolescents (ages 11–18) with cancer.

Format, Administration, and Scoring

The PIE consists of 40 statements that ask the adolescent to rate his/her agreement on a 5-point Likert scale (i.e., five boxes with "disagree" and "agree" as endpoints). Instructions on the scale indicate for adolescents to mark the box that best explains how they currently feel. Sample statements include:

> I only tell people about my illness if I really have to.
> My parents treat me like a baby.
> I can't see my friends as often as I like.

The most recent version of the PIE consists of 10 subscales: physical appearance, interference with activity, disclosure, school, peer rejection, parental behavior, manipulation, preoccupation with illness, food, and treatment. Questions related to the adolescent's physical symptoms or health status have been purposefully omitted from the scale. Scores are calculated separately for each subscale, with each item's score ranging from 1 to 5. A PIE total score is also calculated. The scale was designed as a self-report instrument and has a reading level appropriate for the specified age range. There is also a parent version (see separate description in Chapter 10), and a version for children ages 6 to 11 is reportedly being developed.

Psychometric Information

Items for the PIE were generated from semistructured interviews with children and adolescents. Children either in the midst of, or having recently completed treatment for, cancer were asked to describe areas in their lives that were most difficult for them. Specific statements of the PIE scale were then generated based on these responses, which included 78 items. The standardization sample included 41 adolescents. Internal consistency estimates (Cronbach's alpha) for the nine subscales ranged from .59 to .84. Adolescent and parent ratings were significantly correlated with one another for seven of the nine scales. Descriptive data for the standardization sample on each subscale of the PIE and the total PIE score are provided by the authors.

Four of the PIE scales correlated significantly with other measures of psychological symptomatology. According to the authors of the PIE, six items were added subsequent to the initial analyses; four items yielding an additional "treatment" subscale and two items added to the physical appearance subscale.

Comment

The PIE is a self-report measure of an adolescent's perception of his/her illness across 10 domains. The scale objectively asks adolescents about their adjustment to illness, rather than relying entirely on parent or physician report. Although adequate construct validity has been reported by the authors, specific measures with which the PIE scale has been found to be significantly correlated have not been cited. Descriptive statistics of the standardization sample exist; however, one should use caution when comparing other children's data to those provided given the small number of children ($n = 41$) in the initial sample. A few items have been added to the original measure, and it is unclear from descriptions of the revised instrument whether these items have been tested psychometrically. Furthermore, if this scale is administered to adolescents who have undergone treatment, four items must be removed from the scale. Strengths of this measure are the high concordance rate between adolescents and parents and the high internal consistency of the subscales. Although the measure was designed for use with adolescents having cancer, its general wording may permit flexibility in its use with adolescents who have other types of chronic health conditions. Given its recent development, future research incorporating the PIE scale will likely help discern its strengths and limitations.

Relevant References

Eiser, C., Havermans, T., Craft, A., & Kernahan, J. (1995). Development of a measure to assess the perceived illness experience after treatment for cancer. *Archives of Disease in Childhood, 72,* 302–307.

Personal Adjustment and Role Skills Scale (PARS-III)

R. B. Ellsworth, 1977

Manual and Address Information

There is a manual. Direct inquiries to: Ruth E. K. Stein, Department of Pediatrics, Albert Einstein College of Medicine, 1300 Morris Park Avenue, Bronx, NY 10461.

Purpose

The PARS-III was developed to measure the psychosocial adjustment of children with chronic physical illness in six areas associated with patterns of childhood maladjustment.

Format, Administration, and Scoring

The PARS-III contains 28 items designed to be completed by an adult who knows the child well, such as a parent or a teacher. Items pertain to one of six areas: peer relations, dependency, hostility, productivity, anxiety-depression, and withdrawal. Questions focus on children's competencies rather than on their deviancy or pathology. Somatic items that can potentially influence chronically ill children's ratings of maladjustment have been eliminated.

The PARS-III can be administered in either an interview or self-report format, and may be completed in less than 10 minutes. Using a 4-point rating scale ("never or rarely," "sometimes," "often," and "always or almost always") respondents indicate the frequency with which the child engages in the specified behavior. The total score for the measure is the sum of all scores, ranging from 28 to 112. Higher scores indicate better psychological functioning.

Psychometric Information

Evolving from earlier versions of the PARS, the PARS-III was standardized using a sample of 450 children ages 5 to 18 having chronic physical conditions and three comparison samples of healthy children. The sample resulted from four separate investigations with the Research Consortium on Chronic Illness in Childhood, with data collection occurring in four different states. Few psychometric differences emerged between the four studies, and data were therefore combined for subsequent analyses. Reliability estimates for the total score ranged from .88 to .90 and were somewhat lower for the subscales, ranging from .70 to .80. The authors reported that the high correlations of the PARS-III with the Child Behavior Checklist and other measures of psychosocial functioning in children provide support for its concurrent validity. Construct validity for the PARS-III was partially supported by a principal components factor analysis. The six factors reportedly explained 17% of the variance with all items having factor loading above .50 and most above .70.

Comment

The PARS-III appears to be a useful instrument with adequate reliability and validity for assessing the psychosocial functioning of school-age children having chronic illness and no cognitive impairments. It is brief, easily scored, and provides the clinician with information regarding domains that may be of particular concern for children with chronic physical conditions (dependency, hostility, and withdrawal). A distinct advantage of using the PARS-III with a group of chronically ill children is that the scale excludes somatic items that may inflate estimates of dysfunction in children who are physically ill. In addition, the PARS-III has been shown to be sensitive to change over time and has been used to assess treatment effects.

Relevant References

Ellsworth, R. B. (1977). *Progress report on developing the children's PARS Scale.* Roanoke, VA: Institute for Program Evaluation.

Stein, R. E. K., & Jessop, D. J. (1984). Does pediatric home care make a difference for children with chronic illness: Findings from the Pediatric Ambulatory Care Treatment Study. *Pediatrics, 73*, 845–853.

Walker, D. K., Stein, R. E. K., Perrin, E. C., & Jessop, D. J. (1990). Assessing psychosocial adjustment of children with chronic illness: A review of the technical properties of the PARS-III. *Journal of Developmental and Behavioral Pediatrics, 11*, 116–121.

Post-Hospitalization Behavior Questionnaire (PHBQ)

D. Vernon, 1966

Manual and Address Information

No manual. Direct inquiries to: David Vernon, 707 Fullerton Avenue, Chicago, IL 60630.

Purpose

The PHBQ was designed to assess changes in a child's typical behavior by comparing behavior before hospitalization with behavior during the first week after hospitalization.

Format, Administration, and Scoring

The PHBQ is a 26-item questionnaire designed to be completed by the parent of a hospitalized child in order to assess changes in a child's behavior. For each item, the parent compares the child's behavior before hospitalization with the child's behavior during the first week after being hospitalized. Prehospitalization and posthospitalization behaviors are rated concurrently along a 5-point Likert scale (1 = never present to 5 = occurs daily). Sample items include:

Does your child seem to avoid or be afraid of new things?
Does your child make a fuss about going to bed at night?
Does your child seem to be afraid or shy around strangers?

Psychometric Information

The initial standardization sample consisted of the parents of 387 children (ages 1 month–16 years) recently discharged from a hospital. Factor analysis yielded six different types of responses to hospitalization and illness: (I) General Anxiety and Regression, (II) Separation Anxiety, (III) Anxiety About Sleep, (IV) Eating Disturbance, (V) Aggression Toward Authority, and (VI) Apathy-Withdrawal. Children between the ages of 6 months and 4 years were most likely to experience distress after hospitalization, particularly with regard to separation anxiety. In addition, those children having more lengthy hospital stays (2–3 weeks) were more prone to psychological upset, including increased sleep anxiety and aggression toward authority, than children with stays of a shorter duration. Prior hospitalizations, sex, birth order, and degree of experienced pain were found to have no relationship with any type of responses to hospitalization.

Agreement between PHBQ total scores and independent ratings of nondirective parent interviews is provided by the authors in support of the measure's validity. Correlations of PHBQ equivalent forms was .65, and inter-rater reliability was .95 for mental health professionals.

Comment

Measuring the effects of hospitalization is clearly an issue relevant to health care providers who treat and study children. The PBHQ is a measure developed in the early years of the field of pediatric psychology as a nondisease-specific measure to assess the effects of hospitalization. Despite somewhat limited published research on the PBHQ, it has promising psychometric properties and potential for assessment in child health care. Further research on this measure should focus on the development of a more geographically and ethnically diverse standardization sample.

Relevant References

Rae, W. A., Worchel, F. F., Upchurch, J., Sanner, J. H., & Daniel, C. A. (1988). The psychosocial impact of play on hospitalized children. *Journal of Pediatric Psychology, 14,* 617–627.

Vernon, D., Schulman, J. L., & Foley, J. M. (1966). Changes in children's behavior after hospitalization. *American Journal of Diseases of Children, 111,* 581–593.

General Observations and Recommendations

In concert with the increasing drive within the child health literature toward the use of pediatric or illness-specific assessment tools (La Greca & Lemanek, 1996), our reviews indicate that such measures within the realm of adjustment are certainly a work in progress. While many measures reviewed in this chapter were developed quite recently, others that were first used many years ago continue to have a relatively limited amount of information related to their utility. Reviews in this chapter demonstrate, however, that researchers are on their way to making progress in terms of assessing how illness impacts a child. Furthermore, there is a cadre of measures that tap the multiple perspectives of children, their parents, and health care professionals.

Overall, there is a need to continue the development, validation, and refinement of measures to assess the adaptation of children with chronic health conditions. Significant progress has been achieved in a relatively short time, although several considerations appear to be of continued importance in furthering the development of adjustment measures. Defining the construct of adjustment continues to be a significant challenge. Though some researchers have differentiated adjustment from other constructs (e.g., quality of life, coping), many similarities remain (Perrin, Ayoub, & Willett, 1993). Furthermore, some researchers have questioned the distinction between adjustment and constructs such as social competence or social functioning. Future studies examining the relationship between measures of adjustment and those tapping other constructs will assist in providing conceptual clarity in this regard.

Finding an appropriate degree of specificity has been another difficulty in the mission of developing clinically useful pediatric-specific assessment instruments. For example, while several of the measures described were designed for use with children who have a specific chronic health condition, many of the authors encouraged researchers and clinicians to extend use of the instrument to children with other chronic health conditions. Similarly, we reviewed measures that offer a global assessment of adjustment, as well as those that focus on one particular domain or context, such as a pediatric hospital or school setting. As child health clinicians, we must carefully consider a multimethod, multi-perspective, and contextual approach to our assessment of children's adaptation to chronic health conditions. Furthermore, as we continue to develop and implement intervention programs designed to enhance the psychological adaptation of children with illness, we must exert caution in selecting assessment tools that effectively capture change over time.

It is interesting to note that instruments assessing children's adjustment have, for the most part, focused predominantly on the negative aspects of chronic conditions. Children with chronic health conditions (e.g., diabetes, cancer, cystic fibrosis) often have shared with us their perceptions that there are benefits to living with illness and complex medical regimens. Recently, for instance, a 12-year-old girl with leukemia discussed with one of the authors (Rodrigue) the social benefits she had experienced while living with cancer for the last 3 years. These perceived benefits included her improved relationship with her older brother, increased empathy for other children with chronic health problems, and new friendships following a cancer camp experience. One future direction for child health assessment research might be the development and validation of more competency-based measures of children's adjustment.

References

Cadman, D., Boyle, M., Szatmari, P., & Offord, D. R. (1987). Chronic illness, disability, and mental and social well-being: Findings of the Ontario Child Health Study. *Pediatrics, 79,* 505–512.

Eiser, C. (1990). *Chronic childhood disease: An introduction to psychological theory and research.* Cambridge, England: Cambridge University Press.

Garrison, W. T., & McQuiston, S. (1989). *Chronic illness during childhood and adolescence: Psychological aspects.* Newbury Park, CA: Sage.

La Greca, A. M., & Lemanek, K. L. (1996). Editorial: Assessment as a process in pediatric psychology. *Journal of Pediatric Psychology, 21,* 137–151.

Lavigne, J. V., & Faier-Routman, J. (1992). Psychological adjustment to pediatric physical disorders: A meta-analytic review. *Journal of Pediatric Psychology, 17,* 133–157.

Perrin, E. C., Ayoub, C. C., & Willett, J. B. (1993). In the eyes of the beholder: Family and maternal influences on perceptions of adjustment of children with a chronic illness. *Journal of Developmental and Behavioral Pediatrics, 14,* 94–105.

Wallander, J. L., & Thompson, R. J., Jr. (1995). Psychosocial adjustment of children with chronic physical conditions. In M. C. Roberts (Ed.), *Handbook of pediatric psychology* (2nd ed.) (pp. 124–141). New York: Guilford Press.

Chapter 5

Stress and Coping

RANDI M. STREISAND

Stress and coping have received much attention in the child health literature. At present, we are fortunate to have a wide variety of measures that assess these constructs in several different ways. While the precise definitions of stress and coping are often debated, most researchers concur that stress is an interaction between external and internal factors (Bernard & Krupat, 1994) and is experienced when a situation or event is appraised as having specific demands that exceed one's available resources (Lazarus & Folkman, 1984). The measurement of stress may include child self-report, parent or other adult report (e.g., nurse), major life events (e.g., parents' divorce, moving, sickness), observed distress, fear, or even pain. Some researchers have used physiological arousal (e.g., galvanic skin response, heart rate, blood pressure) or sociological indicators as well.

Despite the seeming importance of children's own appraisals of stressful situations, self-reports of very young children (e.g., those under age 8) are often viewed with skepticism due to their potentially compromised reliability and validity. As such, most research and clinical assessments combine child self-report with parent or health care provider report, or direct observation of the child's behavior. Developmental issues, such as the age of the child at the time of the assessment, as well as his/her capacity for formal thought, mentation, and self-reflection, are important considerations in assessing a child's perceived level of stress. Child-oriented measures with appropriate normative data that permit age-based comparisons are therefore critical when working with these youngsters.

With regard to coping, health professionals typically define coping as the strategies one uses for handling stressful situations. Several different types of coping have been described, with most strategies falling into one of two categories: problem-focused and emotion-focused. Problem-focused coping strategies are those that attempt to change some aspect of the environment or situation. Emotion-focused coping strategies are those that incorporate all efforts used to manage the negative emotions associated with the situation or event. Most scientist-practitioners classify coping strategies within this dichotomy, and several strategies within each type have also been examined. For example, problem-focused strategies may include problem-solving, confrontive, approach, and active methods. In contrast, emotion-focused strategies have been thought to include denial, avoidance, distraction, wishful thinking, self-blame, and expression of feelings. Given the multitude of resources available to individuals to handle stress, the assessment of coping can be a complex and challenging task for the clinician.

Determining how children cope with chronic health conditions has become increasingly important as research findings have linked several coping strategies to more favorable behavioral health outcomes. Although results are not unequivocal, there is some evidence to indicate that problem-focused, or more active, coping styles may predict better adjustment in certain situations (e.g., when a stressor is changeable). However, active coping may not work for everyone, and it has been suggested that individual coping styles should be considered when designing pediatric interventions (Christiano & Russ, 1998; Peterson, 1989).

Instruments that measure coping differ in their focus. Some are situation-specific, while others examine more general coping patterns. Thus, when choosing an assessment tool, one must match their clinical or research objectives with the degree of specificity of the measure. How a child copes with a specific situation (e.g., lumbar puncture) may be very different from how he or she handles an ongoing or chronic stressor (e.g., terminal illness in a parent; Spirito, Stark, & Knapp, 1992). For example, a teenage girl with asthma may use very different strategies in coping with her complex medication regimen than with hearing that she must quit her softball team due to an exacerbation of her symptoms. If the clinician is primarily interested in determining how a child is coping with a particular treatment or regimen, the assessment measure should be specific. Similarly, if one is interested in a more global assessment of all available coping skills, then a general measure may be more appropriate.

There has also been much discussion related to coping as a trait versus coping as a process. Coping has been found to vary with time and situation (Compas, Worsham, & Ey, 1992; Miller, Roussi, Caputo, & Kraus, 1995). As a child with a chronic health condition grows, he/she might develop and use new coping skills. Assessment measures that can be used throughout childhood and adolescence are very helpful in assessing how appraisal and coping strategies change over time.

This chapter reviews stress and coping measures. The instruments described in the following pages have been limited to psychological measures of stress including life events, child self-report, parent report, and observation. The authors of several of the measures we reviewed made a strong effort to attend to the developmental level of the child by using age appropriate test stimuli (Fear Faces Scale, Hospital Scare Scale) or using multiple versions for different age levels (Kidcope, RISCS).

REVIEWS

Children's Concern Scale (CCS)

J. K. Austin, 1996

Manual and Address Information

No manual. Direct inquiries to: Joan K. Austin, Indiana University School of Nursing, 1111 Middle Drive, Indianapolis, IN, 46202-5107, iszd100@iupui.edu.

Purpose

The CCS was designed to assess children's concerns after experiencing their first seizures.

Format, Administration, and Scoring

The CCS is a 15-item self-report measure for children with epilepsy, 8–15 years old. It consists of 13 items to which children rate their concerns about having epilepsy. Items are on a 5-point Likert scale, with scores ranging from 1 (all the time) to 5 (never). The two remaining items are open-ended and allow children to identify a specific concern that he/she might have, and also to rate the frequency of the concern using the same 5-point scale. Specific information on administration and scoring is not available. Sample items include:

> I worry about my friends knowing that I have seizures.
> I worry that I might get sicker.
> I worry about when I will have another seizure.

Psychometric Information

The CCS was developed in a study examining parents and children within the first few months following the onset of a seizure disorder. Parents of 60 children ages 4 to 15 years old were interviewed several times within 4 months of the child's first seizure. Through interviews, which were conducted via telephone, qualitative data focusing on concerns/worries and family needs were gathered. Results of interviews with parents were reportedly content-analyzed to identify common concerns and needs, and this information was then used in constructing the CCS. A shortened version of the CCS was empirically evaluated in an investigation of children with new-onset seizures. Internal consistency of the shortened measure was found to be .80 at 3 months and .73 at 6 months after seizure onset. This version of the CCS was significantly negatively correlated with the Children's Attitude

Toward Illness Scale, which the authors provided as preliminary support for its concurrent validity.

Comment

The CCS is a short, easy to complete questionnaire. No formal analysis of the reading level of the measure has been reported. While items appear to be face valid, no psychometric data on the complete version of the CCS have been reported. There have been only limited findings of reliability and validity, and these were based on a shortened version of the questionnaire. The CCS may be helpful in assessing concerns in children with epilepsy in clinical settings. However, further examination of the psychometric properties of the scale is warranted prior to its more widespread clinical use.

Relevant References

Austin, J. K., & Dunn, D. W. (1996). Assessing children's concerns about epilepsy. *Clinical Nursing Practice in Epilepsy, 3*, 11–12.

Austin, J. K., Oruche, U. M., Dunn, D. W., & Levstek, D. A. (1995). New-onset childhood seizures: Parents' concerns and needs. *Clinical Nursing Practice in Epilepsy, 2*, 8–10.

Coping Health Inventory for Children (CHIC)

J. K. Austin, 1991

Manual and Address Information

No manual. Direct inquiries to: Joan K. Austin, Indiana University School of Nursing, 1111 Middle Drive, Indianapolis, IN, 46202-5107, iszd100@iupui.edu.

Purpose

The CHIC is a paper-and-pencil measure that is completed by parents of children 8 through 12 years old. It was designed to assess the general pattern of coping by children with chronic illness.

Format, Administration, and Scoring

Limited information is available on the CHIC's format, administration, and scoring. Generally, the measure consists of 45 non–illness-specific items covering five coping patterns: develops competence and optimism; feels different and withdraws; is irritable, moody, and acts out; complies with treatment; and seeks support. Parents rate each item using a 5-point Likert scale ranging from "never" to "always." Several items are reverse scored. Sample items include:

> Says health problem is his/her fault.
> Cries or acts sad and mopey after illness episodes.
> Talks with friends about health problems.

Psychometric Information

The literature on child adaptation to illness and child/adult coping was surveyed in developing items for the CHIC. Both parents and children (with either epilepsy or asthma) were asked to describe coping behaviors as the second step in the development of the questionnaire. The coping behaviors were grouped into five coping patterns, and generated items were then reviewed by a multidisciplinary panel for clarity and content validity. A 46-item version of the CHIC was then administered to 30 parents of children with either epilepsy or asthma, ages 8 to 12. Their responses suggested the rewording and addition of several items, resulting in a 49-item version. A second sample of 74 parents of similar children was administered the 49-item version of the CHIC to examine test-retest reliability (range = .57–.91).

A third larger standardization sample (372 parents, 254 children) focused on examining construct validity. In addition to the CHIC, parents completed the Child Behavior Checklist and children completed the Piers-Harris Children's Self-Concept Scale and the Child Attitude Toward Illness Scale. A positive relationship between self-concept and attitude scores and one of the CHIC subscales (i.e., develops competence and optimism), and a negative relationship between self-concept and attitudes and the remaining coping subscales was provided by the authors as partial support of construct validity. All other correlations were reported to be in the direction predicted by the authors. Factor analysis supported a five-factor solution (explaining an estimated .84 of the variance), and internal consistency was greater than .70 for all factors.

Comment

The CHIC is a non–illness-specific measure for assessing children's (ages 8–12) coping with chronic illness. The CHIC's use with pediatric populations other than asthma and epilepsy, as well as with a broad age range of children, has not been explored. The CHIC relies on parent report of children's coping. Development of the measure was extensive, with multiple pilot samples providing data to assist in shaping the final version of the questionnaire. Preliminary reports suggest satisfactory psychometric properties. The CHIC seems to be a useful instrument for both clinical and research settings, particularly when the parents' perspective is sought, and it may be especially helpful in discerning changes in children's coping styles resulting from interventions.

Relevant References

Austin, J. K., Patterson, J. M., & Huberty, T. J. (1991). Development of the coping health inventory for children. *Journal of Pediatric Nursing, 16,* 166–174.

Coping Strategies Inventory (CSI)

D. L. Tobin, 1989

Manual and Address Information

There is a manual. Direct inquiries to: David L. Tobin, Eating Disorders Program, The University of Chicago Physicians Group, 5327 North Sheridan, Chicago, IL 60640.

Purpose

The CSI is a paper-and-pencil measure that is completed by both parents and children to assess children's coping.

Format, Administration, and Scoring

The original CSI has 72 items, although a shorter version has been developed. The CSI can be completed independently by parents and children, or it can be read aloud. There are eight subscales: problem solving, cognitive restructuring, expression of emotion, social support, problem avoidance, wishful thinking, self-criticism, and social withdrawal. Second-level factors include problem-focused engagement, problem-focused disengagement, emotion-focused engagement, and emotion-focused disengagement. There are also two broad band factors (engagement and disengagement). Respondents answer items on a 5-point Likert scale (1 = not at all true to 5 = extremely true). Children and parents are presented with a particular scenario and asked to consider how they would cope with such a situation. Sample items include:

> I let my emotions out.
> I spent more time alone.
> I went along as if nothing was happening.
> I hoped a miracle would happen.

Psychometric Information

The CSI was standardized on a group of college students, yet psychometric data using younger samples of children have also been reported. The CSI has been used with both healthy children and children with chronic illness. The measure was standardized on multiple large samples of college students who generated a coping stressor to use as a reference for answering questions. A hierarchical factor analysis yielded an eight-factor solution. Internal consistency alphas ranged from .71 to .94. Test-retest reliability correlations ranged from .67 to .83.

A shorter version of the CSI with 32 of the original items has been used with several pediatric populations. In a study examining the impact of sickle cell anemia on coping, knowledge, and parental discipline, 4 items on each of the eight subscales were used. Items with the strongest factor loadings from the original standardization sample were retained. Children and parents have responded to both 3- and 5-point Likert scales with the shorter version. Evidence for internal consistency was provided by the authors. Concurrent validity of the shorter version of CSI was suggested, with moderate to high correlations between the CSI and another standardized measure of children's coping (Kidcope). Furthermore, descriptive data have been reported for pediatric samples.

Comment

The CSI is a measure that can be used in either an independent self-report or interview format. Both children and parents can respond to the CSI, and it has been used with healthy and chronically ill child populations. It can be adapted for use with various clinical scenarios, asking respondents to consider a particular scenario (e.g., coping with cancer treatments) in completing the questionnaire. There are two versions of the CSI (72 items, 32 items). With both versions, psychometric data indicate adequate reliability and validity, and normative data have been reported. Factor analyses, computed on the longer version, support an eight-factor structure; the factor structure of the shorter version has not been examined. Similarly, the longer version has not been standardized for use with younger or pediatric samples. Furthermore, the CSI has been used with both children and college-age students, yet a formal investigation of the CSI's reading level (either version) has not been reported. At this time, given the adequate psychometric properties of the 32-item version and its psychometric stability with pediatric populations, this shorter version appears to hold the most utility for child health professionals in busy clinical settings. Overall, the CSI offers both clinicians and researchers a comprehensive assessment of children's coping strategies.

Relevant References

Armstrong, F. D., Lemanek, K. L., Pegelow, C. H., Gonzalez, J. C., & Martinez, A. (1993). Impact of lifestyle disruption on parent and child coping, knowledge, and parental discipline in children with sickle cell anemia. *Children's Health Care, 22,* 189–203.

Tobin, D. L., Holroyd, K. A., & Reynolds, R. V. C. (1984). *User's manual for the Coping Strategies Inventory.* Unpublished manuscript, Ohio University, Athens.

Tobin, D. L., Holroyd, K. A., Reynolds, R. V., & Wigal, J. K. (1989). The hierarchical factor structure of the Coping Strategies Inventory. *Cognitive Therapy and Research, 13,* 343–361.

Fear Faces Scale (Fear Self-Report Scale, or Fear-SR)

E. Katz, 1981

Manual and Address Information

No manual. Direct inquiries to: Ernest R. Katz, Children's Center for Cancer and Blood Diseases, Children's Hospital of Los Angeles, 4650 Sunset Boulevard, MS 99, Los Angeles, CA 90027.

Purpose

The Fear-SR was developed to provide a simple, child friendly, assessment of children's fear related to medical procedures.

Format, Administration, and Scoring

The Fear-SR has been used with children as young as 4 years old. Although it was specifically designed for use with children undergoing invasive procedures for cancer, the measure is not illness-specific. A one-question self-report assessment tool, the Fear-SR consists of seven simple faces ranging incrementally from smiling (Face 1) to sad (Face 7). Children are told to look at the faces, with Face 1 representing "not being scared at all" to Face 7 representing the "most scared possible." For example, when used following a procedure, children are asked to choose the face that best shows how scared they were during the procedure.

Psychometric Information

The Fear-SR has been used in multiple investigations of children's behavioral distress during invasive procedures. In addition to describing children's fear, the Fear-SR has been used as a dependent measure in interventions tailored for decreasing children's procedure-related distress. Descriptive data with multiple-child cancer populations have been reported. The Fear-SR's correlation with a psychometrically sound measure of observational distress (Procedural Behavior Rating Scale), and other self-report measures of anxiety and pain, have been provided as evidence of concurrent validity. Differences between scores on the Fear-SR and a similarly designed tool measuring children's pain has been reported as evidence of discriminant validity. Gender differences have not been reported, although scores on the Fear-SR have been reliably found to decrease with age.

Comment

The Fear-SR is a one-item visual instrument used to assess children's appraisal of their fear during medical procedures. Its format is child-friendly and easy to administer. The Fear-SR has been used in several studies, and some descriptive data are available. It has been used primarily with children undergoing cancer treatments; yet it appears that the measure could easily be adapted for use in assessing children's fear of other medical procedures. Validity has been demonstrated by its significant correlation with a reliable measure of children's observational distress. Although the information gained may be somewhat limited, the Fear-SR provides a useful estimate of children's procedural fear, particularly when other more costly or time-intensive measures are not easily obtained.

Relevant References

Katz, E. R. (1982). Behavioral approaches to pain and distress in children with cancer. In *Western States Conference on Cancer Rehabilitation Conference Proceedings*. Palo Alto, CA: Bull.

Katz, E. R., Kellerman, J., Sharp, B., Siegel, S. E., Marsten, A. R., & Hirshman, J. E. (1982). B-endorphin and acute behavioral distress in children with leukemia. *Journal of Nervous and Mental Diseases, 170,* 72–77.

Katz, E. R., Kellerman, J., & Siegel, S. E. (1982, March). *Self-report and observational measurement of acute pain, fear, and behavioral distress in children with leukemia.* Paper presented at the Annual Meeting of the Society for Behavioral Medicine, Chicago.

Hospital Fears Questionnaire (HFQ)

M. C. Roberts, 1981

Manual and Address Information

No manual. Direct inquiries to: Michael C. Roberts, Clinical Child Psychology Program, Dole Human Development Center, University of Kansas, Lawrence, KS 66045, (913) 864-3580, mcrob@falcon.cc.ukans.edu.

Purpose

The HFQ was developed to assess children's medical fears, particularly in studies of hospital preparation and modeling. Specifically, the HFQ is a measurement of state of anxiety in medical situations.

Format, Administration, and Scoring

The HFQ is a self-report measure that originally consisted of nine items. Other researchers have since adapted the questionnaire, resulting in five- or eight-item versions as well. The items can be administered verbally or given in a paper-and-pencil format. In addition, it has been administered both individually and in groups. Children rate their degree of fear on a "fear thermometer" ranging from 1 (not afraid at all) to 5 (very afraid). For the nine-item version, scores range from 9 to 45. Sample items include:

> How afraid are you of taking medicine?
> How afraid are you of being in strange places?
> How afraid are you of doctors and nurses?

Psychometric Information

The HFQ was developed using face-valid items related to feeling scared of medical or hospital situations. Several researchers who have used the measure have had it reviewed by health professionals, but the questionnaire has not been psychometrically evaluated. It was created to complement the Medical Fears Subscale of the Fear Survey Schedule for Children that has known psychometric stability. The HFQ has been used in multiple studies, and concurrent validity with such anxiety measures as the Children's Manifest Anxiety Scale and the Fear Survey Scale for Children has been demonstrated.

Comment

The HFQ is a short, easy to use, face-valid method of assessing a child's fear related to medical situations or hospitalizations. Aside from its reported concurrent validity with other self-report measures of anxiety, psychometric properties of the measure are unknown. Although the HFQ has not been standardized, it has been used with a variety of pediatric populations. It shows promise and utility as a quick, cost-effective assessment of children's medical-related fears, although additional validation studies are needed.

Relevant References

Elkins, P. D., & Roberts, M. C. (1984). A preliminary evaluation of hospital preparations for nonpatient children: Primary prevention in a "let's pretend hospital." *Children's Health Care, 13,* 31–36.

Roberts, M. C., Wurtele, S. K., Boone, R. R., Ginther, L. J., & Elkins, P. D. (1981). Reduction of medical fears by use of modeling: A preventive application in a general population of children. *Journal of Pediatric Psychology, 6,* 293–300.

Siaw, S. N., Stephens, L. R., & Holmes, S. S. (1986). Knowledge about medical instruments and reported anxiety in pediatric surgery patients. *Children's Health Care, 14,* 134–141.

Hospital Fears Rating Scale (HFRS)

B. G. Melamed, 1975

Manual and Address Information

No manual. The measure has been previously published in the *Dictionary of Behavioral Assessment Techniques* (Melamed & Lumley, 1988). Direct inquiries to: Barbara G. Melamed, 1300 Morris Park Avenue, Albert Einstein College of Medicine, Bronx, NY, 10461, (718) 430-3968.

Purpose

The HFRS was developed to measure situational anxiety associated with medical/hospital concerns as part of a multidimensional approach to fear assessment.

Format, Administration, and Scoring

The HFRS consists of 25 items arranged in a self-report format. Using a 5-point Likert scale (1 = no fear at all to 5 = highly afraid), children rate how fearful they are in response to each item. For younger children, a visual aid or "Fear Thermometer" may be used to assist them in responding to items. Higher "temperatures" on the Fear Thermometer signify increased fearfulness. The total score is obtained by summing the values for the 16 medically related items.

Psychometric Information

Eight of the 25 items were taken from the Medical Fears subscale of the Fear Survey Schedule for Children (FSS-FC). These items refer to: fear of sharp objects; having to go to the hospital, the doctor, or the dentist; getting a shot; getting a haircut; getting sick; and deep water or the ocean. An additional 8 face-valid items were included for measuring hospital fears. These included germs, the sight of blood, being alone without your parents, having an operation, getting a cut or injury, getting sick at school, not being able to breathe, and people wearing masks. The 9 remaining items, not related to the medical setting yet believed to be fear inducing for some children, were included in order to make the scale less recognizable as an exclusive measure of hospital fears. These filler items include fear of spiders, making mistakes, going to bed in the dark, dogs, flying in an airplane, punishment, and thunderstorms.

Test-retest reliability has consistently been estimated at the .75-level. More investigators have utilized the HFRS and have demonstrated the validity of the measure as an assessment tool for situational fear and anxiety related to the medical setting. For example, a group of children participating in an intervention designed to better prepare them for surgery were found to report significantly fewer fears both prior to and after surgery as compared to a group viewing an unrelated film. Regardless of experimental condition, younger children were found to report more fears. The authors have also noted that higher fear levels have been positively correlated with the number of disruptive behaviors while in the operating room (.48) and the time spent in recovery (.54).

Comment

While the HFRS appears to be a valid measurement tool for the assessment of children's fears related to the medical setting, more research needs to be conducted regarding its reliability, as well as in the development of age-appropriate norms. The authors suggest using the HFRS as one instrument in a battery of assessment measures in order to better determine which variables are most relevant for examination and treatment.

Relevant References

Faust, J., & Melamed, B. G. (1984). Influence of arousal, previous experience, and age on surgery preparation of same day surgery and in-hospital pediatric patients. *Journal of Consulting and Clinical Psychology, 52,* 359–365.

Melamed, B. G., Dearborn, M., & Hermecz, D. A. (1983). Necessary considerations for surgery preparation: Age and experience. *Psychosomatic Medicine, 45,* 517–525.

Melamed, B. G., & Lumley, M. A. (1988). Hospital Fears Rating Scale. In M. Hersen & A. Bellack, (Eds.), *Directory of behavioral assessment techniques.* New York: Pergamon Press.

Melamed, B. G., & Siegel, L. J. (1975). Reduction of anxiety in children facing hospitalization and surgery by use of filmed modeling. *Journal of Consulting and Clinical Psychology, 43,* 511–521.

Hospital Stress Scale (HSS)

E. Bossert, 1994

Manual and Address Information

No manual. Direct inquiries to: Elizabeth Bossert, School of Nursing, Loma Linda University, Loma Linda, CA 92350, (909) 824-4360, ext. 45449.

Purpose

A self-report measure, the HSS was developed to assess children's perception of the stressfulness of the global event of hospitalization.

Format, Administration, and Scoring

The HSS is a one-item word-graphic measure consisting of a 10-centimeter horizontal line with anchor points at each end. Proportionally from left to right, though not anchored, are the following descriptions: not upset, little upset, medium upset, large upset, and worst possible upset. Children are asked "When you think about everything that has happened to you since you have been in the hospital, how upset has it made you?" The descriptive words under the line are read aloud to the child, who is asked to mark his/her appropriate response. Scoring entails measuring the distance between the left anchor point and where the mark has been made (in millimeters), with a possible score of 0 to 100. Prior to administering this measure, children are asked a nonrelated question (e.g., pertaining to likes/dislikes of subjects in school) presented in a similar format in order to familiarize them with responding to the instrument.

Psychometric Information

The HSS was designed for use in a study investigating the influence of health status, gender, and trait anxiety on stress in hospitalized children ages 8 through 11. Eighty-two children with chronic and acute illnesses completed the measure. The format of the HSS was developed based on research related to children's responses on different types of rating scales. A panel of pediatric nurse researchers established the measure's face validity. The mean of hospitalized children used in the original standardization sample was 49.6 millimeters (SD = 33.3) with responses ranging from 0 to 100 millimeters. Specific means for gender and type of illness have also been provided. The HSS has been reported to be significantly correlated with a reliable measure of trait anxiety in children (STAIC).

Comment

The HSS is a one-item word-graphic instrument used to assess children's appraisal of the stressfulness of the global event of hospitalization. Its format is child-friendly and easy to administer. The HSS has been used with an adequate sample of hospitalized children, and descriptive data have been reported. Furthermore, some validity of the measure has been demonstrated by its significant correlation with a reliable measure of children's anxiety. While its scope may be somewhat limited, the HSS appears to provide a useful estimate of the stressfulness of children's hospitalization, particularly when other more costly or time-intensive measures are not warranted. The HSS seems to be particularly useful in clinical situations.

Relevant References

Bossert, E. (1994). Stress appraisals of hospitalized school-age children. *Children's Health Care, 23,* 33–49.

Kidcope

A. Spirito, 1988

Manual and Address Information

There is a manual. Direct inquiries to: Anthony Spirito, Child and Family Psychiatry, Rhode Island Hospital, 593 Eddy Street, Providence, RI 02903, (401) 444-4515, anthony_spirito@brown.edu.

Purpose

The Kidcope was developed as a brief paper-and-pencil self-report measure of children and adolescents' use of coping strategies. It was designed to assist examination of the process of children's coping within pediatric populations.

Format, Administration, and Scoring

There are two versions of the Kidcope, a younger version for ages 7 through 12 (15 items), and an older version for adolescents ages 13 through 18 (10 items). The older version consists of 1 item for each of 10 coping strategies: distraction, social withdrawal, cognitive restructuring, self-criticism, blaming others, problem-solving, emotional regulation, wishful thinking, social support, and resignation. The younger version also has 10 main strategies, yet has 2 items (versus only 1) for several strategies.

The Kidcope has been used in multiple studies, and has specifically been used to examine children's coping strategies during hospitalization, related to chronic illness, related to assisting friends with illnesses, and following suicide attempts. In terms of administration, the authors suggest that the younger version of the Kidcope should be completed in an interview format, while older children can respond on their own. Children are either provided with a specific stressor (e.g., hospital or illness-specific), or are asked to generate their own stressor. They are then told to keep the specific stressor in mind while responding to items. Each item has two scales: frequency ("Did you do this?"), and efficacy ("How much did it help?"). For the younger version of the frequency scale, children respond either "yes" or "no," while older children respond using a 4-point Likert scale (0 = not at all to 3 = almost all the time). Both children and adolescents answer the efficacy scale only after giving a frequency response greater than zero. The efficacy scale consists of 3 points for the younger version (0 = not at all to 2 = a lot), and 4 points for the older version (0 = not at all to 3 = very much).

Scoring differs depending on the version, with scores being summed for both frequency and efficacy for the older version. Younger children's responses are scored by identifying the one of two items per coping strategy that yielded the highest frequency rating, and using that corresponding efficacy score. Examples of scoring have been provided by the authors. Sample items include:

> I kept quiet about a problem.
> I wished the problem had never happened.
> I turned to my family, friends, or other adults to make me feel better.
> I tried to see the good side of things.

Psychometric Information

Initial development of the Kidcope consisted of generating 24 items considered to be reflective of common coping styles. A factor analysis conducted on responses from 134 high school students revealed six factors with 13 items loading .50 or above on any given factor. As a result of difficulty in interpreting factors, the development of a brief scale with specific factors was abandoned, and 10 common coping strategies from the literature were selected.

The 10-item version was then administered to numerous samples, most of which consisted of healthy adolescents. Two smaller pediatric samples were also used in the standardization of the Kidcope. Compiling results from each of these samples (total N over 330) indicates variable test-retest reliability, depending on test-retest interval. Shorter intervals (3–7 days) yielded correlations ranging from .41 to .83, while longer intervals (up to 10 weeks) yielded correlations ranging from .15 to .43. Moderate correlations between the Kidcope and another standardized measure of children's coping (e.g., Coping Strategies Inventory) have been reported as evidence of concurrent validity. Internal consistency of the measure has not been reported because it is not predicted to be high given that the items tap different coping strategies. Preliminary analyses have revealed that the items can be grouped into two main strategies: positive/approach and negative/avoidance.

Comment

The Kidcope is a brief and easily administered questionnaire that appears to be useful in assessing children and adolescents' use of different coping strategies. The Kidcope has been used successfully by multiple investigators, and in institutions other than where it was developed. Furthermore, it has been used for both general stressors with healthy children, and with specific stressors for hospitalized children or children with chronic health conditions. Two versions allow for use with a wide age range of children (7–18), yet no formal investigation of the measure's reading level has been reported. There are 10 coping strategies that are commonly used and reported, yet results from factor analyses have been mixed. Indeed, the original authors have suggested that researchers conduct factor analyses independently for each sample. Test-retest reliabilities have ranged from low to moderately high, and concurrent validity has been demonstrated. Overall, the

Kidcope is an innovative measure and it appears to be a good choice for use in both clinical and research contexts.

Relevant References

Spirito, A. (1996). Commentary: Pitfalls in the use of brief screening measures of coping. *Journal of Pediatric Psychology, 21,* 573–575.

Spirito, A., Overholser, J., & Stark, L. J. (1989). Common problems and coping strategies: Findings with adolescent suicide attempters. *Journal of Abnormal Child Psychology, 17,* 213–221.

Spirito, A., Stark, L. J., & Williams, C. (1988). Development of a brief checklist to assess coping in pediatric patients. *Journal of Pediatric Psychology, 13,* 555–574.

Life Events Checklist (LEC)

J. H. Johnson, 1980

Manual and Address Information

No manual. Direct inquiries to: James H. Johnson, Department of Clinical and Health Psychology, P.O. Box 100165, University of Florida Health Science Center, Gainesville, FL 32610, (352) 395-0490, jjohnson@hp.ufl.edu.

Purpose

The LEC was designed to assess life stress, defined in terms of reported life changes, in children and adolescents.

Format, Administration, and Scoring

The LEC consists of 46 life events representative of life changes frequently experienced by children and adolescents. Additionally, four spaces are provided for indicating significant events that have occurred but are not included on the scale. The scale is very similar to the Life Events Record, yet it possesses the added distinction of assessing positive and negative changes separately. The format is also similar to the Life Experiences Survey, a measure of life stress developed for adults. Children are asked to indicate which of the events on the scale they have experienced during the past year, whether they would rate the event as "good" or "bad," and the degree to which each event has impacted their lives. Impact ratings range from 0 (no effect) to 3 (great effect). Positive and negative change scores are obtained by summing the ratings of the events judged to be positive versus negative. Some of the events listed on the scale include: moving to a new home, new brother or sister, serious illness or injury of family member, parents separated, parent getting a new job, joining a new club, making the honor roll, failing a grade, and making an athletic team.

Psychometric Information

The initial life events scores were obtained from a sample of 97 adolescents drawn from the general population (53% female) ranging in age from 13 to 17 years old. Both males and females reported similar levels of negative life events, averaging 5.06 and 6.94, respectively. Females reported significantly higher positive life change scores than did males, although this finding has not remained consistent across studies.

Test-retest reliabilities (2-week interval) for the positive and negative change scores were .69 and .72, respectively. The authors noted that this is in light of the fact events may have actually been experienced by some children during this period. Positive and negative life change scores from the LEC were found to correlate significantly with a range of instruments reflective of both physical health and psychological adjustment.

The discriminant validity of the LEC was examined in an investigation that compared LEC scores between a group of 25 male adolescent sex offenders seen in a clinical setting and a group from the general population matched on the age and sex variables. Interestingly, the mean negative change scores for the clinic group were nearly three times larger than the comparison group.

Comment

The LEC has been used in several investigations with satisfactory reliability and validity. It has been used with both medically ill and healthy children and its four write-in blanks allow for respondents to indicate the experience of specific life events. Length of administration and reading level of the measure have not been reported. Similarly, its use with ethnically diverse populations is uncertain. Overall, the LEC appears to be a useful measure for assessing life stress in older children and adolescents. Furthermore, it holds a distinct advantage over other life-events measures in that positive and negative life-change events are assessed separately and this differentiation appears to be empirically supported.

Relevant References

Brand, A. H., & Johnson, J. H. (1982). Note on the reliability of the Life Events Checklist. *Psychological Reports, 50,* 1274.

Brand, A. H., Johnson, J. H., & Johnson, S. B. (1986). Life stress and diabetic control in children and adolescents with insulin-dependent diabetes. *Journal of Pediatric Psychology, 11,* 481–495.

Johnson, J. H. (1986). *Life events as stressors in childhood and adolescence.* Beverly Hills, CA: Sage.

Johnson, J. H., & McCutcheon, S. (1980). Assessing life stress in older children and adolescents: Development of the Life Events Checklist. In I. G. Sarason & C. D. Spielberger (Eds.), *Stress and anxiety* (Vol. 7), Washington, DC: Hemisphere.

Medical Experiences Questionnaire (MEQ)

J. T. Pate, 1996

Manual and Address Information

No manual. Direct inquiries to: Ronald T. Blount, Department of Psychology, University of Georgia, Psychology Building, Athens, GA 30602-3013, (706) 542-3012, rlblount@uga.cc.uga.edu.

Purpose

The MEQ was designed to measure child and adult medical experiences, attitudes, and coping strategies. The measure can be completed by adolescents or adults.

Format, Administration, and Scoring

As a 67-item self-report paper-and-pencil questionnaire, the MEQ can be completed in about 15 to 20 minutes. The measure taps retrospective reports of childhood fears, pain, and coping strategies associated with common medical experiences. In addition, there are parallel items assessing these same dimensions based on medical experiences as an adult. Current avoidance of medical situations is also measured. Adults respond to each item using a 5-point Likert-type scale (1 = very painful / fearful / effective / almost always to 5 = not at all painful / fearful / effective / never). Sample childhood items include:

As a child, how afraid were you of . . ." (childhood fears)
. . . going to the doctors for an office visit?
. . . going to the dentist?
. . . getting a shot?
As a child, how painful was it for you to . . . (childhood pain)
. . . get a shot?
. . . have blood drawn?
. . . have a cavity filled?
As a child, did you . . . (childhood coping effectiveness)
. . . try to relax or breathe deeply during a medical treatment?
. . . joke around with staff?
. . . tell yourself it would be over soon?

Composite scores are obtained for childhood and adult medical fears (seven items each), childhood and adult pain (five items each), childhood and adult coping effectiveness (six items each), and avoidance of medical situations (four items). Additional items are used to obtain relevant demographic information.

Psychometric Information

The measure was used with 147 (43 male, 104 female) predominantly White undergraduate students in a study examining the relationship between temperament, childhood medical experiences, and current medical experiences. More childhood pain was significantly correlated with more childhood fears and less childhood coping effectiveness. More childhood medical fear was significantly associated with more medical fears, more pain, lower coping effectiveness, and more avoidance of medical situations as adults. Greater childhood coping effectiveness was significantly related to higher coping effectiveness, less adult fear, less adult pain, and less avoidance of medical situations in adulthood. Different childhood medical experiences significantly predicted adult medical fears, pain, coping effectiveness, and avoidance.

Internal consistency estimates were reported as follows: childhood medical fear (.85), childhood pain (.85), childhood coping effectiveness (.71), adult medical fear (.84), adult pain (.87), adult coping effectiveness (.76), and avoidance of medical situations (.51).

Comment

The MEQ is in its initial stages of development and, therefore, requires further study of its psychometric properties. Preliminary data suggest that internal consistency is adequate, with the exception of the avoidance composite, but validity data are very much needed. Information about scale construction is needed, also. The reliance on retrospective reports of childhood medical experiences presents some unique problems of interpretation. Although the MEQ is not a child health measure completed by children or their parents, we have included it here because it is potentially useful in cross-sectional studies examining the relationship between childhood medical experiences and adult behaviors in various medical situations.

Relevant References

Pate, J. T., Blount, R. L., Cohen, L. L., & Smith, A. J. (1996). Childhood medical experiences and temperament as predictors of adult functioning in medical situations. *Children's Health Care, 25,* 281–298.

Medical Fear Questionnaire (MFQ)

M. Broome, 1986

Manual and Address Information

No manual. Direct inquiries to: Marion E. Broome, BE 113, School of Nursing, Medical College of Georgia, Augusta, GA 30912.

Purpose

The MFQ was designed to assess children's perception of fear associated with various medical situations, and was specifically developed to investigate the relationship between reported and observed fear of children in low- and high-threat medical situations.

Format, Administration, and Scoring

The MFQ is a paper-and-pencil measure that is completed by children as young as 4 years old and can be completed with or without an adult's assistance. It contains 12 items that are worded in a 3-point Likert scale. Children rate how fearful they are of each situation represented by items (1 = not at all, 2 = a little, and 3 = a lot). A total score is derived by summing the ratings on each of the 12 items. Sample items include:

> I am afraid of having to get a shot from the nurse or doctor.
> I am afraid of the white coat nurses and doctors wear.
> I am afraid of lying down on the table in the doctor's office.

Psychometric Information

Items on the MFQ were rationally derived from the authors' experiences working with children in a health care setting. The standardization sample included 128 4- to 7-year-old children who were undergoing a preschool health screening. The sample was ethnically diverse. Internal consistency was reported as .84. Test-retest reliabilities were not reported. Descriptive data for the sample have been reported, and suggest good variability in scores. Furthermore, the MFQ's correlation with a psychometrically reliable measure of children's observed behavior (i.e., Child Behavior Observation Rating Scale) was provided as evidence of concurrent validity.

Comment

The MFQ appears to be useful both clinically and as a pre-post measure of the efficacy of interventions. Items are general enough to be of use with children both in and out of the hospital, and with a variety of chronic health conditions. The measure is straightforward and appears to be relatively easy to use. It has been used with children as young as 4 years old, yet no systematic investigation of its reading level has been reported. However, this may not be particularly relevant if the measure was administered verbally by a clinician or investigator because most of the items appear to be developmentally appropriate even for very young children. The standardization sample included a diverse group of children suggesting generalizability of results. Preliminary psychometric data appear promising, and further analyses and replication of these findings will enhance the utility of the measure.

Relevant References

Broome, M. E. (1986). The relationship between children's fears and behavior during a painful event. *Children's Health Care, 14*, 142–145.

Role-Play Inventory of Situations and Coping Strategies (RISCS)

A. L. Quittner, 1996

Manual and Address Information

There is a manual. Direct inquiries to: Alexandra L. Quittner, Department of Clinical and Health Psychology, P.O. Box 100165, University of Florida Health Science Center, Gainesville, FL 32610-0165, (352) 395-0490, aquittne@hp.ufl.edu.

Purpose

Based on a context-specific conceptualization of the stress and coping process, the RISCS was developed to assess the coping skills of children and adolescents with a chronic illness and their parents.

Format, Administration, and Scoring

There are currently four versions of the RISCS. One is for adolescents with cystic fibrosis (CF; ages 12–18), one for school-age children with CF (ages 6–11), one for parents of adolescents with CF, and one for parents of school-age children with CF. Furthermore, there are separate versions for parents depending on the sex of their child (the only difference in the versions is the wording, i.e., son/daughter/he/she). While administration, format, and so forth are similar for each of the versions, this summary focuses on the RISCS version for parents of school-age children.

The RISCS consists of 31 written and audiotaped vignettes representing frequent and difficult problem situations in each of 11 domains: medications and treatment, routines, spouse, outside activities, discipline, peers, school, medical care, finances, siblings, and mealtimes. Coping efficacy across these situations is assessed through each of the 31 items. The RISCS is individually administered. After listening to the audiotaped vignette, parents are asked to give their immediate coping response, which is recorded on audiotape. Respondents then complete a rating form that asks about the frequency and difficulty of each situation for that particular parent. Both are rated on a 5-point scale with frequency/difficulty ranging from "not at all" to "almost all the time"/ "extremely."

Responses are then scored using empirically derived ratings and prototypic responses provided in the manual. Vignettes are scored on a 4-point Likert scale ranging from "extremely competent" to "extremely incompetent." Scores can be obtained for either the total measure (maximum score 124), or for individual domains. An example vignette is: "Your child asks for a snack in the evening. You say, 'Have some cheese and crackers, but be sure to take your enzymes!' Later you go into the kitchen and he's finished the snack but has forgotten his enzymes. He says, 'It's just a snack. I don't really need them.' You are tired of constantly reminding him and wish he would be more responsible. What would you say or do in this situation?"

Psychometric Information

The RISCS was developed using a five-phase plan: situational analysis, item development, response enumeration, response evaluation, and instrument development. A large sample of parents and health care providers were first interviewed in order to obtain a diverse list of problem situations. A total of 1,725 problematic situations were elicited and subsequently categorized into 97 nonredundant items, categorized into the 11 domains. Problems were categorized into domains by the authors, and inter-rater reliability was found to be .80.

Vignettes based on 31 problems most commonly identified as difficult were then constructed, with each of the 11 domains being represented by at least one vignette. The 31-item RISCS was then piloted on four parents of school-age children with CF in order to obtain feedback related to clarity and the relevance of each item.

A panel of 38 independent judges (i.e., psychologists, parents, and pulmonologists) was used to derive competence ratings for each of the 31 vignettes. The judges' ratings were compiled to construct a comprehensive rater's manual.

Predictive validity for problem situations of the RISCS was investigated in the initial sample for the development of the measure. In addition to responding to interviews about most difficult problem situations, parents also completed a standardized measure of depression (CES-D) and one of role strain (Who Does What?). RISCS responses indicative of more problems were related to greater role strain, and more problem situations on the RISCS were also related to greater depressive symptomatology as indicated by mothers.

Comment

The RISCS is a unique tool for the assessment of coping across a variety of domains for parents of children with CF. There are parallel versions of the RISCS for use with parents of adolescents, and also one for children and adolescents report. While the RISCS is relatively time-consuming in its administration and scoring, it improves on other formatted questionnaires by allowing more flexibility in responses. The RISCS was developed in a comprehensive manner, with careful evaluation at each phase of development. While preliminary reports suggest good predictive validity, other investigations of reliability and validity have not been reported. Further examination of the measure's psychometric properties are currently underway in the context of an intervention study. Similarly, they are reportedly investigating the utility of the RISCS with children who have other chronic health conditions. Overall, the precision with which the measure was developed, the extensive manual guiding scoring procedures, and reports that further empirical evaluation of the measure are underway suggest that the RISCS will likely prove to be quite useful in assessing parents' coping in both clinical and empirical settings.

Relevant References

DiGirolamo, A. M., Quittner, A. L., Ackerman, V., & Stevens, J. (1997). Identification and assessment of ongoing stressors in adolescents with a chronic illness: An application of the behavior-analytic model. *Journal of Clinical Child Psychology, 26*, 53–66.

Quittner, A. L. (1996). *Role-Play Inventory of Situations & Coping Strategies.* Indiana University, Bloomington, Indiana.

Quittner, A. L., Tolbert, V. E., Regoli, M. J., Orenstein, D., Hollingsworth, J. L., & Eigen, H. (1996). Development of the Role-Play Inventory of Situations and Coping Strategies (RISCS) for parents of children with cystic fibrosis. *Journal of Pediatric Psychology, 21*, 209–235.

Wager, L., & Quittner, A. L. (May, 1998). Using the RISCS role-play measure to compare mothers and fathers of adolescents with cystic fibrosis. Poster presented at the Great Lakes Regional Conference on Child Health Psychology.

Waldron/Varni Pediatric Pain Coping Inventory (PPCI)

J. W. Varni, 1996

Manual and Address Information

No manual. Direct inquiries to: James W. Varni, Psychosocial Research Program, Children's Hospital and Health Center, 3030 Children's Way, San Diego, CA 92123-4226, (619) 495-4939, jvarni@chsd.org.

Purpose

The PPCI was designed to assess the pain coping strategies of children, adolescents, and their parents.

Format, Administration, and Scoring

This self-administered, paper-and-pencil questionnaire contains 41 coping strategies sometimes used by children and adolescents who experience pain. Using a

3-point rating scale (0 = never, 1 = sometimes, 2 = often), respondents indicate how often they use each of the coping strategies when they feel pain or hurt. The PPCI has been used with children ages 5 to 18. There are three versions of the PPCI (Child, Adolescent, Parent) that are identical except for developmentally appropriate wording changes to the Child version and the use of the third person tense in the Parent version. Scores are obtained for five factor-analytically derived subscales: Cognitive Self-Instruction, Seek Social Support, Strive to Rest and Be Alone, Cognitive Refocusing, and Problem-Solving Self-Efficacy. Total administration time is about 15 minutes. Sample items include:

> Tell myself to be brave. (Cognitive Self-Instruction)
> Have my mother, father, or friend sit with me. (Seek Social Support)
> Go to bed. (Strive to Rest and Be Alone)
> Watch TV. (Cognitive Refocusing)
> Put ice or heat on the sore spots. (Problem-Solving Self-Efficacy)

Psychometric Information

The PPCI was developed within the Biobehavioral Model of Pediatric Pain and is part of a theory-driven pediatric pain research program. Items were generated and revised by reviews of the pediatric and adult pain literatures and feedback by nationally recognized pediatric pain experts. Five a priori scales of the items were developed (Cognitive Self-Instruction, Problem-Solving, Distraction, Seeks Social Support, and Catastrophizing/Helplessness) and subsequently evaluated. The initial PPCI sample included 187 children and adolescents (5–16 years old) with musculoskeletal pain secondary to rheumatologic disease (e.g., juvenile rheumatoid arthritis, systemic lupus erythematosus, dermatomyositis, spondyloarthopathy). The sample was predominantly female (71%), White (66%; 12% Hispanic, 8% African American, 5% Asian, 9% Other), and middle class.

Internal consistency reliability (Cronbach's alpha) was .85 for the total PPCI scale. Alpha coefficients for the a priori subscales were .74 for Cognitive Self-Instruction, .67 for Problem-Solving, .66 for Distraction, .66 for Seeks Social Support, and .57 for Catastrophizing/Helplessness. Alpha coefficients for the factor-analytically derived subscales were .77 for Cognitive Self-Instruction, .74 for Seeks Social Support, .73 for Strive to Rest and Be Alone, .68 for Cognitive Refocusing, and .67 for Problem-Solving Self-Efficacy. Scores on the subscales Strive to Rest and Be Alone and Cognitive Refocusing were most consistently associated with pain intensity (patient- and parent-reported) and psychological or behavioral adjustment (anxiety, self-esteem, internalizing problems).

Comment

The PPCI is a new and theoretically driven measure of strategies used by children and adolescents to cope with pain. Its initial psychometric evaluation suggests good internal consistency reliability for the overall measure and fair to good internal consistency reliability for the a priori and factor-analytically derived subscales. The scaling format is sensitive to the cognitive development of young children. Additionally, the three versions allow for its use with children of varying ages and their parents. More research is needed to examine test-retest reliability, construct validity, and factor structure stability for each of the three PPCI versions separately and across multiple patient populations (e.g., age, disease type, acute and chronic pain). Furthermore, its applicability to children representing various ethnic minorities should be further examined to determine its utility with these populations.

Relevant References

Varni, J. W., Waldron, S. A., Gragg, R. A., Rapoff, M. A., Bernstein, B. H., Lindsley, C. B., & Newcomb, M. D. (1996). Development of the Waldron/Varni Pediatric Pain Coping Inventory. *Pain, 67*, 141–150.

General Observations and Recommendations

Despite the growing number of theories related to both stress and coping within the arena of children's health, a comparatively smaller number of assessment tools exist. Measures reviewed indicate that different groups of investigators may often use different definitions of stress and/or coping, highlighting the importance of determining the most appropriate measure for each particular clinical case or research question. As with each topic area discussed in this handbook, much of the success of future assessment of stress and coping will rely on our ability to adequately define and operationalize distinct constructs.

Several points must be considered in the future development of assessment tools within the area of stress and coping. First, careful consideration must be given to developmental issues. While some authors have examined the reading levels of their instruments or have developed different versions for younger and older children, most have not. Second, the assessment of children's coping and the provision of psychological services to facilitate adaptive coping are arguably two of the most common reasons that pediatricians refer children with chronic health conditions to pediatric psychologists, social workers, and psychiatrists. Further evaluation of the predictive validity of stress and coping measures is desperately needed and would facilitate the clinician's selection of instruments that are most sensitive to change. Third, closer attention must be paid to the appraisal of stress. In investigations relying on observation or parent report, conclusions about the child's level of stress generally do not consider the appraisal process as an important determinant in the experience of stress. This is an important consideration given that many studies focusing on young children must rely on the report of others.

References

Bernard, L. C., & Krupat, E. (1994). *Health psychology: Biopsychosocial factors in health and illness.* Ft. Worth, TX: Harcourt Brace College Publishers.

Christiano, B., & Russ, S. W. (1998). Matching preparatory intervention to coping style: The effects on children's distress in the dental setting. *Journal of Pediatric Psychology, 23,* 17–27.

Compas, B. E., Worsham, N. L., & Ey, S. (1992). Conceptual and developmental issues in children's coping with stress. In A. M. La Greca, L. J. Siegel, J. L. Wallander, & C. E. Walker (Eds.), *Stress and coping in child health.* New York: Guilford Press.

Lazarus, R. S., & Folkman, S. (1984). *Stress, appraisal, and coping.* New York: Springer.

Miller, S. M., Roussi, P., Caputo, C., & Kraus, L. (1995). Patterns of children's coping with an aversive dental treatment. *Health Psychology, 14,* 236–246.

Peterson, L. (1989). Coping by children undergoing stressful medical procedures: Some conceptual, methodological, and therapeutic issues. *Journal of Consulting and Clinical Psychology, 57,* 380–387.

Spirito, A., Stark, L. J., & Knapp, L. G. (1992). The assessment of coping in chronically ill children: Implications for clinical practice. In A. M. La Greca, L. J. Siegel, J. L. Wallander, & C. E. Walker (Eds.), *Stress and coping in child health.* New York: Guilford Press.

Chapter 6

Attitudes and Beliefs

RANDI M. STREISAND

The measurement of attitudes and beliefs plays a significant role in the empirical examination of health behaviors. Though these terms are often used interchangeably and reflect similar ideas, the differences between them are noteworthy. Beliefs have been commonly defined as anything that we hold to be true about the world. For example, we hold the beliefs that a wheel and a ball are both round, or that smoking causes lung cancer. Attitudes are beliefs that are associated with a particular feeling, action, or mood. These may include attitudes toward corporal punishment or the quality of one's health care.

In the ever expanding arena of child health prevention, the assessment of attitudes and beliefs has been very helpful in generating and refining explanatory models for health behavior. Consistent with this perspective, the assessment of attitudes and beliefs is considered here to be distinct from other areas discussed in this handbook because it largely focuses on population-based prevention efforts in "healthy" children. For example, health education curriculums in public schools often teach children about the dangers of smoking, sun exposure, and unprotected sexual intercourse in an effort to decrease their risk of certain illnesses. Some school health programs also include education about the benefits of a healthy diet and exercise regimens in an effort to boost resilience. Researchers who design and implement such interventions will often use pre- and post-measures of children's attitudes as an indicator of treatment outcome. Children who do not "like" to use sunscreen may hold negative attitudes about certain aspects of the product (e.g., the bad smell or slippery texture). Measuring positive changes in these negative attitudes may ultimately provide better insights into how to promote skin cancer prevention behaviors.

Attitudes and beliefs play a significant role in many of the major theories of health behavior change. For example, in both the Health Belief Model (Becker,

1974; Rosenstock, 1966) and the Theory of Reasoned Action (Azjen & Fishbein, 1977) attitudes about behavior are thought to mediate the actions that are taken by individuals. Components of the Health Belief Model include perceived susceptibility and severity of the health threat, perceived benefits and barriers to altering one's lifestyle, and self-efficacy of carrying out the behavior changes. Although the precise nature of the relationship between attitudes, behavior, and even knowledge has been somewhat elusive, attitudes have been associated with both knowledge (Maieron, Roberts, & Prentice-Dunn, 1996; Telljohann, Durgin, Everett, & Price, 1996) and behavior change (Fisher, Fisher, Misovich, Kimble, & Malloy, 1996).

The measurement of attitudes and beliefs can encompass each of the individual parts of behavior change models, or may just focus on one aspect of the model. Some researchers measure attitudes on a continuum (e.g., +10 = I love lying in the sun to –10 = I hate lying in the sun) while others classify an individual as having either positive or negative attitudes about a specific situation (e.g., I love lying in the sun *Yes* or *No*).

Given their importance to theoretical model building, a large number of measures assessing children's attitudes and beliefs are currently available, and more are being developed and evaluated. At present, there are assessment tools that target specific chronic health conditions or medical regimen behaviors (i.e., Asthma Attitudes Questionnaire, Attitudes for AIDS Prevention, Diabetes Opinion Survey, Perceptions of Asthma Medication), as well as those that explore attitudes about more general health topics such as physical disabilities (e.g., Chedoke-McMaster Attitudes Toward Children With Handicaps Scale), death (Death Anxiety Questionnaire), and body image and eating (e.g., Children's Eating Attitudes Test, Body Attitude Scale).

As with other areas of assessment, developmental considerations are important within the area of attitudes and beliefs. While young children's reports of their own beliefs may not be reliable or stable over time, the very nature of attitudes and beliefs are such that direct observations are impossible, and an adult's report of a child's attitudes and beliefs may be misleading. However, several measures completed by informants who know the child well may augment the assessment process. For example, parents' own attitudes or beliefs may impact children's beliefs (Johnson & Tercyak, 1995), or their children's treatment. Similarly, attitudes of siblings or peers may play a significant role in how a child with a disability or illness is treated.

In this chapter, we review assessment tools that are both illness-specific and more general, as well as those that focus on child report and parent report. Many of the measures described are revised versions of measures that were originally designed for adults (e.g., Children's Eating Attitudes Test, Death Anxiety Questionnaire), and some measures have been altered from use with a general child population for use within the area of children's health.

REVIEWS

Asthma Attitudes Questionnaire (AAQ)

P. G. Gibson, 1995

Manual and Address Information

No manual. Direct inquiries to: P. Gibson, Respiratory Medicine Unit, John Hunter Hospital, Locked Building 1, Hunter Region Mail Centre, NSW 2310, Australia.

Purpose

The AAQ was developed to assess the attitudes toward asthma in adolescents both with and without asthma.

Format, Administration, and Scoring

A self-report measure, the AAQ can be administered both individually and in groups. The 15-item questionnaire assesses the attitudes toward asthma across four domains: (1) tolerance toward people with asthma (8 questions); (2) locus of control—internal (2 questions); (3) locus of control—powerful others (3 questions); and (4) locus of control—chance (2 questions). Respondents indicate the degree to which they agree with statements using a 6-point Likert scale (1 = strongly disagree to 6 = strongly agree). Representative items include:

> Students play on their asthma.
> School teachers have a negative attitude toward students with asthma.
> Students are embarrassed about using their inhalers in class.
> If someone with asthma takes care of him/herself, he/she can avoid most asthma symptoms.

Psychometric Information

The AAQ was developed for use in a large-scale investigation of 13- to 14-year-olds' knowledge, attitudes, and quality of life related to asthma. Questions comprising the locus of control domains were based on prior work with an asthma-specific locus of control questionnaire. Items for the tolerance domain resulted from information gained during an adolescent focus group, an asthma support group, and clinical experience. Items were screened for face validity by a multidisciplinary team, and then used in pilot testing. A very large sample (n = 4,161) of students completed the AAQ. The sample was comprised of adolescents with and without asthma. Knowledge about asthma was significantly correlated with each of the four AAQ domains. Descriptive data have been provided for a subset of the items, but no overall means for domains or individual items have been reported. Similarly, tests of reliability, validity, and internal consistency have not been reported.

Comment

The AAQ is a self-report measure consisting of four domains intended to assess adolescents' tolerance and locus of control in relation to asthma. The AAQ has been used with a very large sample in an investigation of the relationship of asthma knowledge, attitudes, and quality of life. Although the instrument has been found to be significantly correlated with a reliable asthma knowledge measure, no other psychometric data have been reported. Furthermore, its use with children younger than 13 to 14 years old is uncertain. Further validation of the AAQ as an assessment tool in both clinical and research settings is warranted.

Relevant References

Gibson, P. G., Henry, D. A., Francis, L. (1993). Association between availability of nonprescription Beta agonist inhalers and undertreatment of asthma. *British Medical Journal, 306,* 1514–1518.

Gibson, P. G., Henry, R. L., Vimpani, G. V., & Halliday, J. (1995). Asthma knowledge, attitudes, and quality of life in adolescents. *Archive of Diseases in Childhood, 73,* 321–326.

Attitude Toward Disabled Persons Scales (ATDP)

H. E. Yuker, 1970

Manual and Address Information

There is a manual ($10.00). Direct inquiries to: Ruth Mangles, Psychology Department, Hofstra University, Hempstead, NY 11549.

Purpose

The ATDP is a paper-and-pencil measure that is completed by able-bodied adults to assess their attitudes toward handicapped children. The ATDP has been modified for the specific use of assessing differences between medical students and undergraduates in their attitudes toward childhood cancer.

Format, Administration, and Scoring

The ATDP comprises 19 items to which adults indicate their attitudes toward the psychosocial development and behavior of children with handicapping conditions.

The measure can be administered individually or in a group format. Higher scores suggest more positive attitudes. A modification of this scale replaced referents to disabled with "children with cancer." In addition, this revision included 4 additional items to assess general familiarity with childhood cancer.

Psychometric Information

Internal consistency of the ATDP has been reported to be .88, and test-retest reliabilities have ranged from .66 to .89. In the modified version used specifically to assess attitudes relevant to childhood cancer, internal consistency for the 19 items and additional 4 items was .92. Teachers' attitudes as measured by the ATDP were not found to be related to students' attraction toward peers with handicaps. In a study examining differences in attitudes between undergraduates and medical students, there were no differences between groups in attitudes related to children with cancer.

Comment

The ATDP appears to be easy to complete. Reports suggest acceptable internal consistency and test-retest reliability. It has been used primarily for assessing attitudes toward children with handicapping conditions, and it has been successfully modified for use with a specific pediatric illness as well. Overall, the ATDP can be useful for clinicians or researchers interested in examining adults' attitudes toward children who are ill or have handicaps. Furthermore, the measure may be useful when working with teachers who may interact with children with handicaps within a school setting. Given the limited information related to the scale's psychometric properties, future investigations incorporating the ATDP will indicate its utility as an assessment tool in research.

Relevant References

Yuker, H. E. (1988). *Attitudes toward persons with disabilities.* New York: Springer Publishing Co.

Yuker, H. E., Block, J. R., & Younng, J. H. (1970). *The measurement of attitudes toward disabled persons.* Albertson, NY: INA MEND Institute at Human Resources Center.

Attitudes for AIDS Prevention

V. Slonim-Nevo, 1992

Manual and Address Information

No manual. Direct inquiries to: Slonim-Nevo, Ben-Gurion University of the Negev, Department of Social Work, 84105 Beer Sheva, Israel, or Wendy Auslander,

Washington University, George Warren Brown School of Social Work, Campus Box 1196, St. Louis, MO, 63130.

Purpose

The Attitudes for AIDS Prevention questionnaire was designed to assess adolescents' attitudes across the following domains: condom use, IV drug use, multiple sexual partners, personal susceptibility, and self-efficacy.

Format, Administration, and Scoring

The Attitudes for AIDS Prevention questionnaire consists of 23 items to which adolescents respond using a 4-point scale (1 = strongly agree to 4 = strongly disagree). The measure can be administered individually as a self-report, or as a combined interview and self-report in small groups of 5 to 10 adolescents. The role of the interviewer in the group format is to read items and clarify questions. The authors reported that pilot testing suggested adolescents' preference for the combination method as opposed to either self-report or interview alone.

The Attitudes for AIDS Prevention questionnaire is scored by summing adolescents' responses across the 23 items and then dividing by 23. Several items are reverse scored, and higher scores reflect more positive attitudes toward AIDS prevention. Sample items include:

> I think people my age who have sex should use condoms.
> It is better not to shoot up drugs because of the AIDS virus.
> I can do things to make sure that I don't get AIDS.
> Women should ask their partner to use condoms.

Psychometric Information

An early version of the Attitudes for AIDS Prevention questionnaire consisted of 28 items based on information gained through a large-scale literature review of existing AIDS surveys. The original standardization sample consisted of 45 adolescents ages 10 to 11 living in a residential center. The original scale reportedly had adequate internal consistency and test-retest reliability, yet a principal components analysis revealed numerous factors accounting for small amounts of the variance. The authors then subjected the measure to an item analysis, and 5 items were deleted. Results of the principal components and item analyses contributed to the authors' decision to score the Attitudes for AIDS Prevention questionnaire as one total score versus separate factors.

The 23-item final version of the Attitudes for AIDS Prevention questionnaire was standardized on another group of adolescents (n = 358; ages 11–18) living in residential centers. Adolescents were ethnically diverse and were in residential centers for either abuse/neglect or juvenile delinquency. The Attitudes for AIDS

Prevention questionnaire was used to examine the relationship between attitudes and specific behaviors, as well as adolescents' intent to engage in risky behaviors. Internal consistency was reported to be .84 and test-retest reliability (4-week interval) was .82. Evidence of construct validity was provided by the authors who found that Attitudes for AIDS Prevention scores were significantly positively correlated with intentions to engage in risky behaviors and AIDS knowledge. Descriptive data also have been provided.

Comment

The Attitudes for AIDS Prevention questionnaire is easy to complete, yet the authors suggest lending assistance via a group format for its completion. Development of the measure has included examinations of its psychometric properties, with appropriate revisions due to specific results. Adequate reliability has been reported, and findings suggest construct validity as well. The Attitudes for AIDS Prevention questionnaire has been used only with adolescents living in residential centers, and its utility with other populations, as well as with younger children, should be examined. Relatedly, before utilized in a self-report format, investigation of the reading level of the questionnaire should be completed. Overall, the Attitudes for AIDS Prevention questionnaire is a useful instrument for both clinicians and researchers examining attitudes toward AIDS. Psychometric data and the use of a large standardization sample greatly improve on the existing literature and will allow for researchers to use a common measure in order to generalize findings across settings.

Relevant References

Paniagua, F. A., O'Boyle, M., Wagner, K. D., Ramirez, S. Z., Holmes, W. D., Nieto, J. F., & Smith, E. M. (1994). AIDS-related items for developing an AIDS questionnaire for children and adolescents. *Journal of Adolescent Research, 9,* 311–339.

Slonim-Nevo, V., Auslander, W. F., & Ozawa, M. N. (1991). Knowledge, attitudes and behaviors related to AIDS among youth in residential centers: Results from an exploratory study. *Journal of Adolescence, 14,* 17–33.

Body Attitude Scale (BAS)

R. M. Lerne, 1973

Manual and Address Information

No manual. Address unknown.

Purpose

The BAS, largely adapted from earlier scales by Rosen and Ross (1968), was developed to assess the relationship between older adolescents' body image and self-concept, taking relative contribution of selected aspects of the body into account.

Format, Administration, and Scoring

The BAS can be administered both individually and in groups. It consists of four separate self-report scales. The first three scales are comprised of a list of 24 body characteristics. On the first scale, adolescents rate each characteristic on a 5-point Likert scale (1 = very dissatisfied to 5 = very satisfied) as to how satisfied they are with the appearance of each characteristic in terms of their own body. On the second scale, adolescents rate each body part as to how important it is to them, and on the third scale adolescents rate each body characteristic in terms of its importance in determining the physical attractiveness of members of the opposite sex.

The fourth scale consists of 16 bipolar dimensions of self-concept presented in an adjective checklist format. Adolescents indicate the degree to which each adjective describes them (1 = word on right end of continuum is most like me to 5 = word on left end of continuum is most like me).

The BAS is scored by summing Likert responses separately for each of the first three scales. Computing correlations between responses to the fourth scale and the other scales provides information on the relationship between satisfaction and attractiveness and self-concept.

Psychometric Information

The BAS was standardized on a sample of undergraduate students (n = 308), and was then used with a different group of undergraduates (n = 242). Descriptive data have been reported for each of these samples, separately for each of the four subscales, as well as for each individual body characteristic. Tests of reliability, validity, or internal consistency have not been reported.

Comment

The BAS has been used in assessing characteristics of attractiveness and body satisfaction in undergraduate populations. Psychometric data for the BAS have not been reported. Furthermore, its utility with younger adolescent or child populations, in addition to groups of people with chronic health conditions, is uncertain. While the BAS may provide useful clinical information, especially with adolescents whose chronic health conditions may impact body image, further validation studies are warranted before its use in clinical settings can be recommended.

Relevant References

Lerner, R. M., & Karabenick, S. A. (1974). Physical attractiveness, body attitudes, and self-concept in late adolescents. *Journal of Youth and Adolescence, 3,* 307–316.

Lerner, R. M., Karabenick, S. A., & Stuart, J. L. (1973). Relations among physical attractiveness, body attitudes, and self-concept in male and female college students. *Journal of Psychology, 85,* 119–129.

Rosen, G. M., & Ross, A. O. (1968). Relationship of body image to self-concept. *Journal of Consulting and Clinical Psychology, 32,* 100.

Chedoke-McMaster Attitudes Toward Children With Handicaps (CATCH) Scale

P. L. Rosenbaum, 1986

Manual and Address Information

No manual. Direct inquiries to: Peter Rosenbaum, Neurodevelopmental Clinical Research Unit, McMaster University, Building T-16, Room 126, 128 Main Street, West Hamilton, Ontario, Canada L8S 4L4, rosenbau@fhs.mcmaster.ca.

Purpose

The CATCH scale was developed as a paper-and-pencil children's self-report measure of attitudes toward peers with handicaps. It was designed as part of a research program examining the integration of children with disabilities into schools and other community programs.

Format, Administration, and Scoring

The CATCH consists of 36 items to which children respond on a 5-point Likert scale (strongly disagree, disagree, can't decide, agree, strongly agree). It can be administered on an individual basis or in a group format, but generally it has been done with oral instructions from an adult. Questionnaire instructions specifically ask children what they think or feel about children with handicaps. Although a brief definition of this term is provided, the child is instructed to interpret this term as they understand it. A stimulus condition is not specified. The child is instructed to read each statement and to place an X over the box that best describes how they feel about the statement. Two sample items are provided to familiarize the child with the questionnaire format. In addition, the questionnaire solicits information about whether the respondent has a handicap, has a friend or family member with a handicap, or has talked to or played with a child who is handicapped in the last week. The CATCH takes approximately 20 minutes to complete.

CATCH items are randomly ordered, but with alternating positive and negative statements. Individual item scores range from 0 to 4, and negative statements are inversely coded. Factor and total scores are obtained by adding the item scores, dividing the sum by the number of items, and multiplying by 10. Standardized scores range from 0 to 40, with high scores reflecting more positive attitudes. Example items include:

> I feel sorry for handicapped children.
> I would invite a handicapped child to my birthday party.
> Handicapped children don't like to make friends.
> I feel upset when I see a handicapped child.

Psychometric Information

Development of the CATCH was guided by a three-component model in which attitudes are believed to have affective, behavioral intention and cognitive components. A pool of statements reflecting these three attitude components was generated on the basis of children's (ages 9–13) common experiences and feelings. Grammar and reading levels were assessed by teachers and principals, some items were subsequently reworded and/or dropped, and the preliminary measure was pretested on a group of children. The CATCH, comprising 12 items in each component, was initially standardized on a sample of 304 children (boys and girls) in fifth through eight grades in four Ontario public schools. Factor analysis findings supported a two- (vs. three) component model of attitudes. One factor comprised affective and behavioral intention items, while the other factor contained cognitive items. Consequently, only total scores have been used in subsequent studies.

Regarding internal consistency, alpha coefficient for the CATCH total score was .90. Test-retest reliability was .73 for the CATCH total score and was computed using a convenience sample of 64 fifth to seventh graders at one school after a 1-month interval. The authors indicate that this relatively low test-retest reliability estimate may have occurred because children in this sample were informed that 8 children with multiple handicaps were about to be integrated into the school.

Regarding construct validation, the CATCH has been found to detect differences in attitudes according to gender, experience with a friend with a disability, and interest in being involved with a child who has a disability. Girls, children with a friend with a handicap, and children with recent contact with a peer with a disability had more positive attitudes, and total CATCH score was correlated .52 with expressed interest in being friends with a child with a handicap. Also, children randomized to participate in a "buddy" program in which they were paired with a peer with a disability demonstrated a significant increase in CATCH total scores over a 3-month period, compared with controls. Child's perceived self-esteem and social status, and parents' socioeconomic status were not found to be associated with children's attitudes toward peers with handicaps using the CATCH.

Comment

The CATCH is a relatively brief and easily administered questionnaire that appears to be very useful in assessing children's attitudes toward peers with disabilities. The CATCH has been used predominantly with White children ages 9 to 13 years old and, consequently, has limited generalizability to other populations. While the items appear appropriate for use with young adolescents, a computerized analysis of reading level is necessary before using this measure with younger children. Also, the CATCH has been used almost exclusively in school settings in which children with severe handicaps are already integrated into everyday activities. Further research is needed to assess its applicability and utility with more diverse populations. The CATCH has demonstrated excellent internal consistency. However, the factor structure and test-retest reliability warrant additional investigation. Although two factors emerged in the initial standardization study, subsequent studies have reported exclusively on CATCH total scores. Indeed, total scores appear to distinguish children along several important dimensions (thus yielding excellent construct validity); yet factor scores may prove beneficial in detecting differential changes in behavioral intention, cognition, and affect following the implementation of school-based programs designed to enhance attitudes toward children with disabilities.

Relevant References

Rosenbaum, P. L., Armstrong, R. W., & King, S. M. (1986). Children's attitudes toward disabled peers: A self-report measure. *Journal of Pediatric Psychology, 11,* 517–530.

Rosenbaum, P. L., & King, S. M. (1992). *Attitudes toward disabled children: An approach to measuring, improving and understanding the attitudes of able-bodied children.* Research Report #92-1, The Neurodevelopmental Clinical Research Unit, McMaster University, Hamilton, Ontario, Canada.

Child Attitude Toward Illness Scale (CATIS)

J. K. Austin, 1993

Manual and Address Information

No manual. Direct inquiries to: Joan K. Austin, Department of Psychiatry, Mental Health, and Nursing, Indiana University School of Nursing, 1111 Middle Drive, Indianapolis, IN 46202-5243, (317) 274-8254, iszd100@iupui.edu.

Purpose

The CATIS was developed to assess how favorably or unfavorably children feel about having a chronic physical condition.

Format, Administration, and Scoring

The CATIS is a self-report measure that has been used with children ages 8 to 17. It consists of 13 items on which children rate their feelings about having a condition on a 5-point Likert scale, both what the feelings are like (e.g., good to bad, fair to unfair, sad to happy) and how often the feelings occur (e.g., never to very often). It is not specific to any illness or chronic health condition, and has been used with children with asthma, epilepsy, and diabetes. The measure reportedly has a third-grade reading level, and children respond independently with an interviewer nearby to answer questions that may arise. Eight items are reverse scored, and item scores are summed and divided by 13 to yield one total score (ranging from 1–5). Higher scores indicate more favorable attitudes toward illness. Example items include:

> How bad or good do you feel it is to have (chronic condition)?
>
> How often do you feel sad about being sick?
>
> How often do you feel different from others because of your (chronic condition)?

Psychometric Information

Initial items of the CATIS were developed from literature reviews and authors' experiences. There were 16 original items that were thought to measure children's attitudes toward their illness, but the number of items was subsequently reduced to 13 following psychometric evaluation. Internal consistency reliabilities have ranged from .77 to .89, and test-retest reliability (2-week interval) ranging from .77 to .80. Regarding construct validity of the CATIS, the authors noted that children's attitudes were significantly negatively correlated with measures of psychosocial adaptation, depression, and behavior problems. Furthermore, children's attitudes were strongly positively correlated with self-concept. Factor analysis revealed support of a one-factor structure accounting for 53% of the variance. Descriptive data have been reported for children with asthma, epilepsy, and diabetes.

Comment

The CATIS is an easy to complete questionnaire assessing children's attitudes toward illness. It has been used with children and adolescents and is reportedly written at a third-grade level. The CATIS is non–illness-specific, and has been used with children with asthma, epilepsy, and diabetes. Given that questions are relevant to other chronic health conditions, its use with other samples should be evaluated. The authors used two standardization samples, one relatively small and the other adequately large, and the measure has been used in other investigations as well. Limited demographic information on the samples have been reported. Examination of psychometric properties of the measure indicate good internal consistency and good construct validity. Preliminary results of test-retest reliability were also satisfactory. Overall, the CATIS appears to be valuable for both clinicians and researchers interested in examining children's own attitudes toward living with a chronic condition.

Relevant References

Austin, J. K. (1996). A model of family adaptation to new-onset childhood epilepsy. *Journal of Neuroscience Nursing, 28,* 82–92.

Austin, J. K., Dunn, D. W., Huster, G. A., & Rose, D. F. (in press). Development of scales to measure psychosocial care needs of children with seizures and their parents. *Journal of Neuroscience Nursing.*

Austin, J. K., & Huberty, T. J. (1993). Development of the child attitude toward illness scale. *Journal of Pediatric Psychology, 18,* 467–480.

Child Satisfaction Questionnaire (CSQ)

L. Rifkin, 1988

Manual and Address Information

No manual. Direct inquiries to: Catherine C. Lewis, University of California at San Francisco, 400 Parnassus Avenue, A-204, Box 0314, San Francisco, CA 94143.

Purpose

Developed for use with 6- to 14-year-old children, the CSQ assesses satisfaction with physicians following a well-child medical office visit.

Format, Administration, Scoring

The CSQ is a self-administered (for children with adequate reading skills) or interviewer administered (for younger children) 12-item questionnaire. It is administered immediately after a child's medical outpatient office visit. Children read each item and indicate their level of agreement using a 5-point Likert-type scale (1 = not at all true to 5 = really a lot). Size-graded circles are used to assist nonreaders in responding to the items. All items are positively worded and their aggregate yields a total CSQ score (range = 12–60). Administration time is approximately 15 minutes. Sample items include:

> I got along well with this doctor.
> The doctor explained things so I could remember them.
> When I was done seeing the doctor, I felt better about my health.
> This doctor understood what I was trying to say.

The authors reported that a 19-item version of the CSQ can be used with adolescents and may add important information about their satisfaction with the physician's communication skills. The additional 7 items are all negatively worded and were deleted from the final CSQ version because younger children had difficulty understanding them. Preliminary factor analysis of the 19-item version yielded two factors: Physician-Child Rapport and Physician Communication Skills.

Psychometric Information

CSQ items initially were generated from adult patient and parent satisfaction measures, children's attitudes measures, and interviews with children and health professionals. A panel of pediatricians and psychologists reviewed the items for appropriateness and a 44-item measure was subsequently field tested with 75 children (ages 6–14) following an ambulatory pediatric clinic visit. Ethnicity breakdown was as follows: 43% White, 25% Black, 17% Hispanic, and 12% Asian.

Internal consistency (Cronbach's alpha) was .89 for both the 12-item and 19-item versions, and .89 for the two subscales of the 19-item CSQ. The authors reported some preliminary evidence for an association between CSQ scores and a measure of physician attributes.

Comment

While we agree that the measurement of children's satisfaction with health care services represents an important aspect of clinical care and outcome assessment, we cannot recommend the CSQ for clinical use at this time. In reviewing the items and response format it is not entirely convincing that the CSQ actually measures satisfaction rather than some other aspect of the child-physician interaction. Indeed, the measure may simply be mislabeled. Furthermore, the authors noted that the factor analysis of the CSQ was performed on only 75 children and, consequently, should be considered very exploratory in nature. Clarification of its content and construct validity is necessary, and additional psychometric evaluation of the CSQ versions (numerical rating scale, size-graded circle version, 19-item version, 12-item version) with larger and more diverse samples of children should be undertaken.

Relevant References

Rifkin, L., Wolf, M. H., Lewis, C. C., & Pantell, R. H. (1988). Children's perceptions of physicians and medical care: Two measures. *Journal of Pediatric Psychology, 13,* 247–254.

Child Vulnerability Scale (CVS)

M. Thomasgard, 1995; B. W. C. Forsyth, 1996

Manual and Address Information

No manual. Direct inquiries to: Michael Thomasgard, Behavioral-Developmental Pediatrics, Columbus Children's Hospital, 700 Children's Drive, Columbus, OH 43205-2696.

Purpose

The CVS is a paper-and-pencil measure that is completed by parents of children ages 4 to 8. It was designed to measure parents' perceptions of their child's vulnerability, related to both the vulnerable child syndrome and general concerns about a child's health.

Format, Administration, and Scoring

The CVS has been used with healthy children as well as those with chronic health conditions, and it also has been used to examine the relationship between parental overprotection and parental perception of child vulnerability to illness or injury. The most recent version of the CVS consists of eight items to which parents respond on a 4-point Likert scale (0 = definitely false to 3 = definitely true). The eight items are summed to yield one total score, and higher scores reflect increased vulnerability. A cut-off score of greater than or equal to 10 has been suggested to indicate high vulnerability. Sample items include:

> In general my child seems less healthy than other children.
> I get concerned about circles under my child's eyes.
> My child seems to have more accidents and injuries than other children.

Psychometric Information

The CVS was first used in an investigation of mothers' perception of children's vulnerability in a sample of children hospitalized for infection. The scale originally consisted of 12 items. The 12-item version was used in other studies, both with healthy and physically ill children. However, until recently no formal investigation of the measure's psychometric properties had been completed. In an attempt to standardize the CVS, 1,095 mothers' responses to the 12-item measure were examined. Correlations between items and the two factors considered to contribute to perception of vulnerability were computed. Analyses indicated that 3 items did not correlate significantly with either factor, and that 1 of the items with a weak correlation added little information to the total score. As a result, the scale was revised to contain 8 items.

Internal consistency of the 8-item measure has been reported to be .73 and .74 across two separate studies, and test-retest reliability was found to be .84. Concurrent validity of the CVS was examined through correlations with child behavior problems as measured by the Child Behavior Checklist and number of medical office visits by the child. Both were found to be significantly associated with scores on the CVS. CVS scores also have been found to positively correlate with a measure of parental overprotectiveness.

Comment

The CVS is a short, easy to complete self-report measure that can be used for assessing parents' views related to the vulnerability of their child. The most appropriate age ranges for its use are unclear, yet items suggest children must be at least close to 2 years old. Its use with parents of adolescents has not been reported. It has been administered to multiple large samples of parents of children with varying degrees of illnesses (healthy through hospitalized for infections). Results across several studies indicate very acceptable internal consistency and reliability, and concurrent validity as well. Standardization samples have primarily consisted of parents utilizing health care for their child, limiting the measure's external validity. Overall, the CVS appears to be a useful instrument in clinical and research settings in which one is interested in examining parents' perceptions of their child's vulnerability.

Relevant References

Forsyth, B., Horwitz, S. M., Leventhal, J. M., Burger, J., & Leaf, P. J. (1996). The Child Vulnerability Scale: An instrument to measure parental perceptions of child vulnerability. *Journal of Pediatric Psychology, 21,* 89–101.

Thomasgard, M., & Metz, W. P. (1995). The vulnerable child syndrome revisited. *Journal of Developmental and Behavioral Pediatrics, 16,* 47–53.

Children's Eating Attitude Test (ChEAT)

M. J. Maloney, 1988

Manual and Address Information

No manual. Direct inquiries to: Michael J. Maloney, Department of Psychiatry, Children's Hospital Medical Center, 333 Burnet Avenue, Cincinnati, OH 45229-3039, (513) 559-4788.

Purpose

The ChEAT is a modified version of the Eating Attitude Test (EAT). It was designed to assess eating attitudes (i.e., food preoccupation, anorexia, bulimia, concerns about being overweight) in children ages 8 through 13.

Format, Administration, and Scoring

The ChEAT is a 26-item self-report questionnaire. Children respond to statements on a 6-point Likert scale (always through never). The ChEAT can be administered individually or in a group format, and reportedly takes approximately 35 minutes to complete. Extreme responses in the anorexic direction are scored as a 3 (engage in dieting behavior: always = 3), with the next symptomatic choice scored as a 2, and the next scored as a 1. The remaining three choices are scored as a 0. Item scores are totaled (possible total scores range from 0–78) and scores ≥20 are suggestive of anorexia nervosa. Sample items include:

> I am scared about being overweight.
> I think a lot about being thinner.
> I feel uncomfortable after eating sweets.
> I have the urge to vomit after eating.

Psychometric Information

The ChEAT was developed as a modification of the original 40-item EAT. A factor analysis of the EAT, designed for use by adults and adolescents, indicated that 14 of the original items did not load on any of the EAT's three factors (avoidance of high-caloric foods and preoccupation with being thin, bulimia and food preoccupation, and self-control of eating). The language and wording of the remaining 26 items were simplified for use with younger children, resulting in the ChEAT. For example, "preoccupied" was changed to "think a lot about."

Satisfactory psychometric properties of the EAT had been demonstrated prior to its revision. Analyses have also been conducted on the ChEAT, using data from 318 elementary school children divided between the third, fourth, fifth, and sixth grades in one investigation, and 308 middle school girls in another study. The test-retest reliability of the ChEAT was found to be .81. Internal consistency reliability coefficients exceeded .68 across grades, with the exception of one statement that was removed from one investigation, and three statements that were removed by other investigators. In general, higher internal consistencies were seen in responses of older children. Regarding concurrent validity, higher ChEAT scores were significantly correlated with weight management and body dissatisfaction.

A factor analysis using the 26-item version of the ChEAT indicated seven factors that accounted for 61% of the variance. In examining the variance accounted for by each factor, in addition to each item's loadings, four main factors emerged: dieting, restricting and purging, food preoccupation, and oral control.

Comment

The ChEAT is an easy to use self-report instrument that appears to be a developmentally appropriate modification of the EAT. It aids in the assessment of food preoccupation, dieting patterns, and eating attitudes in children. Although the language of the EAT was specifically modified for children in forming the ChEAT, analyses of reading levels of the new instrument have not been reported. Given the higher internal consistencies for older children, it appears that the measure may be more appropriate for use with children ages 8 to 11, or adolescents. The ChEAT was standardized on two groups of "non–clinic-referred" school children, thereby limiting investigation of its predictive utility in clinical populations. Future research incorporating other populations (i.e., adolescents with anorexia or bulimia) would allow for the testing of its utility as a clinical or diagnostic tool. Similar to the EAT, satisfactory reliability and internal consistency have been demonstrated for the ChEAT. Results indicate, however, that the 23-item version may be more reliable in terms of its internal consistency. Furthermore, the authors currently suggest a cut-off score for anorexia, yet provide no definitive scoring information related to other types of eating disorders.

Relevant References

Maloney, M. J., McGuire, J. B., & Daniels, S. R. (1988). Reliability testing of a children's version of the Eating Attitude Test. *Journal of the American Academy of Child and Adolescent Psychiatry, 27,* 541–543.

Smolak, L., & Levine, M. (1994). Psychometric properties of the Children's Eating Attitudes Test. *International Journal of Eating Disorders, 16,* 275–282.

Children's Health Care Attitudes Questionnaire (CHCAQ)

J. P. Bush, 1987

Manual and Address Information

No manual. Direct inquiries to: Joseph P. Bush, The Fielding Institute, 2112 Santa Barbara Street, Santa Barbara, CA 93105-3538, (805) 687-1099, jbush@fielding.edu.

Purpose

The CHCAQ was developed to assess children's attitudes toward different areas of health care including providers, settings, and procedures. Specifically, authors of the measure were interested in investigating the effect of attitude on both the approach of children's health care situations and their overall experiences.

Format, Administration, and Scoring

The CHCAQ is a 24-item self-report measure. For younger children, the measure may be verbally administered. In their standardization sample, the authors found that many children under the age of 9 required assistance in completing the CHCAQ. Together with another measure of pain perceptions, the CHCAQ took an average of 12 minutes to complete. Ninety-five percent of children over the age of 5 were reportedly able to complete the measure with assistance.

The CHCAQ consists of eight items on each of three dimensions: like-dislike, attributed effectiveness-ineffectiveness, and approach-avoidance. Attitudes toward doctors, dentists, nurses, hospitals, medicine, shots, blood tests, and surgery are assessed within each dimension. Items are on a 5-point multiple-choice/Likert-scale format. In addition to the written response choices, children are presented with many pictures and graphic symbols to aid their understanding of the questions. For example, like-dislike questions are accompanied with an array of five faces ranging from a smile to a frown.

Sample items include:

How do you like taking medicine?

a. I really hate it.
b. I don't like it.
c. I don't like it or hate it.
d. I like it.
e. I really like it a lot.

When people are sick and the doctor gives them a shot, what happens?

a. It always helps them.
b. It usually helps them.
c. It might help them or it might not.
d. It usually makes them worse.
e. They get worse.

Psychometric Information

The CHCAQ was first used in an investigation of children's health care attitudes and their perceptions of pain. Three hundred-eight children (ages 5–19) were included in the standardization sample. Means and standard deviations have been reported for five different age groups. A factor analysis was conducted and the three dimensions were found to account for 35% of the variance.

Internal consistency estimates for the CHCAQ factors across several studies have ranged from .57 to .80, and test-retest reliability (2-week interval) has ranged from .69 to .84. Regarding construct validity, results have suggested that children who rate stimuli as more painful on the CHCAQ like health care less and are more avoidant of health care, and children with more negative health care attitudes are likely to report more distress during medical treatment. Children's scores across the different CHCAQ scales also were found to be mediated by different intrinsic and extrinsic variables, with no one variable consistently correlating with all scales. Also, studies have found a positive relationship between CHCAQ scores and mothers' health care attitudes using a modification of the CHCAQ.

Comment

The CHCAQ is a child-friendly measure that allows assessment of a wide age range of children. It is easily administered, requiring approximately 10 minutes to complete. Although data on ages most likely to need assistance have been gathered, a formal investigation of the reading level of the questionnaire has not been reported. Preliminary psychometric data across several samples have shown adequate reliability and validity, and normative data have been reported. Further assessment of the CHCAQ's psychometric properties with more diverse samples will provide further validation of the measure's utility. For instance, the studies to date have used children recruited at a science museum health fair, private school setting, and pediatrician well-child visit. Extending its use to the inpatient pediatric setting or with children who have chronic health conditions would provide more useful information about its ecological validity. Moreover, examination of its cultural specificity is needed. Overall, the CHCAQ is a useful assessment tool and should facilitate research designed to enhance our understanding of how children perceive specific aspects of their health care.

Relevant References

Bachanas, P. J., & Roberts, M. C. (1995). Factors affecting children's attitudes toward health care and responses to stressful medical procedures. *Journal of Pediatric Psychology, 20,* 261–275.

Bush, J. P., & Holmbeck, G. N. (1987). Children's attitudes about health care: Initial development of a questionnaire. *Journal of Pediatric Psychology, 12,* 429–443.

Hackworth, S. R., & McMahon, R. J. (1991). Factors mediating children's health care attitudes. *Journal of Pediatric Psychology, 16,* 69–85.

Children's Health Locus of Control Scale (CHLC)

G. S. Parcel, 1978

Manual and Address Information

No manual. Direct inquiries to: G. S. Parcel, School Health Programs, University of Texas Medical Branch, Galveston, TX, 77550.

Purpose

The CHLC scale was designed to assess children's locus of control related to several aspects of health.

Format, Administration, and Scoring

The CHLC is a paper-and-pencil measure consisting of 20 items that children respond to as either "true" or "false." Responses indicating an internal locus of control are scored a 2 and those in the external direction are assigned a 1. All 20 items are summed to yield one total score. Higher scores indicate orientation to a more internal health locus of control. The CHLC scale has been administered to children ages 5 to 16, yet it is unclear if children are supposed to read it independently, or complete the measure with assistance. Sample items include:

> Good health comes from being lucky.
> It is my mother's job to keep me from getting sick.
> I can do many things to prevent accidents.

Psychometric Information

The CHLC scale was first examined using a sample of 168 children, ages 7 to 12. The scale originally consisted of 30 items to which children responded their agreement (yes or no). Item analysis indicated low discrimination between internal and external control for 10 of the items, resulting in their elimination. The revised 20-item questionnaire was then standardized on a second group of children (ages 7–12). A factor analysis revealed three main factors: powerful others, chance control, and internal control. The wording of several items was then adjusted due to relatively low factor loadings for those items. Regarding internal consistency, Kuder-Richardson coefficients ranging from .72 to .75 were reported. Test-retest reliability (6-week interval) was .62. There has also been support for construct validity, with low to moderate correlations between the CHLC scale and a standardized measure of children's general locus of control (Nowicki-Strickland Internal-External Control Scale). The CHLC has been used with pediatric samples, and was specifically employed in an investigation of the relationship between illness-related concept attainment and perceived control over health. Means and standard deviations for both healthy and chronically ill children have been reported for four different age groups.

Comment

The CHLC scale is a self-report measure for assessment of a wide age range of children. The format of its administration with younger children is unclear, and formal investigation of the measure's reading level has not been reported. Psychometric data utilizing an adequate sample indicate acceptable reliability and validity, and normative data have been reported. Furthermore, the measure has been used successfully with both healthy and chronically ill children. Overall, the CHLC scale is a useful means of exploring children's locus of control related to health issues. It appears to be promising for use both in clinical and research settings.

Relevant References

Parcel, G. S., & Meyer, M. P. (1978). Development of an instrument to measure children's health locus of control. *Health Education Monographs, 6*, 149–159.

Shagena, M. M., Sandler, H. K., & Perrin, E. C. (1988). Concepts of illness and perception of control in healthy children and in children with chronic illness. *Journal of Developmental and Behavioral Pediatrics, 9*, 252–256.

Children's Hope Scale (CHS)

C. R. Snyder, 1994

Manual and Address Information

No manual. Direct inquiries to: C. R. Snyder, Department of Psychology, University of Kansas, Lawrence, KS 66045, (785) 864-9855.

Purpose

The CHS was developed to measure the perceived hope of children and adolescents.

Format, Administration, and Scoring

Developed for use with children ages 8 to 16, the CHS is a downward extension of the adult Hope Scale. It contains six items to which children respond using a Likert-type scale (1 = none of the time to 6 = all of the time). A factor analysis yielded one factor that measures the agency component (three items) of hope and one factor that measures the pathways component of hope (three items). A child's belief that a goal can be met is referred to as agency, whereas a child's perception that available strategies can be used to achieve a goal is referred to as pathways. Sample items include:

> When I have a problem, I can come up with lots of ways to solve it.
> I think the things I have done in the past will help me in the future.

Psychometric Information

The CHS has been used with children who have psychological disorders and chronic health conditions (e.g., sickle cell disease) and with children without chronic conditions. Internal consistency estimates have ranged from .70 to .86, and 1-month test-retest reliability has ranged from .71 to .73. Regarding convergent validity, the CHS is positively correlated with measures of children's perceived self-competence (.22–.59), parental hope (.37–.53), children's internal locus of control (.29–.35), and academic achievement (.50), and negatively correlated with anxiety (−.23 — −.34) and depression (−.04 — −.48). There is some empirical evidence that children's coping strategies moderate the relationship between hope and anxiety, with high hope and more active coping strategies being associated with less anxiety.

Comment

The CHS is a recently developed instrument designed to measure a construct in children that has been found to be significantly related to better physical health in adults. This is an important new development when one considers that hope is a relatively stable construct by middle childhood. Preliminary psychometric data on the CHS are encouraging, although additional validation studies with different pediatric populations are needed. Larger sample sizes should be incorporated into such studies and consideration should be given to examining developmental differences in the hope construct.

Relevant References

Lewis, H. A., & Kliewer, W. (1996). Hope, coping, and adjustment among children with sickle cell disease: Tests of mediator and moderator models. *Journal of Pediatric Psychology, 21*, 25–41.

Snyder, C. R., Rapoff, M., Ware, L., Hoza, B., Pelham, W. E., Danovsky, M., Highberger, L.,

Rubinstein, H., & Stahl, K. J. (1994, October). *The development and validation of the Children's Hope Scale.* Presented at the first Kansas Conference in Clinical Child Psychology, Lawrence, KS.

Death Anxiety Questionnaire (DAQ)

H. R. Conte, 1975

Manual and Address Information

No manual. Direct inquiries to: H. R. Conte, Department of Psychiatry, Bronx Municipal Hospital Center, Pelham Parkway South & Eastchester Road, Bronx, NY 10461.

Purpose

The DAQ was designed to assess a wide variety of feelings separate from general anxiety that may be related to death and dying. It was developed for use by healthy individuals of all ages (primarily adults).

Format, Administration, and Scoring

The DAQ is a self-report measure consisting of 15 items related to attitudes about death and dying. Respondents indicate the degree that they worry about each of the items (0 = not at all to 2 = very much). The final shortened version with 15 items has a range of scores from 0 to 30. Sample items include:

> Do you worry that dying may be very painful?
>
> Does the thought of leaving loved ones behind when you die disturb you?
>
> Do you worry that those you care about may not remember you after your death?

Psychometric Information

There were 24 items on the original version of the DAQ. Original items were developed from open-ended interviews with senior citizens, and college and graduate students. Item analyses eliminated items that assisted little in discrimination among individuals, resulting in 15 items. Split-half reliability was then examined and was found to be .76. Item-total correlations ranged from .18 to .74.

A second analysis of the DAQ based on responses from graduate students found 2-week test-retest reliability to be .87. A principal components factor analysis revealed five factors that accounted for 64.3% of the variance, four of which were easily labeled: fear of the unknown aspects of death (five items), fear of suffering involved in the process of dying (three items), fear of loneliness at the time of death (two items), and reflects interpersonal aspects of death anxiety (three items). Concurrent validity was evaluated by examining the correlation between the DAQ and the Albert Einstein College of Medicine Depression Scale (.74) and Taylor Manifest Anxiety Scale (.53).

Comment

The DAQ is a short paper-and-pencil instrument designed to assess anxiety related to attitudes of death and dying. The measure appears to be face valid, and has undergone several tests of its reliability and validity resulting in satisfactory test-retest reliability, split-half reliability, and concurrent validity. The DAQ was originally developed for use with adults without chronic disease; yet it has also been used in a study examining death and dying in children with cancer. The DAQ was reportedly adapted for its use with children, but psychometric properties of the revised child version have not been reported. Similarly, it is unclear how much the wording of questions was changed, and for what ages and reading level the revised DAQ is most appropriate. In addition, given that the measure was initially designed for use with adults without chronic disease, differences between people with and without chronic disease have not been reported. Caution should therefore be used when applying the DAQ to either an ill or a child population. Psychometric properties of the DAQ would need to be evaluated prior to using the measure in either of such situations.

Relevant References

Conte, H. R., Weiner, M. B., & Plutchik, R. (1982). Measuring death anxiety: Conceptual, psychometric, and factor-analytic aspects. *Journal of Personality and Social Psychology, 43,* 775–785.

Koocher, G. P., O'Malley, J. E., Gogan, J. L., & Foster, D. J. (1980). Psychological adjustment among pediatric cancer survivors. *Journal of Child Psychology and Psychiatry, 21,* 163–173.

Diabetes Opinion Survey (DOS)

S. B. Johnson, 1985

Manual and Address Information

No manual. Direct inquiries to: Suzanne B. Johnson, Center for Pediatric Psychology and Family Studies, P.O. Box 100165, University of Florida Health Science Center, Gainesville, FL 32610-1065, (352) 395-0490, sjohnson@hp.ufl.edu.

Purpose

The DOS was developed to assess diabetes-specific attitudes of children and adolescents. A similar measure, the Parents Diabetes Opinion Survey (PDOS), was developed specifically for parents.

Format, Administration, and Scoring

The self-administered DOS (35 items) and PDOS (55 items) contain statements to which children and parents indicate their level of agreement or disagreement using a 5-point scale (1 = strongly agree to 5 = strongly disagree). Factor analysis of the DOS has identified five constructs:

Stigma (eight items): how different child feels from peers; feels others treat him/her differently

Rule Orientation (eight items): how rigidly child adheres to rules about managing diabetes

Sick Role (five items): needs special attention or treatment because of diabetes

Family Interruption (nine items): how disruptive diabetes has been on child's parents and family

Divine Intervention (five items): how child feels about diabetes as punishment for sins and whether God can cure diabetes

Factor analysis of the PDOS has identified eight constructs:

Manipulativeness (nine items): extent to which parent perceives child as using diabetes to manipulate others

Rule Orientation/High Supervision (nine items): adherence to strict rules about managing diabetes

Stigma (seven items): extent to which parent feels self, child, or family is treated differently by others

Divine Intervention (five items): beliefs that child's diabetes is a religious test or that God can cure diabetes

Attitudes Toward Medical Staff (seven items): how parent feels toward health care staff

Reactions: Observation/Detection (six items): extent to which parent believes she/he can identify blood glucose highs and lows in child

Sweet Consumption (three items): extent to which parent believes child should be allowed to have sweets

Family Interruption (nine items): how disruptive diabetes has been on parents and family

In addition to the foregoing scales, the DOS and PDOS both contain a Lie Scale. Scores are obtained by summing the items within each scale, with lower scores reflecting greater acknowledgment of the attitude assessed. Administration time is approximately 10 minutes for both versions.

Psychometric Information

Items were generated from clinical literature reviews and interviews with patients and health providers. Initially, the authors developed 152 items and 10 concepts for the DOS, administered it to 157 children and adolescents, revised it, and administered the revision to a new sample of 155 children and adolescents. Subsequent factor analysis on data from 281 children and adolescents (ages 6–19) yielded a five-factor solution. The PDOS was developed in the same manner (138 items) and administered to over 750 parents (mothers and fathers) of children with diabetes across three samples. Factor analysis of the PDOS produced eight factors.

Internal consistency reliabilities (Cronbach's alpha) for the DOS have been reported as follows: Stigma (.76–.83), Rule Orientation (.73–.81), Sick Role (.63–.72), Family Interruption (.70 to .79), and Divine Intervention (.76–.84). Alpha coefficients for the PDOS range as follows: Manipulativeness (.83–.87), Rule Orientation/High Supervision (.69–.78), Stigma (.69–.85), Divine Intervention (.79–.88), Attitudes Toward Medical Staff (.67–.79), Reactions: Observation/Detection (.64–.71), Sweet Consumption (.69–.77), and Family Interruption (.76–.86).

Comment

Both the DOS and PDOS have undergone considerable empirical scrutiny since their development in 1985. Generally, they are valid and reliable measures of children's and parents' attitudes toward diabetes. Some scales appear to have consistently good internal consistency (DOS Stigma, DOS and PDOS Divine Intervention, PDOS Manipulativeness, PDOS Family Interruption), whereas others have yielded alpha coefficients lower than desirable (DOS Sick Role, PDOS Reactions: Observation/Detection). Test-retest reliability have not been reported, although longitudinal studies using these instruments have been conducted. Unfortunately, sample characteristics have not been specified and it is not possible to determine the degree to which the factor structures of the DOS and PDOS are stable across culturally diverse groups of children and parents. Given the prominence of child and parent attitudes in several health-related conceptual models, the DOS and PDOS provide researchers and clinicians with well-developed tools for measuring disease-specific attitudes and beliefs.

Relevant References

Johnson, S. B. (1995). Managing insulin-dependent diabetes mellitus in adolescence: A developmental perspective. In J. L. Wallander & L. J. Siegel (Eds.), *Adolescent health problems: Behavioral perspectives* (pp. 265–288). NY: Guilford Press.

Enuresis Nuisance and Tolerance Scales

R. T. T. Morgan, 1975

Manual and Address Information

No manual. Address unknown.

Purpose

The Enuresis Nuisance and Tolerance Scales were developed in order to assess parental attitudes toward enuresis.

Format, Administration, and Scoring

The Enuresis Nuisance and Tolerance Scales are self-report measures completed by parents of children with enuresis. The Tolerance Scale is comprised of 20 items to which parents respond either "yes" or "no." Each item is assigned a scale value, and the parents' score is the median scale value of all items that are responded to with a "yes"; higher scores are indicative of intolerance.

The Nuisance Scale consists of 25 items to which parents are asked to indicate whether situations are considered worse to deal with than enuresis. The greater number of problems marked to be worse to deal with indicate a lower enuresis nuisance value.

Sample items include:

> Children could stop wetting the bed if they tried hard enough.
>
> I try to help him (her) to not be upset by his (her) bedwetting.
>
> I worry more about my child's happiness than about a few extra sheets to wash.

Psychometric Information

The Tolerance Scale was initially completed by 134 mothers of enuretic children. Demographic composition of the standardization sample is unknown. Scale values were assigned on the basis of item-ratings by 40 independent judges (student social workers). Quartiles of median scale values were computed and split-half reliability was found to be .43. The Nuisance Scale was standardized on 108 mothers of enuretic children. Frequencies of items selected as being worse to deal with than enuresis were computed. No other tests of reliability, validity, or internal consistency have been reported.

Comment

The Enuresis Nuisance and Tolerance Scales are self-report measures used to assess parental attitudes of enuresis. The scales have been used in various treatment programs and research studies. Tolerance has been found to be related to socioeconomic status and premature withdrawal from treatment. Nuisance has been correlated with type of enuresis and children's anxiety. Although the Enuresis Nuisance and Tolerance Scales have provided significant contributions in terms of parental attitudes in the treatment of enuresis, further examination of reliability and validity is warranted. Specifically, internal consistencies, and concurrent and divergent validities have not been reported. Furthermore, little information is known about the use of these scales with ethnically diverse populations.

Relevant References

Morgan, R. T. T., & Young, G. C. (1975). Parental attitudes and the conditioning treatment of childhood enuresis. *Behavior Research and Therapy, 13,* 197–199.

Intentions to Engage in AIDS-Risk Situations

V. Slonim-Nevo, 1996

Manual and Address Information

No manual. Direct inquiries to: Slonim-Nevo, Ben-Gurion University of the Negev, Department of Social Work, 84105 Beer Sheva, Israel, or Wendy Auslander, Washington University, George Warren Brown School of Social Work, Campus Box 1196, St. Louis, MO, 63130.

Purpose

The Intentions to Engage in AIDS-Risk Situations questionnaire was designed to assess adolescents' coping during high-risk situations, including unsafe sexual intercourse, intravenous drug use, and pressure to take drugs and drink alcohol.

Format, Administration, and Scoring

The Intentions to Engage in AIDS-Risk Situations questionnaire consists of nine items or short scenarios to which adolescents indicate their ability to resist peer influence, as well as skills in dealing with problems related to risky sexual activity and drug use. Items are on a 3-point forced-choice scale. Adolescents are instructed to choose only one of three possible answers: one correct response exhibiting good skills in coping with the high-risk situation, one incorrect response that could potentially lead to unsafe sex or drug use, or one response indicating that the respondent did not know how to deal with the scenario. Total score is the number of correct responses across the nine items, with higher scores indicating greater coping ability in high-risk situations. One sample item includes:

> You and your partner are having sex. You prefer to use a condom, but your partner says that condoms make sex less fun and refuses to use them. What will you do?

1. Agree to have sex without a condom.
2. Explain why you want to use a condom and refuse to have sex without it.
3. You are not sure how to handle this.

Psychometric Information

The original version of the Intentions to Engage in AIDS-Risk Situations questionnaire consisted of 12 items or situations. Scenarios were developed through pilot work with youths in foster care including formal and informal assessments, and discussions with counselors and staff. The measure was standardized on a group of 358 adolescents (ages 11–18) living in a residential center. Adolescents had been placed in the residential center for both abuse/neglect and juvenile delinquency. A principal components analysis resulted in a single-factor solution, using 9 of the 12 items and accounting for 44% of the variance. The 3 items were eliminated due to low loadings on the single factor and because they lowered the alpha for the entire measure when included. Internal consistency and test-retest reliability for the 9-item version were .84 and .86, respectively. Descriptive data for the sample have been provided. Scores on the Intentions to Engage in AIDS-Risk Situations questionnaire were significantly correlated with measures of adolescents' behaviors.

Comment

Descriptions of specific administration and reading level of the Intentions to Engage in AIDS-Risk Situations questionnaire have not been reported. While the measure has been used with adolescents ages 11 to 18, situations may be unfamiliar to younger adolescents, and help with administration may be necessary. The Intentions to Engage in AIDS-Risk Situations questionnaire has been standardized on a large sample of adolescents, yet results are not yet generalizable beyond a residential population. However, the authors have noted that the scale has been used with in- and out-of-school adolescents in Zambia and also with adolescents in foster care, but these data are not yet published. Reliability of the measure is very satisfactory. Overall, the Intentions to Engage in AIDS-Risk Situations questionnaire is a useful instrument for both clinicians and researchers examining adolescents' intentions to engage in such behaviors.

Relevant References

Paniagua, F. A., O'Boyle, M., Wagner, K. D., Ramirez, S. Z., Holmes, W. D., Nieto, J. F., & Smith, E. M. (1994). AIDS-related items for developing an AIDS questionnaire for children and adolescents. *Journal of Adolescent Research, 9,* 311–339.

Slonim-Nevo, V., Auslander, W. F., & Ozawa, M. N. (1995). Educational options and AIDS-related behaviors among troubled adolescents. *Journal of Pediatric Psychology, 20,* 41–60.

Slonim-Nevo, V., Auslander, W. F., & Ozawa, M. N. (1996). The long-term impact of AIDS-preventive interventions for delinquent and abused adolescents. *Journal of Adolescence, 31,* 409–421.

Parent Participation Attitude Scale (PPAS)

F. Seidl, 1967

Manual and Address Information

No manual. Direct inquiries to: Frederick W. Seidl, 359 Baldy Hall, University of Buffalo, Buffalo, NY, 14260.

Purpose

The PPAS was designed to measure attitudes of nursing personnel toward parent participation in hospital pediatric programs for children between the ages of 1 and 4.

Format, Administration, and Scoring

The PPAS is a 24-item self-report measure that is administered to nursing personnel. The respondent is asked to rate 24 statements concerning parent participation in hospital pediatric programs on a 4-point Likert scale (A = strongly agree to D = strongly disagree). Sample items include:

> The nurse-patient relationship is frequently enhanced by parental involvement.
> When death occurs, it is usually better for parents to be absent from the room.
> Generally, parents should not be told the diagnosis and the implications of the diagnosis in terminal cases.
> Parents should be allowed to visit the hospital whenever they wish.

Psychometric Information

The 24 items were generated via a review of the literature and nurse-judge validation. Gill (1987) documented the construct validity of the PPAS. Eight factors/constructs were labeled as parental visiting, homelike atmosphere, parental adjustment, parental support-child negative condition, parental comforting, emotional support-child accompaniment, and emotional support-parent.

The PPAS was standardized on 231 nursing personnel at the Children's Hospital of Buffalo, New York. The sample consisted of 75 nurses aides, 27 practical nurses, 99 staff nurses, 16 head nurses, and 14 instructors, supervisors, and administrators. Data were also collected on the family life cycle of the respondents' families. Split-half reliability was .37, and internal consistency was measured to be .75.

Comment

Although the PPAS was developed over 30 years ago, limited information about its use is available. There are psychometric concerns in terms of the measure's internal consistency as a tool for the assessment of attitudes of nursing personnel toward parent participation. Further studies on the reliability and validity on this scale would be useful prior to its use for either clinical or research purposes.

Relevant References

Gill, K. M. (1987). Nurses' attitudes toward parent participation: Personal and professional characteristics. *Children's Health Care, 15,* 149–151.

Seidle, F. W., & Pillitteri, A. (1967). Development of an attitude scale on parent perception. *Nursing Research, 16,* 71–73.

Parental Attitudes Toward Children with Handicaps (PATCH) Questionnaire

P. L. Rosenbaum, 1987

Manual and Address Information

No manual. Direct inquiries to: Peter Rosenbaum, Neurodevelopmental Clinical Research Unit, McMaster University, Building T-16, Room 126, 128 Main Street, West Hamilton, Ontario, Canada L8S 4L4, rosenbau@fhs.mcmaster.ca.

Purpose

The PATCH questionnaire is a paper-and-pencil measure that is completed by parents of able-bodied children to assess their attitudes toward children with handicapping conditions. It was designed to examine the relationship between parental and children's attitudes toward children with disabilities, and to assess changes in parental attitudes as a function of their children's experiences with peers who have disabilities.

Format, Administration, and Scoring

The PATCH comprises 30 items to which parents of preadolescent children respond on a 5-point Likert scale (0 = strongly disagree to 4 = strongly agree). Group administration seems possible, although all published reports describe individual administration of the measure. Parents are asked to indicate their agreement or disagreement with the statements containing references to children with handicaps. The authors acknowledge that some controversy exists in the use of the term *handicapped* (vs. *disabled* or *impaired*), although the term is used by the World Health Organization to refer to the social consequences of disability or impairment. Essentially, they have attempted to avoid reference to a specific disability or disorder by using the more generic *handicapped* term. It is noteworthy that the PATCH has been translated into Italian and Portuguese. Two sample items are provided to familiarize the parent with the questionnaire format. The questionnaire also asks parents to indicate if they know someone who is disabled (spouse, relative, friend). The questionnaire takes approximately 10 minutes to complete.

The PATCH questionnaire contains an equal number of positively and negatively worded items. Individual item scores range from 0 to 4, and negative statements are inversely coded. A total score is obtained by adding the item scores, dividing by the number of items, and multiplying by 10. Higher scores reflect more positive attitudes. Example items include:

> I would be pleased if a handicapped child invited my son or daughter to his/her house.
> I would feel comfortable talking to a handicapped child I didn't know.
> I feel sorry for handicapped children.
> Handicapped children are a burden to their families.

Psychometric Information

The PATCH questionnaire was adapted from a children's attitude measure (CATCH) and is based on a three-component conceptual model comprising affective, behavioral intention, and cognitive dimensions. The development of items appears to have been conceptually driven although information about how many items were in the original pool and how they were maintained or discarded has not been specified. The initial standardization sample comprised approximately 1,700 mothers and fathers of children in fifth through eighth grades in Hamilton, Ontario. Principal components factor analysis revealed that affective and behavioral intention items loaded together, whereas items in the cognitive dimension aggregated separately. However, the authors indicate that the total score is the most meaningful unit of analysis. Distribution of scores was approximately normal for both mothers and fathers. Internal consistency analyses showed an alpha coefficient of .88 and a split-half coefficient of .85.

The authors provide support for construct validity. Specifically, hypotheses regarding the relationship between attitudes and gender and familiarity with a person with disabilities were supported. Mothers reported significantly more favorable attitudes than fathers, and parents who knew an individual with a disability had higher PATCH scores than those who did not know a person with a disability.

Comment

The PATCH is easy to complete, requires very little time, and samples a broad range of common experiences that parents and their children may encounter. The authors included a large standardization sample with mixed ethnicity. Furthermore, preliminary results suggest very acceptable internal consistency and good construct and discriminant validity. Its use has been limited to parents of preadolescent children (fifth through eighth grades) and, therefore, its utility with younger and older children should be further examined. Also, test-retest data have not been reported. Overall, the PATCH questionnaire is a useful instrument that would be of interest to clinicians and researchers examining attitudes toward children who are impaired, disabled, or handicapped.

Relevant References

King, S. M., Rosenbaum, P. L., Armstrong, R. W., & Milner, R. (1989). An epidemiological study of children's attitudes toward disability. *Developmental Medicine and Child Neurology, 31,* 237–245.

Rosenbaum, P. L., Armstrong, R. W., & King, S. M. (1987). Parental attitudes toward children with handicaps: New perspectives with a new measure. *Journal of Developmental and Behavioral Pediatrics, 8,* 327–334.

Parental Health Belief Scales

B. J. Tinsley, 1989

Manual and Address Information

No manual. Direct inquiries to: Barbara Tinsley, Healthy Families Project, Mail Stop 142, University of California, Riverside, CA 92521, (909) 787-3889, tinsley@ucrac1.ucr.edu.

Purpose

The PHB scales were designed to assess mothers' health locus of control beliefs.

Format, Administration, and Scoring

The PHB scales were developed through the modification of Parcel and Meyer's Children's Health Locus of Control Scales (1978) by rewording items to reference parents instead of children. The PHB focuses on three dimensions thought to be important in determining health locus of control: (a) mother's degree of perceived control with respect to their child's health, (b) the extent to which mothers believe that "chance" or (c) "powerful others" affect their child's health. The scale consists of 20 items to which mothers respond on a Likert scale from 1 to 6. Example items include:

> It's my job as a mother to keep my child from getting sick.
> I can do many things to fight illness in my child.
> Only a doctor or nurse keeps my child from getting sick.

Scoring information has not been provided.

Psychometric Information

The PHB scales were used in an investigation of the relationships among mothers' health locus of control beliefs, utilization of childhood preventive health services, and child health status. Specific description of administration procedures, time required to complete the measure, or reading level have not been reported. The scale was administered to 88 mothers (White and African American, low to middle income) of children ages 1 week through 20 months old. All infants were born at term without serious illness. The PHB scales were found to have test-retest reliability at the .96 level (.83–1.00 across individual items). No other reliability or validity data for the measure are reported.

Comment

Psychometric data on the PHB scales are limited to test-retest reliability, which has been indicated to be high, although the time interval was not specified. No other information related to the reliability or validity of the measure has been reported. The measure does appear to be face valid, and it was standardized on an ethnically diverse population. However, its use with older children or children with illnesses has not yet been examined. Further examination of the measure's psychometric properties, as well as its use with the previously mentioned populations is warranted prior to its use as a reliable assessment tool.

Relevant References

Howell-Koren, P. R., & Tinsley, B. R. (1990). The relationships among maternal health locus of control beliefs and expectations, pediatrician-mother communication, and maternal satisfaction with well-infant care. *Health Communication, 2,* 233–253.

Tinsley, B. J., & Holtgrave, D. R. (1989). Maternal health locus of control beliefs, utilization of childhood preventive health services, and infant health. *Journal of Developmental and Behavioral Pediatrics, 10,* 236–241.

Perceptions of Asthma Medication Scale (PAM)

L. M. DePaola, 1997

Manual and Address Information

No manual. Direct inquiries to: Michael C. Roberts, Clinical Child Psychology Program, Dole Human Development Center, University of Kansas, Lawrence, KS 66045, mroberts@ukans.edu.

Purpose

The PAM was developed to assess the perceptions that children with asthma and their parents have about the benefits and drawbacks of asthma medication.

Format, Administration, and Scoring

There are two versions of this instrument: Child's Perceptions of Asthma Medication Scale (C-PAM; 26 items) and Parent's Perceptions of Asthma Medication Scale (P-PAM; 23 items). Both PAM versions use the same 5-point Likert format (1 = really do not agree to 5 = really do agree) and are comprised of two factor-analytically derived subscales, Drawbacks (C-PAM, 15 items; P-PAM, 14 items) and Benefits (C-PAM, 11 items; P-PAM, 9 items). The Drawbacks factor assesses the perceived negative consequences of asthma medications, including side effects, financial burden, and inconvenience. The Benefits factor, on the other hand, measures the perceived efficacy of asthma medications, including better health, preventing symptom exacerbation, and staying out of the hospital.

Factor scores are derived by summing and averaging item scores within factors. Reading level analysis showed that the C-PAM is written at the fourth grade level whereas the P-PAM is written at the seventh grade level. Approximate administration time is 7 to 10 minutes. Sample items include:

Drawbacks Factor

Every time I take my asthma medicine, I get sick with asthma anyway. (C-PAM)

The asthma medicine makes it hard for me to think. (C-PAM)

My child has mood swings and I think it's because of the asthma medicine. (P-PAM)

My child says the asthma medicine tastes bad. (P-PAM)

Benefits Factor

The asthma medicine keeps me from having to go to the hospital. (C-PAM)

I feel better when I have the asthma medicine with me. (C-PAM)

The asthma medicine will keep my child well most of the time. (P-PAM)

My child's asthma medicine is good at preventing attacks. (P-PAM)

The PAM has also been modified for use in a population of children with ADHD.

Psychometric Information

The development of the PAM was driven conceptually by two components of the Health Belief Model: perceived drawbacks and perceived benefits. Initially, the developers generated items by interviewing 18 children with a range of severity of asthma and their mothers. Items were subsequently modified following panel (six immunology/allergy specialists) review and pilot tested with 17 children (ages 9–15) and their mothers. Test-retest reliability with this sample of 17 child-mother dyads was .81 for the C-PAM and .87 for the P-PAM.

Separate factor analyses were conducted on the two versions using a sample of 162 children (ages 8–16; 58% boys; 62% White, 33% Black) with asthma and their mothers, and these analyses yielded four factors for each version. However, two factors for both versions were eliminated because of their poor interpretability. The developers reported that the retained items all had factor loadings of .30 or above. Cronbach alpha coefficients were reported to exceed .70 for all factors, although specific values were not provided. Factor scores were significantly correlated for C-PAM ($r = .36$), but not for P-PAM ($r = .09$), and C-PAM and P-PAM scores were significantly correlated (Drawbacks, $r = .30$; Benefits, $r = .25$). Regarding the relationship between PAM scores and medical indices, Drawbacks factor scores were significantly predicted by asthma severity and number of side effects, while Benefits factor scores were predicted by asthma severity but not number of side effects.

Comment

As clinicians, we often find it necessary to examine the perceptions that children and parents hold toward their medication regimen. This is an especially important clinical objective given the high rate of nonadherence with medication in some illness populations (e.g., asthma). The PAM is the first conceptually driven assessment tool specifically developed and evaluated to measure such perceptions about medications, and it has promise as a brief, cost-effective addition to the asthma clinic assessment protocol. Since many child health conditions are treated with medications, the PAM could be modeled in developing similar medication perception questionnaires for use with other patient populations. The PAM may have practical utility in facilitating the development of appropriate education interventions. The developers included both Whites and Blacks in their sample, although ethnic similarities or differences were not presented. Examination of ethnic-specific perceptions would be an important step in the continued development of the PAM since cultural factors are likely to influence children's and parents' perceived benefits and drawbacks to medications. Overall, more detailed reliability and validity would increase its utility.

Relevant References

DePaola, L. M., Roberts, M. C., Blaiss, M. S., Frick, P. J., & McNeal, R. E. (1997). Mothers' and children's perceptions of asthma medication. *Children's Health Care, 26,* 265–283.

McNeal, R. E. (1995, May). Mother's and children's perceptions of medication for children with attention deficit hyperactivity disorder. Unpublished master's thesis, University of Kansas, Lawrence, KS.

General Observations and Recommendations

We have included assessment tools that refer to both general health and specific illness/regimen. Measures reviewed here that focused on more general topics within attitudes and beliefs (i.e., body image, death, and disabilities) clearly do not include all available measures published to date. Instead, we have focused on those with a particular relevance to health. Instruments reviewed overall indicate the great surge of assessment within this area. While some measures were developed only recently, others that have existed for many years are now being more closely examined. The constructs of attitudes and beliefs are overarching, with influences that affect several areas within the health of children. However, we believe that authors of measures reviewed in this chapter have worked particularly hard to limit the scope of their measurement, examining specific information about children's attitudes.

Based on our review of the instruments in this chapter, we have chosen to highlight several issues. First, many of the instruments are revised versions of measures originally developed for use with adults. While many measures report standardized scores for a group of children, the age appropriateness of several measures remains undelineated. Specifically, few measures reported reading levels and even fewer described administration processes in which children were assisted. Second, despite the failure to directly assess reading level of the instruments, most measures reviewed are, on the surface, very child-friendly. This is a unique challenge in that direct observational assessment is not possible, and most assessment of attitudes and beliefs thereby relies on child self-report. Future measures might explore the use of sample items to familiarize children with the assessment tool. Similarly, if possible, the use of visual stimuli may also assist in making measures more developmentally appropriate.

Third, the measures presented demonstrate an outstanding beginning to assessment of attitudes and beliefs in children's health. Future research on existing measures will speak to psychometric properties and further examine a measure's utility. Studies incorporating more diverse populations will also expand the generalizability of findings. Finally, while this chapter does not completely capture all available instruments assessing attitudes and beliefs, many specific topics that should be the focus of assessment within children's health were notably absent. For example, measures pertaining to sun exposure, smoking, and diet and exercise were not reviewed.

References

Ajzen, I., & Fishbein, M. (1977). Attitude-behavior relations: A theoretical analysis and review of empirical research. *Psychological Bulletin, 84,* 888–918.

Becker, M. H. (Ed.). (1974). *The Health Belief Model and personal health behavior.* Thorofare, NJ: Charles B. Slack.

Johnson, S. B., & Tercyak, K. P. (1995). Psychological impact of islet cell antibody screening for IDDM on children, adults, and their family members. *Diabetes Care, 18,* 1370–1372.

Maieron, M. J., Roberts, M. C., & Prentice-Dunn, S. (1996). Children's perceptions of peers with AIDS: Assessing the impact of contagion information, perceived similarity, and illness conceptualization. *Journal of Pediatric Psychology, 21,* 321–333.

Telljohann, S. K., Durgin, J., Everett, S. A., & Price, J. H. (1996). Third grade students' general health knowledge, attitudes and behaviors. *American Journal of Health Behavior, 20,* 20–29.

Chapter 7

Pediatric Pain and Childhood Injury

JAMES R. RODRIGUE

Pain and injury are universal phenomena and all individuals first experience them during childhood. There have been several important advances in pain measurement during the past several years, including the development of sophisticated observational systems for young children and the proliferation of questionnaire methods for older children and adolescents. Although childhood injury represents the source of pain for a substantial number of children, scant attention has been paid to the development and validation of measurement tools to assess factors associated with injury susceptibility and severity. In this chapter, we review assessment methods that have been developed to assess pediatric pain and childhood injury. We have chosen to focus predominantly on those questionnaires that have been developed during the past decade, although we provide reviews of several behavioral measures that have been extensively studied. First, however, let us provide a few introductory comments about pediatric pain and childhood injury.

Pediatric Pain

While numerous volumes have been published on the topic of pain, most delegate childhood pain to a solitary chapter and only a few have focused exclusively on pain in children (e.g., Bush & Harkins, 1991; McGrath, 1990; McGrath & Unruh, 1987; Ross & Ross, 1988; Schechter, Berde, & Yaster, 1993). The books that do exist are excellent and provide state of the art reviews of scientific studies and effective clinical interventions. Despite its universality, childhood pain was only recently considered distinct from the pain experienced by adults, and the nursing community was the first to recognize it as a clinical problem in desperate need of study. The clinical complexity of assessing children's pain was evident to nurses, pediatricians, pediatric psychologists, and child psychiatrists who were in need of documenting clinical symptomatology, selecting appropriate interventions, and determining treatment effectiveness. Consequently, numerous methods for evaluating the pain and distress experienced by infants, children, and adolescents have been developed and evaluated during the past 10 to 15 years. Despite this increased attention to the development of pain assessment tools, most child health professionals remain unaware of their existence or are unfamiliar with their clinical utility. Their underutilization in medical settings has been implicated as a primary cause of inadequate pain management for children (Beyer & Byers, 1985; Bush & Harkins, 1991).

There are many reasons why pain is one of the most difficult constructs to assess in children. First, pain is a subjective experience and it includes sensory, affective, and evaluative components. Indeed, its expression is influenced by multiple physiological, intrapersonal, interpersonal, and environmental factors. Second, the assessment of pain is further complicated by its various types and origins. For instance, childhood pain may be either acute or chronic and brought on by medical procedures, disease, traumatic injury, or, in some instances, ambiguous factors (Varni, 1984). Third, the relevance of cognitive and psychosocial development, particularly regarding the development of children's pain concepts, language, and memory, necessitates that a developmental framework to childhood pain assessment be used. Fourth, difficulties and inconsistencies in defining pain have hampered pain assessment (Karoly, 1991). While "pain" may be the operative word and the intended focus of assessment, it is not always clear what is being measured. Is the clinician or researcher targeting pain intensity, suffering, general distress, pain sensation, pain behaviors, or pain complaints?

Several different assessment strategies have been developed for use with children. These include interview methods, self-report methods, pain diaries and self-monitoring systems, direct observation methods, physiochemical methods, projective and drawing methods, and informant judgment/rating procedures (Karoly, 1991). Interview methods include those face-to-face assessments that target children's sensory and affective experiences (e.g., location, intensity, duration and frequency, anxiety, frustration, fear), cognitive factors (e.g., appraisal and understanding of pain source and consequences, perceived control, expectations), behavioral factors (e.g., coping strategies, overt distress, parents' behaviors, physical activities and limitations), and other relevant clinical factors such as the relationships with health professionals (McGrath & Hillier, 1996). While interviews can be unstructured, those that are semistructured or structured are most commonly used.

Self-report methods are used with children as young as 2 years old, although the complexity of the assessment tool increases as children grow older because older children are capable of rating pain frequency and intensity. Visual analogue scales, facial affective scales, pain thermometers, and various types of questionnaires have been developed and validated in recent years and are increasingly used in clinical settings. It is important to emphasize that such measurement tools focus predominantly on the assessment of pain intensity. Pain diaries and self-monitoring systems have been incorporated into some self-report measures to extend the assessment beyond pain intensity and duration, although their utility with young children is very limited. Furthermore, a few multidimensional assessment instruments have been developed to tap other highly relevant aspects of children's pain experiences (i.e., nonpain symptoms, pain coping strategies, stressful life events). Generally, self-report methods have several advantages including their ease of administration, convenience, efficiency, and cost-effectiveness, although most childhood pain experts advocate a multidimensional approach to pain assessment.

Unlike older children and adolescents, infants and very young children are incapable of providing reliable verbal reports of their subjective pain experiences. Consequently, several excellent behavioral observation and coding systems have been developed to assess the occurrence and frequency of pain-related behaviors. Behavioral measures include those that focus on general diffuse movements, limb withdrawal, facial expression and changes, vocalizations, torso movements, crying, and changes in functional activity. More sophisticated systems have also been developed to examine the sequential interaction patterns between distressed children and adults during painful medical procedures. Observation techniques have benefited from high levels of interobserver reliability, yet their use is limited by several factors including labor intensity, cost, and training demands. Furthermore, one should be cautioned that it is often difficult to discern the degree to which the behaviors observed are reflections of emotional distress or direct representations of the child's pain experience (McGrath, 1990).

Childhood Injury

Unintentional childhood injury is the leading cause of morbidity and mortality in children and adolescents, and accounts for over one million years of potential life lost by children ages 1 to 19 (Finney et al., 1993; Rodriguez, 1990). Motor vehicle accidents, drownings, burns, falls, firearms, aspiration, suffocation, and poisoning are only a few of the leading accidental injuries that lead to death, disability, disfigurement, and high utilization of health care resources among children. Despite its societal significance, only recently has this frequent threat to the health of children stimulated empirical interest in measuring the psychological, behavioral, and environmental components of injury-risk behavior.

The design and implementation of injury-control strategies have met with variable success. As reviewed by Finney and colleagues (1993), injury-control strategies have ranged from those that are more passive or structural (e.g., legislative regulations, automobile air restraint systems, speed bumps) to ones that are considered more active (e.g., programs to teach home safety and burn prevention, rewarding children for wearing bicycle helmets, acquisition and installation of smoke and carbon monoxide detectors), with multifaceted, community-based approaches that combine structural and behavioral techniques assuming increased prominence.

The proliferation of childhood injury prevention programs and their outcomes necessitates increased consideration of measurement issues. While real measures of injury (e.g., emergency room and hospital records, ICD-9 codes, death certificates) and behavioral observations have obvious benefits and are the preferred measurement choice, they also are limited by inaccurate recording, low base rates, and cost. More indirect, or proxy, measures of injury-risk behavior have been developed and used in injury prevention research, although it is readily acknowledged that such indices also have important limitations (e.g., demand characteristics, errors of memory, misinterpretation of questions).

In this chapter, we review a few injury-related questionnaires that have been developed for use with children and their parents. Our intent in doing so is not to discount the relative value and significance of observational methods, but to provide information relevant to one facet of the multidimensional assessment approach to injury-related behavior in children. Clinicians and researchers interested in a comprehensive review of the key conceptual, methodological, and measurement issues related to childhood injury should read the Society of Pediatric Psychology's Injury Task Force Report (Finney et al., 1993) and the report of the National Committee for Injury Prevention and Control (1989).

REVIEWS

Behavioral Approach-Avoidance and Distress Scale (BAADS)

N. C. Hubert, 1988

Manual and Address Information

No manual. Direct inquiries to: Nancy C. Hubert, 300 Vestaria Office Park, #3200, Birmingham, AL 35216-3753, (205) 822-7348.

Purpose

The BAADS is an observational measure designed to assess children's coping style and distress related to painful medical procedures.

Format, Administration, and Scoring

The BAADS consists of two subscales: Approach-Avoidance and Distress. Each subscale includes five behaviors or situations that are rated on a 5-point scale by a trained observer. On the Approach-Avoidance subscale, a rating of 1 indicates high avoidance (turns away, tries to escape or change situation), and a rating of 5 indicates high approach (looks, touches, questions, initiates involvement). For the Distress subscale, a score of 1 indicates no distress, calm appearance, or no crying, and a rating of 5 indicates extreme distress, agitation, screaming, and/or extreme muscle tension. Summary scores for each subscale range from 5 to 25. Behaviors can be rated both prior to and during procedures.

Psychometric Information

The BAADS was standardized on a sample of 43 children undergoing their first bone marrow aspiration. The children were ethnically diverse and ranged in age from 3 to 11. Internal consistency ranged from .82 to .97. Concurrent validity was demonstrated through correlations of the Distress subscale of the BAADS and the Observational Scale of Behavioral Distress, measures of self-reported fear, and nurses' ratings of children's distress and cooperation. Although inter-rater reliability was not reported in the standardization sample, it has subsequently been demonstrated to be .77 for the Distress subscale and .78 for the Approach-Avoidance subscale.

Comment

The BAADS is an observational measure of children's coping related to painful medical procedures. Overall, it appears to be promising as an assessment tool for coping and distress. The Approach-Avoidance subscale warrants further investigation in terms of its validity, yet satisfactory inter-rater reliability, internal consistency, and validity of both subscales have been demonstrated. The BAADS has successfully been used both prior to and during medical procedures, as well as with a fairly wide age range of children (ages 3–11). Its ease of employment and cost-effectiveness make the BAADS a suitable choice for measuring children's distress.

Relevant References

Bachanas, P. J., & Blount, R. L. (1996). The Behavioral Approach-Avoidance and Distress Scale: An investigation of reliability and validity during painful medical procedures. *Journal of Pediatric Psychology, 21,* 671–681.

Hubert, N. C., Jay, S. M., Saltine, M., & Hays, M. (1988). Approach-avoidance and distress in children undergoing preparation for painful medical procedures. *Journal of Clinical Child Psychology, 17,* 194–202.

Charleston Pediatric Pain Pictures (CPPP)

R. W. Belter, 1988

Manual and Address Information

There is a manual. Direct inquiries to: Ronald W. Belter, Department of Psychology, University of West Florida, 11000 University Parkway, Pensacola, FL 32514, (904) 474-2363, rbelter@uwf.edu.

Purpose

The CPPP is designed to measure children's pain intensity ratings for common hypothetical painful events that occur during childhood.

Format, Administration, and Scoring

The CPPP consists of 17 cartoon picture cards depicting common childhood scenes across medical, play, and home situations. Each card shows a young child, gender nonspecific and without facial expression, engaged in an activity that could be considered painful. Verbal instructions accompany each card and are read to the child who then indicates how much pain they would feel if they were the child depicted. These pain ratings are made by the child using either a visual analog scale or other graphic-rating scale (e.g., Faces Scale, Oucher Scale). Administration time is about 10 to 20 minutes depending upon how many pain rating scales are used.

The CPPP has four subscales for which mean ratings are obtained. These include No Pain (four cards), Low Pain (four cards), Moderate Pain (five cards), and High Pain (four cards). Sample card depictions and their respective subscales include:

> Having temperature taken by a nurse (No Pain)
> Doctor listening to heart (No Pain)
> Having a Band-Aid removed (Low Pain)
> Tripping and falling on the carpet at home (Low Pain)
> Hitting head on table at home (Moderate Pain)
> Scraping knee on sidewalk (Moderate Pain)
> Burning hand on stove at home (High Pain)
> Receiving a shot at the doctor's office (High Pain)

Psychometric Information

The authors initially developed 27 picture cards that were subjected to review and classification (using the four categories previously mentioned) by six child clinicians. Agreement among raters reached 84%, although 10 picture cards were excluded due to poor agreement. Initial study samples included both preschool ($n = 50$) and elementary school-aged ($n = 58$) children who were predominantly White and had no known significant health problems.

Internal consistency (Cronbach's alpha) for the CPPP subscales across both samples ranged from .42 to .63 for the No Pain subscale, .57 to .69 for the Low Pain subscale, .60 to .74 for the Moderate Pain subscale, and .39 to .69 for the High Pain subscale. Test-retest reliability (1 week) with 36 preschoolers across the different pain intensity rating scales ranged from .53 to .72 for the No Pain subscale, .66 for the Low Pain subscale, .54 to .66 for the Moderate Pain subscale, and .57 to .68 for the High Pain subscale.

Assessment of construct validity yielded high intercorrelations among the different pain-intensity rating scales in preschoolers (.62 to .88) and significant associations between pain-intensity ratings and CPPP subscales in both preschoolers and older children (i.e., pain ratings increase from no pain to high pain levels). Preschoolers were able to distinguish no pain from low pain, and moderate pain from high pain, but unable to make the distinction between low and moderate pain levels.

Comment

Studies using the CPPP demonstrate that young children can differentiate between varying levels of pain intensity, although the distinctions are made at a much finer level as children get older. More research is needed to examine test-retest reliability (low for individual items, while high when using composite subscale scores with preschoolers) and construct validity of the CPPP in healthy and pediatric samples representing greater diversity (age, ethnicity, socioeconomic status). The clinical utility of the CPPP at this time is very limited, although the authors note that it can be useful in teaching children how to report and differentiate pain experiences, as well as in identifying children with high pain sensitivity.

Relevant References

Adesman, A. R., & Walco, G. A. (1992). Validation of the Charleston Pediatric Pain Pictures in school-age children. *Journal of Clinical Child Psychology, 21,* 10–13.

Belter, R. W., McIntosh, J. A., Finch, A. J., & Saylor, C. F. (1988). Preschoolers' ability to differentiate levels of pain: Relative efficacy of three self-report measures. *Journal of Clinical Child Psychology, 17,* 329–335.

Child-Adult Medical Procedure Interaction Scale-Revised (CAMPIS-R)

R. L. Blount, 1990

Manual and Address Information

There is a manual. Direct inquiries to: Ronald L. Blount, Department of Psychology, University of Georgia, Athens, GA 30602, (706) 542-3012, rlblount@arches.uga.edu.

Purpose

The CAMPIS-R represents a revision of its initial version that was designed to measure children's distress, nondistress, and coping behaviors, as well as the behavior of parents and medical staff during invasive medical procedures.

Format, Administration, and Scoring

The CAMPIS-R is an observational system used in coding categories of child and adult behaviors during invasive medical procedures, including bone marrow aspirations, lumbar punctures, venipunctures, and immunizations. It has also been used during physical therapy and other medical treatments. Typically, younger children (e.g., ages 4–7) and their interactions with parents and medical staff are videotaped immediately before, during, and after the medical procedure. However, children as old as 13 have been included in investigations by the authors. The videotapes typically are transcribed prior to coding along six dimensions: Child Coping, Child Distress, Child Neutral, Adult Coping Promoting, Adult Distress Promoting, and Adult Neutral. Each of these coding dimensions includes several content codes as indicated below. The coding system is very complex and includes content codes for adult and child vocalizations, affect, and child, parent, and staff behaviors. Nonverbal behaviors have also been included. A proportion, rate, or interval metric can be used in obtaining a score for each coding dimension. The proportion-based metric is determined by dividing the total number of times that a behavior or dimension occurred by the total number of behaviors observed and coded for that person (e.g., child, parent, or staff).

The coding dimensions and content codes for the CAMPIS-R are as follows:

Coding Dimension	*Content Code*
Child Coping	Audible deep breathing Nonprocedural talk Humor Making coping statements
Child Distress	Cry Scream Verbal resistance Request emotional support Verbal fear Verbal pain Verbal emotion Information seeking
Child Neutral	Child informs about status Child's general condition related talk Requests relief from nonprocedural discomfort Assertive procedural verbalizations
Adult Coping Promoting	Nonprocedural talk to child Humor directed to child Command to use coping strategy
Adult Distress Promoting	Reassuring comment Apology Empathic statement Giving control to the child Criticism
Adult Neutral	Nonprocedural talk to adults Humor directed to adults Procedural talk to adults Command to engage in procedural activity Notice of procedure to come Behavioral command to child Checking child's status Child's general condition talk Child's current status talk Praise Command for managing child's behavior

Psychometric Information

The original CAMPIS coding system consisted of 35 content codes (19 for adults, 16 for the child) and was developed for use with young children undergoing bone marrow aspirations and lumbar punctures. Several of the content codes were derived from existing observational systems measuring marital interactions and procedural distress in children. The 35 content codes were subsequently combined into 6 empirically and conceptually derived coding dimensions (i.e., CAMPIS-R). Inter-rater reliability (Cohen's kappa) for the child and adult codes has generally ranged from .65 to .91 across studies.

The CAMPIS-R has been used in several assessment studies and the sequential analysis of behaviors during medical procedures has yielded numerous findings about the interactional patterns among children, parents, and medical staff. Furthermore, there is evidence that the CAMPIS-R codes are sensitive to detecting change in child-adult interaction patterns following interventions designed to increase children's and parents' use of distraction and other coping techniques during painful procedures.

In investigating the concurrent validity of the CAMPIS-R with a sample of 77 children receiving immunization shots, Blount and colleagues (1997) found that the CAMPIS-R codes of Child Coping, Child Distress, Parent/Staff Distress Promoting, and Parent/Staff Coping Promoted were significantly correlated in the hypothesized direction with several observational (i.e., Observational Scale of Behavioral Distress, Behavioral Approach-Avoidance and Distress Scale) and parent-, staff-, and child-report measures (e.g., visual analogue scales of fear and pain) before, during, and after the procedure.

Comment

The CAMPIS-R represents a substantial improvement over assessment tools designed only to capture the presence, intensity, and range of children's pain and distress surrounding various invasive medical procedures. It is a well-developed and frequently studied behavioral coding system that provides an assessment of the coping behaviors, as well as the interactions that occur during medical procedures. The revision includes only 6 coding dimensions for which scores are reported, although the original behavioral categories are still coded and used in deriving scores for the revised dimensions. The CAMPIS-R manual is very detailed and comprehensive, and it provides appropriate operational definitions and examples for each of the behavior categories that are coded. The coding and scoring system is very complex and requires extensive training. Despite its complexity, however, good to excellent levels of inter-rater agreement have been reported. The CAMPIS-R has been used extensively with White and African American children. While most of these children have been preschool or elementary school-age, children as young as 6 months and as old as 13 years have been included. The scale also has been used with children undergoing physical therapy and other acute medical treatments. The CAMPIS-R has not been used to a great extent with Hispanic American or Asian American, older adolescents, to monitor adults' coping or distress behaviors, or with people who speak a language other than English. While comprehensive, the complexity of the CAMPIS-R makes it most useful for research and limited clinical applications. When used in clinical settings with highly distressed children, the focus should be on the relevant child coping and distress behaviors, as well as adults' coping promoting and distress promoting behaviors. For pragmatic reasons, neutral or irrelevant behaviors would have to be ignored. In order to increase the clinical applicability of the CAMPIS-R, a rating-scale version of the scale is currently being developed.

Relevant References

Blount, R. L., Cohen, L. L., Frank, N. C., Bachanas, P. J., Smith, A. J., Manimala, M. R., & Pate, J. T. (1997). The Child-Adult Medical Procedure Interaction Scale-Revised: An assessment of validity. *Journal of Pediatric Psychology, 22,* 73–88.

Blount, R. L., Corbin, S. M., Sturges, J. W., Wolfe, V. V., Prater, J. M., & James, L. D. (1989). The relationship between adults' behavior and child coping and distress during BMA/LP procedures: A sequential analysis. *Behavior Therapy, 20,* 585–601.

Blount, R. L., Powers, S. W., Cotter, M. W., Swan, S. C., & Free, K. (1994). Making the system work: Training pediatric oncology patients to cope and their parents to coach them during BMA/LP procedures. *Behavior Modification, 18,* 6–31.

Blount, R. L., Sturges, J. W., & Powers, S. W. (1990). Analysis of child and adult behavioral variations by phase of medical procedure. *Behavior Therapy, 21,* 33–48.

Child Behavior Observation Rating Scale (CBORS)

S. N. Frankl, 1962

Manual and Address Information

No manual. Address unknown.

Purpose

The CBORS is an observational scale that measures children's behavior during physician visits and medical procedures. It was originally designed to investigate children's anxiety associated with dental care.

Format, Administration, and Scoring

Children's behaviors are recorded during a specific procedure or time frame (e.g., behavior of child during x-ray exam). Four categories of behavior constitute the possible ratings. Children receive one rating for each time or procedure. The four categories include: Definitely negative (e.g., refusal of treatment, crying forcefully), Negative (e.g., reluctant to accept treatment, withdrawn), Positive (e.g., acceptance of treatment, willingness to comply), and Definitely Positive (e.g., good rapport with dentist, laughing and enjoying the situation). Raters watch the procedure live. The majority of ratings for a particular time period characterizes the score for that event. For example, if five events comprise the first visit, three negative and two positive ratings would result in an overall negative score for the first visit.

Psychometric Information

Categories of behavior considered to be "... most explicit, functional, and workable..." were selected for the CBORS. The original sample consisted of 112 mothers of children 3½ to 5½ years old. Children in the standardization sample had not visited a dentist previously. Three raters observed the children and their interactions with the dentist during both their first and second visits. Inter-rater reliability was .97 for the initial standardization sample, and has subsequently been reported to range from .88 to .90. The CBORS has been used in studies with varying procedures and physician visits, yet no other investigations of its validity have been reported.

Comment

The CBORS is an observational measure of children's behavior related to medical and dental situations and procedures. Children ages 3 through 9 have been observed using the CBORS. Raters can view the children either during the procedure or code videotaped interactions. Reports of inter-rater reliability have been high, and the four behavioral categories appear fairly simple to use. Although the measure was originally designed for use within a dental situation, it has been adapted for other medical situations, such as immunizations. The CBORS seems to have been a useful addition to a handful of empirical investigations. However, little psychometric data in addition to inter-rater reliability are available.

Relevant References

Broone, M. E., & Endsley, R. C. (1989). Maternal presence, childrearing practices, and children's responses to an injection. *Research in Nursing & Health, 12,* 229–235.

Frankl, S. N., Shiere, F. R., & Fogels, H. R. (1962). Should the parent remain with the child in the dental operatory? *Journal of Dentistry for Young Children, 29,* 150–163.

Shaw, E., & Routh, D. (1982). Effect of mother presence on children's reaction to aversive procedures. *Journal of Pediatric Psychology, 38,* 33–42.

Children's Hospital of Eastern Ontario Pain Scale (CHEOPS)

P. J. McGrath, 1985

Manual and Address Information

No manual. Direct inquiries to: Patrick J. McGrath, Department of Psychology, Dalhousie University and Pain and Palliative Care Service, Children's Hospital, Ottawa, Ontario, Canada K1H 8L1.

Purpose

The CHEOPS is an observational postoperative pain measure for use with children ages 1 to 12.

Format, Administration, and Scoring

Use of the CHEOPS involves observing a child's behavior during and/or after a medical procedure in 3- to 5-minute intervals. The CHEOPS has six behavior domains for which operational definitions are provided and scores are obtained. The six domains are Cry, Facial, Child Verbal, Torso, Touch, and Legs. Within each domain are specific behaviors that are assigned numerical values ranging from 0 to 3 (0 = behavior that is the antithesis of pain, 1 = behavior that is not indicative of pain and is not the antithesis of pain, 2 = behavior indicating mild or moderate pain, 3 = behavior indicating severe pain). For instance, behavioral descriptors for the Facial domain are: smiling = 0, composed = 1, and grimace = 2, and those for the Child Verbal domain are: positive comments = 0, not talking = 1, non-pain complaints = 1, pain-specific complaints = 2, and both types of complaints = 2. The total possible score ranges from 4 to 13 for each observation interval.

Psychometric Information

The CHEOPS behavioral domains were developed after focused meetings with recovery-room nurses, observations of children in a recovery-room environment, and pilot testing of the measure. Inter-rater reliability (26 children ages 1–5) immediately following different surgical procedures (hernia repair, tonsillectomy, circumcision, hypospadias repair) yielded average agreement exceeding 90% for all six behavior domains: Cry (93.2%, range = 76–100%), Facial (90%; range = 61–100%), Child Verbal (95.5%; range = 95–100%), Torso (90.6%; range = 76–100%), Touch (99.2%; range = 87–100%), and Legs (92%; range = 76–100%). Inter-rater agreement has been reported at similar levels in several other studies.

Using a sample of 30 children (ages 1–7) immediately following circumcision surgery, the authors reported correlations among the six behavior domains ranging from .35 to .81. Also, correlations between CHEOPS scores and nurses' ratings on a visual analog scale ranged from .52 (Torso) to .81 (Total score). Significant reductions in CHEOPS scores following the administration of intravenous narcotics was provided as evidence for construct validity. As a measure of social validation, 88 teachers completed a visual analog scale in response to viewing video clips of children recovering from surgery. The CHEOPS total score correlated .85 with the teachers' ratings.

Comment

The development of the CHEOPS represented one of the first attempts to validate a measure specifically designed to assess postoperative pain in very young children. It has been used very extensively in the study of children's pain and there now are several pain measures that incorporate the CHEOPS behavior dimensions and descriptions. There is adequate data to suggest that it can be used reliably by health professionals in the assessment of children's pain. However, some significant discordance has been reported between CHEOPS scores and the self-reported pain of 3- to 7-year-old children, where the CHEOPS was not detecting pain being reported by children within 36 hours after surgery. Several reviewers of the pediatric pain assessment literature have concluded that, overall, the CHEOPS is a valid tool for assessing short, sharp pain (e.g., venipunctures), although further psychometric work is needed.

Relevant References

McGrath, P. J., Johnson, G., Goodman, J. T., Schillinger, J., Dunn, J., & Chapman, J. (1985). CHEOPS: A behavioral scale for rating postoperative pain in children. In H. L. Fields, R. Dubner, & F. Cervero (Eds.), *Advances in pain research and therapy* (Vol. 9, pp. 395–402). New York: Raven Press.

Children's Pain Inventory (CPI)

P. A. McGrath, 1990

Manual and Address Information

No manual. Direct inquiries to: Patricia A. McGrath, Child Health Research Institute, 800 Commissioners Road East, London, Ontario, Canada N6C 2V5.

Purpose

The CPI provides hypothetical pain situations for which children rate pain intensity and affect. The CPI is used to validate newly developed pain instruments before using them in actual clinical situations.

Format, Administration, and Scoring

The original CPI comprised 30 situations (25 painful, 5 nonpainful) experienced by children in recreational and medical settings. Most of the items could be used with children without serious illness, although several items apply specifically to children with cancer, arthritis, or headaches. A more recent version of the CPI (McGrath et al., 1996) contains 16 painful events varying in nature and degree of tissue damage. Two items are administered to familiarize the child with the measure and pain ratings. Children are then presented with each CPI item and then respond by indicating whether the painful event has ever happened to them, whether it was painful, and if it was painful, how much it hurt and what it felt like. Pain intensity and affective ratings are typically provided using visual analog scales (VAS, numerical or colored) and a Facial Affective Scale (FAS), respectively. Scoring is based on the particular rating tool used. Sample situations described in the CPI include ("Have you ever . . ."):

> Fallen and scraped your knee?
> Had an earache?
> Had an injection (shot) in your arm?
> Burned your hand?
> Had a sore throat?
> Had a stomach ache?

Psychometric Information

Using 104 (51 without headaches, 53 with headaches) 5- to 16-year old children, pain intensity and affective ratings to the CPI situations were obtained using a traditional VAS (black line mounted on white paper) and a newly developed Coloured Analogue Scale (CAS) as well as the FAS. The number of painful situations experienced was positively correlated with age, although pain intensity ratings were negatively associated with age. There were no differences in pain intensity ratings by scale type (VAS versus CAS) or between without headache and headache groups. Painful situations involving significant tissue damage (e.g., burn, broken bone) resulted in significantly higher pain intensity and affective ratings than did those with less or minor tissue damage (e.g., bruise, blister). The authors reported good discriminant validity for both the VAS and CAS, and indicated that they were used rather easily by children. However, the CAS was rated by interviewers as superior to the traditional VAS in ease of use and scoring.

Comment

Additional information about the development of the CPI, including the development and selection of items, would be helpful in assessing its utility in clinical and research settings. It does appear to be a useful tool to use when attempting to validate new pain-rating scales for children since some normative data now are available for children 5 to 16 years old. Furthermore, the CPI could be used as an instructional and practice tool before having children monitor and rate (e.g., at home or in the pediatric clinic) the intensity and affect associated with actual pain experiences.

Relevant References

McGrath, P. A. (1990). *Pain in children: Nature, assessment, and treatment.* New York: Guilford Press.

McGrath, P. A., Seifert, C. E., Speechley, K. N.,

Booth, J. C., Stitt, L., & Gibson, M. C. (1996). A new analogue scale for assessing children's pain: An initial validation study. *Pain, 64,* 435–443.

Faces Pain Scale (FPS)

D. Bieri, 1990

Manual and Address Information

No manual. Direct inquiries to: J. B. Ziegler, Division of Pediatrics, The Prince of Wales Children's Hospital, High Street, Randwick, N.S.W. 2031, Australia.

Purpose

The FPS was developed to assess pain intensity in young children (first and third graders).

Format, Administration, and Scoring

The FPS is a set of seven faces displaying increasing levels of pain intensity or severity. The scale is usually mounted on white cardboard for presentation to the child, who is then asked to select the face that best represents the amount of pain experienced at that time (i.e., "... how much hurt you feel."). Each face corresponds to a numerical value (0 = *no pain* to 6 = *most pain possible*).

Psychometric Information

Development of the FPS occurred in several phases that included children's (first and third graders) drawings of faces representing degrees of pain (no pain to great deal of pain), artists' constructions of the initial scales, pilot testing of the initial sets of faces, children's immediate and delayed recall of the order of faces, and test-retest reliability. A total of 195 first graders and 358 third graders from Sydney, Australia participated in the various phases of scale development.

Two-week test-retest reliability for the same painful episode yielded a rank correlation coefficient of .79 (first-grade children only). Overall agreement between first graders (71–96%) and third graders (86–100%) on the rank ordering of faces as a measure of pain intensity indicated good content validity. Also, in a more recent study, FPS scores discriminated between a local anesthetic cream and a placebo cream in attenuating the pain intensity associated with a needle puncture. FPS scores also discriminated between punctures using needles of two different sizes (i.e., butterfly versus standard cannula).

Comment

The FPS is brief, easy to administer by health professionals, and requires minimal instructions to the child. It addresses some of the weaknesses inherent in other child-report pain measures by not requiring the child to map pain concepts onto another dimension like visual-analog or numeric-rating scales. Also, the FPS uses a neutral face (versus face denoting happiness) as its no-pain anchor point to avoid the pleasure-pain continuum. The use of a 7-point rating scale allows for a more sensitive level of measurement than the more common 5-point scales. The authors note that the FPS has approximately equal intervals between ratings, thus permitting the use of parametric statistics; however, more research is necessary to determine whether this is truly an interval scale. While the scale has been used with children as young as 2, this is not recommended because it has not yet been determined that the FPS can be reliably completed by children younger than 6.

Relevant References

Arts, S. E., Abu-Saad, H. H., Champion, G. D., Crawford, M. R., Fisher, R. J., Juniper, K. H., & Ziegler, J. B. (1994). Age-related response to lidocaine-prilocaine (EMLA) emulsion and effect of music distraction on the pain of intravenous cannulation. *Pediatrics, 93,* 797–801.

Bieri, D., Reeve, R. A., Champion, G. D., Addicoat, L., & Ziegler, J. B. (1990). The Faces Pain Scale for the self-assessment of the severity of pain experienced by children: Development, initial validation, and preliminary investigation for ratio scale properties. *Pain, 41,* 139–150.

Headache Symptom Questionnaire-Revised (HSQ-R)

J. A. Mindell, 1987

Manual and Address Information

No manual. Direct inquiries to: Frank Andrasik, Department of Psychology, University of West Florida, 11000 University Parkway, Pensacola, FL 32514, (850) 474-2041, fandrasi@uwf.edu.

Purpose

The HSQ-R measures the frequency of headache symptoms in children.

Format, Administration, and Scoring

The HSQ-R is a self-administered revision of a previously developed instrument for adult headache patients (Epstein & Abel, 1977). It can be completed by children over 10 years of age and their parents. The HSQ-R contains 20 items reflecting various symptom dimensions commonly associated with both migraine and muscle contraction headaches. Using a 5-point scale (1 = never to 5 = always), respondents indicate the degree to which the symptom dimension is experienced by the child or observed by the child's parent. Factor analysis suggested the presence of four factors: one related to muscle contraction headaches, one related to vascular headaches, one related to classical migraine, and one related to both common migraine and muscle contraction headaches. A total score is obtained and ranges from 20 to 100. Sample items include:

> I awaken with headaches.
> My headache is throbbing or pulsating.
> My headache begins on one side.
> My headache starts in the neck, shoulder, or back of the head.
> I have nausea and/or vomiting with my headache.

Psychometric Information

Sixty-eight children and adolescents (33 males, 35 females) with classic migraines, common migraines, combined migraine-muscle contraction headaches, or muscle contraction headaches seeking psychological treatment for their headaches served as the initial standardization sample. Headache diagnosis was made based on standardized criteria.

No internal consistency data were provided by the authors. Parent-child correspondence across items ranged from .03 ("During a headache the area around my temple(s) becomes swollen, tender and painful.") to .64 ("My headache is so bad I can't do anything when I have a headache."), with 7 items yielding very low agreement (<.20). Discriminative classification analysis accurately classified 66% of the children with headaches, with higher classification rates for children with classic migraine (75%) and muscle contraction headaches (75%).

Comment

Although headaches during childhood are very common and are a major reason for visits to the pediatrician, assessment tools designed to measure headache symptoms in children have not been developed. The HSQ-R is one brief (5 minutes), cost-effective measure of headache symptomatology in children, but it has several important limitations. Caution should be exercised in using the HSQ-R in its present form with children under 12 years of age. Several of the items need rewording to ensure that they are developmentally appropriate (e.g., "My headache is worse at the end of the working day.") and understandable (e.g., "My headache is associated with visual changes like seeing stars, blind spots, double vision and/or intolerance to light.") to even young adolescents. Very little reliability and validity information has been reported, and its sensitivity to cultural factors has not been examined. While the HSQ-R may be helpful eventually in the clinical diagnosis and treatment of headaches in children, further refinement of the items and psychometric study are needed before adopting it as a standard assessment tool in the headache clinic.

Relevant References

Epstein, L. H., & Abel, G. G. (1977). An analysis of biofeedback training effects for tension headache patients. *Behavior Therapy, 8,* 34–47.

Mindell, J. A., & Andrasik, F. (1987). Headache classification and factor analysis with a pediatric population. *Headache, 27,* 96–101.

Injury Behavior Checklist (IBC)

M. L. Speltz, 1990

Manual and Address Information

No manual. Direct inquiries to: Matthew Speltz, 8605 56th Place West, Mukilteo, WA 98275-3125, (206) 368-4949, mspeltz@u.washington.edu.

Purpose

The IBC was developed to assess risky and injurious-type behavior in toddlers and preschool children and to identify mishaps that would not necessarily be brought to a health care professional's attention. It has subsequently been used in children as old as 10.

Format, Administration, and Scoring

Parents or teachers complete the IBC using a 5-point scale (0 = not at all to 4 = very often, more than once a week) to rate the frequency with which 24 behaviors have been observed in the child (ages 2–5) during the past 6 months. A total score (range = 0–96) is obtained by summing the item scores. Sample items include:

Rides bike in unsafe areas.
Puts fingers or objects in electrical sockets or appliances.
Tries to climb on top of furniture, cabinets, etc.
Comes into contact with hot objects.
Teases and/or approaches unfamiliar animals (e.g., dogs).

Psychometric Information

IBC items were generated from discussions with emergency-room staff regarding common injuries among young children, as well as from epidemiological injury reports focusing on toddlers and preschoolers. Predominantly middle-class parents of 253 children (123 girls, 130 boys) ages 2–5 comprised the initial standardization sample. Parents were recruited from a children's hospital (employees and visitors), an emergency room in which treatment had been sought for an unintentional injury, and a preschool.

Internal consistency reliability (Cronbach's alpha) was .87, and test-retest reliability (1 month, n = 30) was .81. Subsequent studies using the IBC have shown similar levels of internal consistency (.84–.92). The ability of the IBC (i.e., nine items) to distinguish between three injury-risk groups (low = no injuries, moderate = one injury, high = two or more injuries) was provided as evidence for convergent validity. Construct validity was demonstrated when IBC scores for 143 young children in one sample and 264 older children in another sample significantly predicted injury-risk group after controlling for relevant demographic variables. Subsequent studies have found that IBC scores are positively correlated with parent reports of injury frequency.

Comment

The IBC adds a measure of injury specificity beyond those measures typically used in studies of child behavior and injury (e.g., Child Behavior Checklist, Connors' Parent Rating Scale). There is good evidence of the total scale's internal consistency, test-retest reliability, and construct validity. Furthermore, it now appears that the IBC can be used with children as old as 10. More research also is needed to examine the psychometric properties and utility of the IBC when completed by other caretakers (e.g., daycare specialists, preschool teachers) for children with more diverse demographic characteristics. The authors note the IBC's potential use as a screening instrument for assessing injury risk in young children, although they appropriately caution that ability of the IBC to predict future injury in children who have not yet been injured has not been determined. The authors, however, are currently tracking children over a 5-year period to examine the prospective validity of the IBC.

Relevant References

Bernardo, L. M. (1996). Parent-reported injury-associated behaviors and life events among injured, ill, and well preschool children. *Journal of Pediatric Nursing, 11*, 100–110.

Potts, R., Martinez, I. G., & Dedmon, A. (1995). Childhood risk taking and injury: Self-report and informant measures. *Journal of Pediatric Psychology, 20*, 5–12.

Potts, R., Martinez, I. G., Dedmon, A., Schwarz, L.,

DiLillo, D., & Swisher, L. (1997). Brief report: Cross-validation of the Injury Behavior Checklist in a school-age sample. *Journal of Pediatric Psychology, 22*, 533–540.

Speltz, M. L., Gonzales, N., Sulzbacher, S., & Quan, L. (1990). Assessment of injury risk in young children: A preliminary study of the Injury Behavior Checklist. *Journal of Pediatric Psychology, 15*, 373–383.

Minor Injury Severity Scale (MISS)

L. Peterson, 1996

Manual and Address Information

No manual. Direct inquiries to: Lizette Peterson, Department of Psychology, 210 McAlester, University of Missouri, Columbia, Missouri 65211, (314) 882-6083, psyltz@mizzou1.missouri.edu.

Purpose

The MISS was developed to measure the degree and severity of tissue damage after a minor childhood injury.

Format, Administration, and Scoring

The MISS is comprised of 22 childhood injury categories that are very specific, descriptive, and quantifiable. These categories include:

Animal scratch/bite	Bruise/bump	Burn
Choke/drown	Crushing injuries	Cut
Electricity	Eye	Firearm/bow
Floor/rug burn	Gymnastics	Joint/bone/muscle
Loss of consciousness	Nosebleeds	Paper cut
Poison	Puncture/splinter	Scrape
Stings	Testicle impact	Tooth injuries
Torn finger/toenails		

Each injury is rated between 0 and 7, with 0 reflecting no apparent tissue damage and 7 indicating death as a result of the injury. Any permanent tissue damage is rated a 6, and ratings between 1 and 5 differ in severity depending on the type of injury coded. Some additional assessment tools are used to determine the most appropriate injury rating. For instance, a visual scale (or bumpometer) is used to measure the amount of swelling caused by an injury and rulers are used to measure the depth and width of tissue damage.

Detailed information about injury events are recorded by parents and children and this information is subsequently used by coders to complete the MISS. The MISS can be completed by lay persons who have no prior medical training, and the ranking system can be learned effectively within a few hours. Parents and children keep detailed, longhand descriptions of injuries so that they can be recalled easily when interviewed at a later date. In addition to the injury type and description, they record emotional reactions and injury site. Children and their parents then are interviewed and asked to recall whether any of the 22 injury types occurred in the preceding 2 weeks.

Psychometric Information

The standardization sample comprised 61 midwestern second-grade children (30 girls, 31 boys) and their mothers. The sample was predominantly White (97%), middle-class, and without developmental disability, chronic illness, or behavioral disorder.

It has been demonstrated that the MISS can be coded reliably (.71) and test-retest stability has been reported to be .99 for mothers and .98 for children. Agreement between mothers and children in their reports of injury severity made within 2 weeks of the injury was .53. There is some preliminary evidence of discriminant validity. The MISS ratings of tissue damage have been shown to be only moderately (but significantly) correlated with several outcome variables, including injury treatment, number of physician visits following the injury, pain intensity and duration, and child's fear and anxiety.

Comment

The MISS shows considerable promise as a measure of minor childhood injuries, which occur at a higher rate and are emotionally distressing to children and parents. While scales exist for measuring major injury events and their severity, the MISS is the only assessment tool that demonstrates sensitivity to minor types of childhood injuries. Accurate and objective classification of childhood injury is possible with this scale. Also, it allows for the assessment of the effects of multiple minor injuries in the same event. It should be emphasized that the MISS focuses on tissue damage, not pain, disability, or fear. The use of other tools (e.g., bumpometer and rulers) allow for the user to maximally operationalize the severity of the childhood injury. The main limitations of the MISS have been noted by the authors and include the need to examine the utility and psychometric properties of the MISS in more diverse samples (e.g., different ages, ethnicities, socioeconomic status, etc.) and settings (e.g., daycare, school, playgrounds). Further examination of inter-observer agreement also is warranted. Finally, the feasibility and cost-effectiveness of training adults to use the MISS in natural settings are presently unknown.

Relevant References

Peterson, L., Bartelstone, J., Kern, T., & Gillies, R. (1995). Parents' socialization of children's injury prevention: Description and some initial parameters. *Child Development, 66,* 224–235.

Peterson, L., Harbeck, C., & Moreno, A. (1993). Measures of children's injuries: Self-reported versus maternal reported events with temporally proximal versus delayed reporting. *Journal of Pediatric Psychology, 18,* 133–147.

Peterson, L., Saldana, L., & Heiblum, N. (1996). Quantifying tissue damage from childhood injury: The Minor Injury Severity Scale. *Journal of Pediatric Psychology, 21,* 251–267.

Modified Behavioral Pain Scale (MBPS)

A. Taddio, 1995

Manual and Address Information

There is a manual. Direct inquiries to: Anna Taddio, Department of Pharmacy, Hospital for Sick Children, 555 University Avenue, Toronto, Ontario, Canada, M5G 1X8, (416) 813-6235.

Purpose

The MBPS is a pain assessment tool designed for use with infants ages 2 to 6 months.

Format, Administration, and Scoring

The MBPS is a downward extension of the Behavioral Pain Score (Robieux et al., 1991) that was developed for use with older infants and toddlers. The MBPS is an observational pain measure designed to assess infant behavior along three dimensions: Facial Expression, Cry, and Movements. Facial Expression behaviors range from definite positive expression (e.g., smiling) to definite negative expression (e.g., furrowed brows, eyes closed tightly); Cry behaviors range from laughing or giggling to full-lunged cry (more than baseline cry); Movement behaviors range from usual movements/activity (or resting/relaxed) to agitation with complex movements involving the head, torso, or other limbs, or rigidity). Ratings along these dimensions are made by trained observers who are provided with operational definitions of the range of targeted behaviors within each dimension. Possible total scores range from 0 to 10, with individual subscale scores for the three dimensions (facial expression, 0–3; cry, 0–4; movements, 0–3).

Psychometric Information

The MBPS was developed in the context of a clinical trial evaluating the efficacy of a local anesthetic in decreasing the pain experience of infants during routine vaccination. Eleven infants were videotaped during routine vaccination and four health professionals (neurologist, pediatrician, pharmacist, physiotherapist) and one lay person subsequently completed the original Behavioral Pain Score scale while reviewing the tapes. Revisions were made on the basis of their comments and were designed to capture changes between baseline and post-vaccination pain experiences. The MBPS was subsequently used in the pain assessment of 96 healthy infants (ages 4–6 months) participating in the clinical trial.

Reliability analyses showed that the three behavioral dimensions were significantly correlated: Facial Expression and Cry ($r = .67$), Facial Expression and Movements ($r = .54$), and Cry and Movements ($r = .48$). Item-total correlations were .66

for Facial Expression, .60 for Cry, and .55 for Movements. Inter-rater agreement (five raters) on a subset of 10 infants yielded intraclass correlation coefficients of .95 for the total score, .89 for Facial Expression, .96 for Cry, and .83 for Movements. Test-retest reliability (one rater re-reviewing videotapes of same 10 infants 12 months later) was reported as .95.

The pediatrician administering the vaccine and a trained observer independently provided ratings of the infants' pain experience using a 0 to 100 mm visual analog scale (VAS). Correlations between the VAS and MBPS scores (.68, trained observer; .74, pediatrician) were provided as evidence of concurrent validity. Significantly lower MBPS scores at baseline (versus post-vaccination) and in the anesthetic group (versus placebo) were reported as evidence for construct validity.

Comment

The MBPS is a promising addition to the pediatric pain assessment toolbox. Its psychometric properties are quite good, although further validation in a more diverse group of infants (e.g., involving other medical procedures, clinical settings, acute and chronically ill infants) is needed. We agree with the authors' comment that the inter-rater reliability of the MBPS should be reevaluated since the scale's original developers served as the raters in this study. Overall, the MBPS appears to be cost-effective, user-friendly, and a valid measure of infant pain behaviors.

Relevant References

Robieux, I., Kumar, R., Radhakrishan, S., & Koren, G. (1991). Assessing pain and analgesia with a lidocaine-prilocaine emulsion in infants and toddlers during venipuncture. *Journal of Pediatrics, 118,* 971–973.

Taddio, A., Nulman, I., Koren, B. S., Stevens, B., & Koren, G. (1995). A revised measure of acute pain in infants. *Journal of Pain and Symptom Management, 10,* 456–463.

Neonatal Infant Pain Scale (NIPS)

J. Lawrence, 1993

Manual and Address Information

No manual. Direct inquiries to: Jocelyn Lawrence, Children's Hospital of Eastern Ontario, 401 Smyth Road, Ottawa, Ontario, Canada K1H 8L1.

Purpose

The NIPS is a downward extension of the Children's Hospital of Eastern Ontario Pain Scale (CHEOPS) and assesses pain in the pre-term and full-term neonate.

Format, Administration, and Scoring

The NIPS is a behavioral-observation pain measurement tool that comprises six behavioral groupings: facial expression, crying, breathing pattern, arm movement, leg movement, and state of arousal. Trained observers rate the neonates along these six dimensions at 1-minute intervals before, during, and/or after medical procedures. Each dimension has behavioral descriptors and operational definitions. Scores within each dimension range from 0 to 1, except for the Cry dimension, which has three descriptors (0, 1, 2). Total 1-minute interval scores range from 0 to 7. Behavioral descriptors for the six dimensions include:

Facial expression (0 = relaxed muscles, 1 = grimace)
Crys (0 = no cry, 1 = whimper, 2 = vigorous cry)
Breathing pattern (0 = relaxed, 1 = change in breathing)
Arms (0 = relaxed/restrained, 1 = flexed/extended)
Legs (0 = relaxed/restrained, 1 = flexed/extended)
State of arousal (0 = sleeping/awake, 1 = fussy)

The NIPS is designed to be used with pre-term neonates (i.e., gestational age <37 weeks) and full-term neonates (gestational age ≥37 weeks through 6 weeks old).

Psychometric Information

Adapted from the CHEOPS, the NIPS dimensions were constructed using behaviors identified by nurses as being reflective of pain in infants during medical procedures. A preliminary version of the scale was used in a study assessing neonates undergoing needle punctures and subsequently revised to accommodate difficulties in observing torso movements. A subsequent study involving 38 infants (27 pre-term, 11 full-term) and 90 needle sticks (capillary, venous, or arterial punctures) yielded internal consistency reliability coefficients (Cronbach's alpha) of .95, .87, and .88 for before, during, and after the procedure, respectively. Inter-rater reliability using two independent observers of 20 needle stick procedures at six 1-minute time intervals (two before, two during, two after procedure) ranged from .92 to .97 (Pearson correlation coefficients).

Construct validity was assessed by examining pain intensity scores before, during, and after the needle sticks on 22 infants, and analyses showed that pain scores at these time periods were significantly different from each other in the expected direction. Also, NIPS scores correlated with nurses' ratings of infant pain on a visual analog scale (range = .53–.84) and provided evidence for concurrent validity.

Comment

The NIPS represents an important adaptation of the CHEOPS, one of the most commonly used behavioral measures of children's pain. The evidence for reliability and construct validity is very preliminary and further evaluation of the NIPS with larger and more diverse samples is warranted. It is possible that a ceiling effect may be common in using the NIPS, as the needle puncture consistently produced scores at the high end of the scale. It may, therefore, not be a clinically useful measure of infant pain for more invasive medical procedures, although future studies may help to determine its utility in this regard. For relatively minor procedures, the NIPS is a brief, easily learned, and cost-effective method for measuring neonatal pain.

Relevant References

Lawrence, J., Alcock, D., McGrath, P., Kay, J., MacMurray, S. B., & Dulberg, C. (1993). The development of a tool to assess neonatal pain. *Neonatal Network, 12,* 59–66.

Observation Scale of Behavioral Distress (OSBD)—Revised

S. M. Jay, 1981

Manual and Address Information

There is a manual. Direct inquiries to: Susan Jay, 11500 West Olympic Boulevard #380, Los Angeles, CA, 90064-1527, (310) 479-8204.

Purpose

A modification of the Procedure Behavior Scale (PBS), the OSBD is an observational scale that measures the behavioral distress of children undergoing medical procedures. The test was originally designed for assessing behaviors indicative of pain and/or anxiety in children undergoing bone marrow aspirations (BMAs) and lumbar punctures (LPs), throughout the course of the procedure.

Format, Administration, and Scoring

The child's behavior is examined for the occurrence of eight specific behaviors considered to be indicative of anxiety and pain: information seeking ("Is the needle in?"), cry (sobbing), scream (shrieks), restraint (child resists and is physically held down), verbal resistance ("Let me loose!"), emotional support ("Momma please"), verbal pain ("It stings"), and flail (throwing arms out randomly). Children's behaviors are recorded in continuous 15-second intervals during four phases of the medical procedure, with clinicians as the providers of rating scores. Intervals are indicated on audiotape that the rater listens to through an earphone while observing the child's behavior. The four phases begin a few minutes prior to the procedure to measure anticipatory distress, and end 1½ minutes after the removal of the needle, to measure post-procedure pain/anxiety. The authors give exact lengths for each phase, yet caution that they are subject to change as a function of an institution's techniques and/or methods for conducting the particular procedure.

Raters can either watch the medical procedure live, or the procedure can be videotaped and coded at a later time. Scores that are derived include unweighted mean-interval category scores, weighted mean-interval category scores, weighted phase scores, and one Total Distress score. The frequencies of each behavior category within each phase are divided by the number of intervals scored in each phase, yielding unweighted mean-interval category scores. Weighted mean-interval category scores are derived by multiplying interval category scores by preassigned intensity weight. Weighted phase scores consist of the weighted mean-interval category scores summed across categories within each phase. The Total Distress score is the sum of the four weighted phase scores.

Psychometric Information

The OSBD was constructed by subjecting 11 original behavioral categories to an item analysis. Separate item analyses were conducted for the total sample and each age group. Categories with very low frequency or low correlations to either behavioral categories or total scores were eliminated. Therefore, criteria for retaining behavioral categories were (a) category scores had to occur for 10% or more of the subjects, and (b) item-total correlation coefficients of category scores had to be ≥.3 for the total sample and/or at least one age group. The item analyses yielded eight behavioral categories that met these criteria.

A measure of internal consistency indicated further evidence for the elimination of three of the original categories, and was .72 for the eight retained behaviors. Percent agreement, calculated by dividing the number of agreements within each interval by the total number of agreements plus disagreements has ranged from 80 to 84%.

Construct validation has been demonstrated in the OSBD's correlation with a standardized measure of children's trait anxiety (State Trait Anxiety Inventory for Children) and also with children's self-ratings of pain. OSBD scores have also been significantly correlated with nurses' ratings of children's anxiety and physiological measures of anxiety.

Comment

The OSBD is an objective measurement of a child's anxiety/pain related to specific medical procedures. The OBSD allows raters to either be present during actual procedures or to later review videotapes of procedures; reports of interrater reliability have been high. Although the measure was designed for use with BMAs and LPs, the authors suggest that it may be modified for use with other medical procedures. However, given the complexity of the recording and scoring procedures, substantial adjustments would be necessary prior to its use with other procedures. Similarly, the scoring or interval-phase process may need to be adjusted depending on institution and/or person administering the procedure. The OSBD has been used successfully in institutions other than where it was developed. Furthermore, it has been used for other procedures, specifically with children with leukemia undergoing intravenous and intramuscular injections. The contribution of the eight behavioral categories have been clearly demonstrated through item analyses and strict inclusion criteria, and they have also been found to be internally consistent. Much attention was paid to both the frequency of occurrence, as well as the intensity of the behavior, during construction of the scoring system. The OSBD has been found to have satisfactory construct validity. Overall, several published studies report using the OSBD, and each has found it to be a useful and valid assessment tool.

Relevant References

Jay, S. M., & Elliott, C. (1981). *Observation Scale of Behavioral Distress-Revised*. Los Angeles: University of Southern California.

Jay, S. M., Elliott, C. (1984). Behavioral observation scales for measuring children's distress: The effects of increased methodological rigor. *Journal of Consulting and Clinical Psychology, 52*, 1106–1107.

Jay, S. M., Ozolins, M., & Elliott, C. H. (1983). Assessment of children's distress during painful medical procedures. *Health Psychology, 2*, 133–147.

Katz, E. R., Kellerman, J., & Siegel, S. (1980). Behavioral distress in children undergoing medical procedures: Developmental considerations. *Journal of Consulting and Clinical Psychology, 48*, 355–369.

Powers, S. W., Blount, R. L., Bachanas, P. J., Cotter, M. W., & Swan, S. C. (1993). Helping preschool leukemia patients and their parents cope during injections. *Journal of Pediatric Psychology, 18*, 681–695.

Oucher Scale

J. E. Beyer, 1984

Manual and Address Information

There is a manual. Direct inquiries to: Judith E. Beyer, School of Nursing, University of Missouri, Kansas City, 2220 Holmes, Kansas City, MO 64108.

Purpose

The Oucher was developed to assess pain intensity in children ages 3 to 12.

Format, Administration, and Scoring

The Oucher is a self-report scale that contains both a vertical numerical scale (0 = no hurt to 100 = the biggest hurt you could ever have) and a corresponding vertical photographic scale mounted together on the same display sheet or card. The numerical scale is presented in 10-unit intervals, while the six photographs are positioned at 20-unit intervals. The photographs depict the same child (4-year-old boy before and after hernia repair) with varying facial expressions reflecting different levels of pain. While original descriptions of the Oucher suggested that the two scales could be used interchangeably, with the pictures serving to cue the child's use of the numerical scale, it is now recognized that the two scales are distinct and should not be used together. Children old enough to grasp the sequential meaning and value of numbers are instructed to use the numerical scale when rating pain intensity, whereas younger children use the photographic scale. Pain scores using the numerical scale range from 0 to 100, whereas scores using the photographic scale range from 0 to 5.

Psychometric Information

In their review of the methodological studies on the Oucher, Beyer, Denyes, and Villarruel (1992) reported evidence for content, convergent, discriminant, and construct validity. Seventy-eight 3- to 7-year-old children showed strong agreement in the sequencing of the six photographs (Kendall's coefficient = .73) and 77% successfully placed five or six of the photographs in the correct sequence. Sequencing agreement varied as a function of age, with younger children (3 years) showing the lowest agreement (Kendall's coefficient = .53) and older children (7 years) yielding the highest agreement (Kendall's coefficient = .99). In a sample of 18 children undergoing surgery, Oucher ratings were lowest before surgery, highest on the day of surgery, and gradually decreased in the 5 days after surgery. Similar patterns of pain ratings were obtained in a sample of 25 children receiving analgesic pain medications. Finally, the Oucher has been shown to correlate with other measures of pain intensity (Poker Chip Tool and visual analog scales; range of gamma coefficients = .70–.98), and there is evidence for alternate forms reliability between a small and large version of the Oucher.

More recently, alternate ethnic forms (Hispanic and African American) of the Oucher have been developed and evaluated. Agreement levels (Kendall's coefficient) for sequencing the photographs was .65 for 112 Hispanic children and .67 for 143 African American children. In a recent study of 104 children (52 Hispanic, 52 African American) having day surgery, the Oucher was highly correlated with a visual analog scale for both ethnic groups (Hispanic numerical scale = .89; Hispanic photographic scale = .96; African American numerical scale = .97; African American photographic scale = .95), but not significantly correlated with a measure of fear. Oucher scores before and after analgesics were given postoperatively showed that Hispanic and African American children using the numerical scale reported significantly higher pain ratings before the administration of analgesics.

Comment

The Oucher is one of the most widely used pain-intensity measures with young children and its psychometric properties have been examined in several dozen studies. It can be used efficiently and cost-effectively in many clinical settings where quick assessment of children's pain is needed, including pediatric outpatient clinics, emergency rooms, and hospital recovery rooms. The newly developed ethnic forms provide culturally sensitive alternatives for Hispanic and African American children, although support for the construct validity of the ethnic forms of the photographic scale is currently lacking. The Oucher does possess some of the same problems that exist in other pain-rating scales, and we still know very little about children's ability to use numerical rating scales. For instance, it is not clear when to administer the photographic scale or the numerical scale. Beyer recommends that children who can count to 100, identify which of two numbers is largest, and successfully complete a Piagetian task be given the numerical scale. However, this approach is time-consuming and not very practical in a busy clinical setting. Finally, it remains unclear whether the photographs more accurately reflect pain intensity or a pain-affective dimension.

Relevant References

Beyer, J. E., & Aradine, C. (1986). Content validity of an instrument to measure young children's perceptions of the intensity of their pain. *Journal of Pediatric Nursing, 1,* 386–395.

Beyer, J. E., & Aradine, C. (1987). Patterns of pediatric pain intensity: A methodological investigation of a self-report scale. *The Clinical Journal of Pain, 3,* 130–141.

Beyer, J. E., & Aradine, C. (1988). The convergent and discriminant validity of a self-report measure of pain intensity for children. *Children's Health Care, 16,* 274–282.

Beyer, J. E., Denyes, M. J., & Villarruel, A. M. (1992). The creation, validation, and continuing development of the Oucher: A measure of pain intensity in children. *Journal of Pediatric Nursing, 7,* 335–346.

Beyer, J. E., & Knott, C. B. (1998). Construct validity estimation for the African-American and Hispanic versions of the Oucher Scale. *Journal of Pediatric Nursing, 13,* 20–31.

Pediatric Pain Questionnaire (PPQ)

J. Varni, 1987

Manual and Address Information

No manual. Direct inquiries to: James W. Varni, Psychosocial Research Program, Children's Hospital and Health Center, 3030 Children's Way, Suite 103, San Diego, CA 92123-4226, (619) 495-4939, jvarni@chsd.org.

Purpose

The PPQ was developed to assess the pain perceptions of children, adolescents, and their parents.

Format, Administration, and Scoring

The PPQ combines interview data and pain-rating scales in measuring the intensity of pain, as well as the sensory, affective, and evaluative qualities of pain experienced by children and adolescents. There are three versions of the PPQ: child form, adolescent form, and parent form. Its use is most appropriate for individuals ages 5 through 18. In addition to the foregoing, the child form also permits the use of charts and colored pencils for children to indicate pain intensity and location. The adolescent and parent forms solicit additional information about pain history, specific symptoms experienced, pain remedies or treatments, and a variety of socioenvironmental situations that may be associated with pain experiences and perceptions. Information about the family's pain history also is obtained from the parent form.

Current pain intensity and worse pain intensity experienced during the preceding week are measured using visual analog scales. On the child form, the visual analog scale (100-mm horizontal line) includes happy and sad faces with anchored pain descriptors that are considered developmentally appropriate for younger children (i.e., not hurting, hurting a whole lot). Two visual analog scales are used with adolescents and parents, and the anchors reflect a more mature cognitive developmental level (e.g., hurting and discomfort; no pain and severe pain). The PPQ also includes a visual analog scale for physicians to complete in assessing the child's current pain intensity. In all versions of the visual analog scale, a vertical line is drawn on the scale continuum to indicate the pain intensity (e.g., no pain to severe pain).

Psychometric Information

Several large studies have reported validity and reliability data on the PPQ, and these have included children and adolescents with arthritis, sickle cell disease, hemophilia, reflex sympathetic dystrophy, and cancer and their parents. Samples were predominantly White, middle- to upper-middle class and the majority of children and adolescents had mild to moderate disease or no apparent disease symptoms. Several studies have reported adequate convergent validity, with moderately high positive correlations between parent, child/adolescent, and physician pain-intensity ratings. The authors report as evidence of construct validity the consistently positive associations between PPQ visual analog scale ratings and several indices of disease severity and activity in children and adolescents, as well as the reductions in PPQ visual analog scale ratings following analgesia administration postoperatively. The functional status of chronically ill children and adolescents has been predicted successfully by PPQ ratings, particularly when used in combination with other important measures. While the nature of pain is highly variable, the PPQ visual analog scales have shown stability (6-month test-retest) in one large sample of children and adolescents with juvenile rheumatoid arthritis whose disease activity was very stable over time.

Comment

The PPQ is a useful and valid assessment tool that combines interview data and rating scales in the measurement of children's pain experiences. In addition to the visual analog scales, important diagnostic and treatment information is obtained regarding the terms used by children and adolescents to describe the sensory and affective components of their pain experiences, the emotional factors that might be associated with pain (e.g., unhappy, anxious, angry, lonely, happy), and activities that might be affected by pain (e.g., schoolwork, seeing friends, sports). While the comprehensive nature of the PPQ permits the solicitation of pain-related information from multiple sources, it does require a considerable amount of time to administer and, consequently, the full version may not be a cost-effective choice in many busy clinical settings. However, the PPQ visual analog scales have been shown to be psychometrically sound, practical, and easy to administer to even very young children. The authors have conducted numerous studies using the PPQ and have a demonstrated commitment to ongoing evaluation of its reliability and validity. In this context, examination of its applicability to more diverse ethnic and socioeconomic groups would provide useful additional information for clinicians and researchers.

Relevant References

Gragg, R. A., Rapoff, M. A., Danovsky, M. B., Lindsley, C. B., Varni, J. W., Waldron, S. A., & Bernstein, B. H. (1996). Assessing chronic musculoskeletal pain associated with rheumatic disease: Further validation of the Pediatric Pain Questionnaire. *Journal of Pediatric Psychology, 21,* 237–250.

Varni, J. W., Rapoff, M. A., Waldron, S. A., Gragg, R. A., Bernstein, B. H., & Lindsley, C. B. (1996). Effects of perceived stress on pediatric chronic pain. *Journal of Behavioral Medicine, 19,* 515–528.

Varni, J. W., Thompson, K. L., & Hanson, V. (1987). The Varni/Thompson Pediatric Pain Questionnaire. I. Chronic musculoskeletal pain in juvenile rheumatoid arthritis. *Pain, 28,* 27–38.

Varni, J. W., Wilcox, K. T., Hanson, V., & Brik, R. (1988). Chronic musculoskeletal pain and functional status in juvenile rheumatoid arthritis: An empirical model. *Pain, 32,* 1–7.

Perception of Procedures Questionnaire (PPQ)

A. Kazak, 1995

Manual and Address Information

No manual. Direct inquiries to: Anne Kazak, Division of Oncology, The Children's Hospital of Philadelphia, 324 South 34th Street, Philadelphia, PA 19104-4399, (215) 590-2220, kazak@kermit.oncol.chop.edu.

Purpose

The PPQ is a brief parent-report measure of distress experienced by children with leukemia before and during medical procedures. This measure also assesses the procedural context, parents' satisfaction with and involvement in their child's medical treatment, and the parents' own distress.

Format, Administration, and Scoring

The PPQ is a 19-item paper-and-pencil questionnaire to which parents respond using a 7-point Likert-type scale. It can be self-administered during the child's clinic appointment or in the convenience of the parent's home. Factor analyses have produced five factors or scales: Parent Satisfaction (6 items); Child Distress: During (5 items); Child Distress: Before (4 items); Parent Distress (2 items); and Parent Involvement (2 items). Separate scores are obtained for each of the factors. Lower scores indicate lower levels of distress and higher levels of parent satisfaction and involvement. Sample items include:

> How satisfied are you with the medical services in the division?
>
> How much distress does your child experience during bone marrow aspirations?
>
> How distressed does your child become on the morning of a visit for a spinal tap?
>
> How distressed do you becoming during bone marrow aspirations?
>
> How actively are you involved during spinal taps, bone marrow aspirations, and administration of chemotherapy?

Psychometric Information

The standardization sample comprised 140 mothers and 96 fathers of children and adolescents with leukemia in first remission who were taking part in a research protocol on interventions for procedural pain (Analgesia Protocol for Procedures in Oncology study). The majority of the children were White (87%; 9% African American) and had received their cancer diagnosis within the preceding 2 years. Cancer treatments included multiagent chemotherapy, lumbar punctures, and bone marrow aspirations.

The PPQ has high internal consistency for both mothers (coefficient alphas for total measure and factors: .89, .95, .91, .84, .92, .91) and fathers (coefficient alphas for total measure and factors: .86, .91, .90, .84, .94, .82). High mother-father correspondence was similarly high for the Child Distress: Before factor (.77) and the Child Distress: During factor (.83).

Concurrent validity was assessed by examining the relationship between PPQ factor scores and the Pediatric Oncology Quality of Life Scale (POQOLS) and the Parenting Stress Index-Short Form (PSI-S). The POQOLS emotional distress factor score was correlated with mothers' PPQ child distress (before = .29 and during = .43) and fathers' PPQ child distress (before = .32) factor scores, and the PSI-S Parent-Child Dysfunctional Interaction score was correlated with mothers' PPQ Child Distress (before = .41 and during = .32) factor scores. Discriminant validity was assessed by correlating the PPQ Child Distress (before and during) factor scores with separate parent and nurse observational ratings of child distress during an actual procedure. Both parents' and nurses' observational ratings were correlated with PPQ Child Distress: During (.34 to .61) factor scores but not with PPQ Child Distress: Before (.06 to .14) factor scores. Parents' self-reported distress during an actual procedure was also correlated with the PPQ Parent Distress factor score (.39 for mothers and .59 for fathers).

Comment

The PPQ is a brief, easily completed parent-report measure of child and parent distress during medical procedures performed throughout the diagnosis and treatment of childhood leukemia. Most of its items are specific to spinal taps and bone marrow aspirations and, consequently, use of the PPQ is presently limited to this chronic illness population. While the development of the PPQ is still in its early stages, this instrument has several strengths. These include its usefulness and strong psychometric properties with both mothers and fathers, its ability to discriminate between procedural distress and anticipatory distress, and its cost-effectiveness. Additional research is needed, however, to assess the predictive validity of the PPQ in detecting changes in child- and parent-procedural distress following appropriate interventions, to more systematically examine developmental differences in child-procedural distress, and to assess its applicability to a more culturally diverse group of children with leukemia and their parents. Despite these relative limitations, the PPQ can easily be integrated into existing clinical and research protocols as a measure of procedural distress from the parent's perspective. As with other parent-report assessment tools, use of the PPQ should be supplemented with measures tapping the child's perception of their own procedural distress.

Relevant References

Kazak, A. E., Boyer, B., Brophy, P., Johnson, K., Scher, C., Covelman, K., & Scott, S. (1995). Parental perceptions of procedure-related distress and family adaptation in childhood leukemia. *Children's Health Care, 24,* 143–158.

Kazak, A. E., Penati, B., Boyer, B., Himelstein, B., Brophy, P., Waibel, M. K., Blackall, G., Daller, R., & Johnson, K. (1996). A randomized controlled prospective outcome study of a psychological and pharmacological intervention protocol for procedural distress in pediatric leukemia. *Journal of Pediatric Psychology, 21,* 615–631.

Kazak, A. E., Penati, B., Waibel, M. C., & Blackall, G. F. (1996). The Perception of Procedures Questionnaire: Psychometric properties of a brief parent report measure of procedural distress. *Journal of Pediatric Psychology, 21,* 195–207.

Kazak, A. E., & Barakat, L. (1997). Parenting stress and quality of life during treatment for childhood leukemia predicts child and parent adjustment after treatment ends. *Journal of Pediatric Psychology, 22,* 749–758.

Scare Scale (SS)

J. E. Beyer, 1988

Manual and Address Information

No manual. Direct inquiries to: Judith E. Beyer, School of Nursing, University of Missouri, Kansas City, 2220 Holmes, Kansas City, MO 64108.

Purpose

The SS is a single-item instrument that was designed to measure children's ratings of fear during various medical situations. Specifically, it was developed to assist in devising pain-management strategies for children.

Format, Administration, and Scoring

The SS has been used with children from ages 3 to 13. The scale consists of one item asking children to indicate how afraid or scared they are *now* in their immediate situation. An example of administration of the SS might be "How afraid are you right now of being in the hospital 2 days after your heart operation?" Intensity of fear is indicated on a 5-point circle scale. Not at all afraid is coded 0. The smallest circle, a little afraid, is coded 1, through the largest circle, very much afraid, coded 4. As opposed to asking children to rate their fear retrospectively, the SS focuses on the child's present experience.

Psychometric Information

The SS has been used in relatively few studies, yet preliminary psychometric data have been reported. One investigation used the SS in examining the relationship between children's pain and their self-reported perceptions of fear. Specific aims of the study included examining the ways in which pain influences children's hospital experience, coping style, and recovery rate. The SS was administered to 79 hospitalized children. School-age children reportedly had little difficulty completing the measure, yet more assistance was needed with younger children. Some reports of difficulty with the meaning of "scared" versus "afraid" were indicated by the authors. The authors reported a moderate correlation between the SS and another standardized measure of hospital-related fears, yet this relationship was weaker for younger children. There was little correlation with the SS and measures of pain.

Comment

The SS is a single-item word and visual instrument used to assess children's fear related to immediate situations. Its format appears to be child-friendly and easy to administer. The SS has been used with an adequate sample of hospitalized children, and different stressors have been used as the "immediate situation." Some construct validity of the measure has been demonstrated by its significant correlation with another measure of children's fear. Descriptive data of the SS have not been reported. Furthermore, the SS's reliability has not been investigated. In terms of its use with such a young population (age 3), it is unclear if results vary depending on the amount of assistance with which children are provided when completing the measure. The SS appears to be useful for assessing fear in various clinical situations. However, its utility as a measure of children's fear in empirical studies is dependent on further investigation of its psychometric properties.

Relevant References

Beyer, J. E., & Aradine, C. R. (1988). Convergent and discriminant validity of a self-report measure of pain intensity for children. *Children's Health Care, 16,* 274–282.

Toddler-Preschooler Postoperative Pain Scale (TPPPS)

S. E. Tarbell, 1992

Manual and Address Information

No manual. Direct inquiries to: Sally E. Tarbell, University of Pittsburgh Cancer Institute, 3600 Forbes Avenue, Suite 405, Pittsburgh, PA 15213, (412) 624-4806, starbell+@pitt.edu..

Purpose

The TPPPS is an observational measure developed to assess postoperative pain in children ages 1 to 5.

Format, Administration, and Scoring

This observational pain measurement tool has seven behavioral items across three categories: Vocal Pain Expression, Facial Pain Expression, and Bodily Pain Expression. Using detailed coding procedures, trained observers rate the child (ages 1–5) in the immediate postoperative period upon awakening from anesthesia. The seven behavioral items are scored as being present (1) or not present (0) during 5-minute time intervals. The number of pain behaviors that were present during a 5-minute interval is summed to yield a total TPPPS score (range = 0–7). Observations are discontinued if the child falls asleep. The TPPPS categories and behavioral items include:

Vocal Pain Expression	Verbal complaint/cry
	Groan/moan/grunt
	Scream
Facial Pain Expression	Pull back mouth
	Squint/close eyes
	Forehead furrow
Bodily Pain Expression	Restless/rub body part

Psychometric Information

TPPPS items were developed through preliminary studies conducted by the authors and other pain researchers. Initially, 15 pain-behavior items were generated, but 6 items were subsequently discarded due to their low frequency of occurrence and low item-to-total correlations. The initial validation sample consisted of 74 predominantly White (95%; 4% Black) 1- to 5-year-old children (15 girls, 59 boys) who were observed during 2- to six 5-minute intervals immediately upon awakening from surgery for inguinal hernia or hydrocele repair.

Internal consistency reliability (Cronbach's alpha) was .88 for the TPPPS scores aggregated across all observation intervals and ranged from .82 to .86 for the individual observation intervals. Inter-rater reliability using 28 children (38% of sample) yielded kappa coefficients ranging from .53 (Forehead furrow) to .78 (Scream).

A significant decrease in TPPPS scores after the administration of postoperative analgesia in 25 children, and higher TPPPS scores in children receiving both intra- and postoperative analgesics and more potent analgesics were provided as evidence for discriminant validity. Regarding concurrent validity, TPPPS scores were positively correlated with nurses' and parents' ratings on a visual analog scale (.36–.55 and .43–.61, respectively) and nurses' ratings on a numerical pain rating scale (.32–.63). Unlike TPPPS scores, nurse- and parent-pain ratings did not distinguish children according to their intraoperative analgesia regimen. Mean TPPPS scores also were significantly correlated with low and high intraoperative systolic blood pressure (.32 and .35, respectively) and the mean postoperative respiratory rate (.35).

Comment

The TPPPS is a broad-band behavioral measure that allows for the assessment of surgical pain in the immediate postoperative recovery period. It appears to be a reliable and valid measure that can be used efficiently by nurses in a recovery room to guide the use and effectiveness of analgesic medication with very young children. The authors have noted that further validation studies are needed because observers in the initial study were not blind to the administration of postoperative analgesics and narcotics were the analgesic of choice, which did not allow for appropriate TPPPS comparisons by analgesic type. It was suggested that a minimum of two 5-minute observation intervals be conducted when using the TPPPS. It is possible that fewer than six observations and shorter time intervals would produce reliable and valid pain ratings, but further empirical scrutiny is needed before drawing this conclusion. Finally, the restricted sample demographics (i.e., mostly White boys undergoing minor surgery) necessitates further evaluation of the TPPPS with children of different ethnicity undergoing a broader range of surgical procedures.

Relevant References

Christiano, B., & Tarbell, S. E. (1998). Brief report: Behavioral correlates of postoperative pain in toddlers and preschoolers. *Journal of Pediatric Psychology, 23,* 149–154.

Tarbell, S. E., Cohen, I. T., & Marsh, J. L. (1992). The Toddler-Preschooler Postoperative Pain Scale: An observational scale for measuring postoperative pain in children aged 1–5—Preliminary report. *Pain, 50,* 273–280.

Tarbell, S. E., Marsh, J. L., & Cohen, I. T. (1991). Reliability and validity of the PAS: A scale for measuring postoperative pain in young children [Abstract 196]. *Journal of Pain and Symptom Management, 6.*

General Observations and Recommendations

The empirical literatures in pediatrics, psychology, and nursing have witnessed an explosion of new assessment tools for measuring pain in children. While we have provided reviews for many such measures, still there are other pain measurement techniques to be found in the anesthesiology, dentistry, and pharmacology literatures. Clearly, progress has been made in the development of valid and reliable pediatric-pain assessment methods, especially for infants and young children. Some instruments (e.g., Pediatric Pain Questionnaire) even extend beyond more traditional self-report questionnaires and incorporate more multidimensional components of pediatric-pain assessment. In reviewing available instruments, we experienced considerable enthusiasm tempered with appropriate caution regarding the future of pediatric-pain and childhood-injury assessment. For instance, we are hopeful that the preponderance of pain measures may lead health professionals to rely less on personal beliefs and attitudes about pain management as they have done in the past (Beyer & Byers, 1985; Ross, Bush, & Crummette, 1991). Nevertheless, we have several observations and recommendations that we share. Many of these same observations and recommendations have been made by notable experts in the field (e.g., Karoly, 1991; McGrath, 1990; Tarnowski & Kaufman, 1988), but we repeat them here hoping that repetition will be helpful in advancing the field.

First, the need to further evaluate existing pediatric-pain measures supersedes the need to develop additional assessment tools at the present time. Researchers must provide additional validity and reliability data on existing pain-assessment tools and such data should include larger samples involving greater representation of children (i.e., developmental level, sex, ethnicity, health condition, etc.). Some instruments reviewed (e.g., Child-Adult Medical Procedure Interaction Scale-Revised) provide excellent examples of the substantive studies that are necessary to effectively document acceptable psychometric properties.

Second, it is essential to document a pediatric-pain instrument's sensitivity to change and cost-effectiveness. These issues are critically important in the development, implementation, and evaluation of pain-management programs for children. Third, attention to cross-validation of the different pain-assessment methodologies is lacking and further assessment in this regard is warranted.

Fourth, a more sophisticated approach to examining the developmental appropriateness of pediatric-pain instruments is necessary. Age is an inaccurate proxy measure for child development, yet it is most commonly used to identify the range of children for whom pain assessment tools are appropriate. It is often difficult to separate pain intensity from distress and emotions in children because of the nature of language and affective development in young children.

Fifth, the most well-developed and validated pain-measurement tools are most appropriate for acute (mostly procedural), but not intermittent or chronic, pain. This is particularly true for behavioral-observation assessment approaches. Additional research is needed to examine the utility of existing measures in assessing chronic childhood pain, especially that which persists in the child's natural environment.

Sixth, while some measures are model-driven, most do not emanate from conceptually-driven assessment methodologies (see Karoly, 1991). The fact that pain is recognized as a multidimensional phenomenon highlights the need for assessment tools to reflect the complexity of its manifestations (e.g., Child-Adult Medical Procedure Interaction Scale-Revised, Pediatric Pain Questionnaire).

Finally, childhood injury researchers have developed new and interesting proxy measures (e.g., Injury Behavior Checklist, Minor Injury Severity Scale), and these questionnaires should prove useful in injury prevention research. Nevertheless, we concur with Finney and colleagues (1993) who concluded that "the development of improved measures of injuries, behaviors, and environmental characteristics that are useful for injury research and program evaluation" (p. 521) is urgently needed.

References

Beyer, J. E., & Byers, M. L. (1985). Knowledge of pediatric pain: The state of the art. *Children's Health Care, 13,* 150–159.

Bush, J. P., & Harkins, S. W. (1991). Conceptual foundations: Pain and child development. In J. P. Bush, & S. W. Harkins. (Eds.), *Children in pain: Clinical and research issues from a developmental perspective* (pp. 1–30). New York: Springer-Verlag.

Bush, J. P., & Harkins, S. W. (Eds.). (1991). *Children in pain: Clinical and research issues from a developmental perspective.* New York: Springer-Verlag.

Finney, J. W., Christophersen, E. R., Friman, P. C., Kalnins, I. V., Maddux, J. E., Peterson, L., Roberts, M. C., & Wolraich, M. (1993). Society of Pediatric Psychology task force report: Pediatric psychology and injury control. *Journal of Pediatric Psychology, 18,* 499–526.

Karoly, P. (1991). Assessment of pediatric pain. In J. P. Bush, & S. W. Harkins. (Eds.), *Children in pain: Clinical and research issues from a developmental perspective* (pp. 59–82). New York: Springer-Verlag.

McGrath, P. A. (1990). *Pain in children: Nature, assessment, and treatment.* New York: Guilford Press.

McGrath, P. A., & Hillier, L. M. (1996). Controlling children's pain. In R. J. Gatchel, & D. C. Turk. (Eds.), *Psychological approaches to pain management: A practitioner's handbook* (pp. 331–370). New York: Guilford Press.

McGrath, P. J., & Unruh, A. (1987). *Pain in children and adolescents.* Amsterdam: Elsevier.

National Committee for Injury Prevention and Control. (1989). *Injury prevention: Meeting the challenge.* New York: Oxford University Press.

Rodriguez, J. G. (1990). Childhood injuries in the United States: A priority issue. *American Journal of Diseases of Children, 144,* 625–626.

Ross, D. M., & Ross, S. A. (1988). *Childhood pain: Current issues, research, and management.* Baltimore: Urban and Schwarzenberg.

Ross, R. S., Bush, J. P., & Crummette, B. D. (1991). Factors affecting nurses' decisions to administer PRN analgesic medication to children after surgery: An analog investigation. *Journal of Pediatric Psychology, 16,* 151–167.

Schechter, N. L., Berde, C. B., & Yaster, M. (Eds.). (1993). *Pain in infants, children, and adolescents.* Baltimore: Williams & Wilkins.

Tarnowski, K. J., & Kaufman, K. L. (1988). Behavioral assessment of pediatric pain. In R. J. Prinz (Ed.), *Advances in behavioral assessment of children and families (Vol. 4)* (pp. 119–158). New York: JAI Press.

Varni, J. (1984). Pediatric pain: A biobehavioral perspective. *Behavior Therapist, 7,* 23–25.

Chapter 8

Quality of Life

JAMES R. RODRIGUE

Quality of life is recognized by child health researchers, clinicians, and policy makers as a primary measure of disease and treatment outcome. While it has not kept pace with that of adults with chronic health conditions, research focusing on quality of life issues in children has increased exponentially in recent years. Improved survival rates for several chronic conditions most frequently are identified as the catalyst propelling the construct of quality of life to the forefront of scientific inquiry. Quality of life assessments are now routinely implemented in clinical trials as well as in more general estimations of population-based health care needs (e.g., Spieth & Harris, 1996). The primary applications of such assessments include those that discriminate among children along various health, illness, and disability parameters; predict prognosis or treatment outcome; and longitudinally evaluate changes in individual children (Jaeschke & Guyatt, 1990).

Athough the field has moved forward and several essential advances have been made in measuring this important health-related construct, researchers and clinicians alike have confronted numerous challenges regarding the conceptualization, definition, and measurement of quality of life in children. Defining what is meant by "quality of life" has been especially difficult. While several authors have noted that a universally accepted definition is lacking (Aaronson, 1988; Spieth & Harris, 1996), most professionals agree that quality of life is multidimensional and incorporates both objective and subjective aspects of disease state, physical symptoms, functional status, and psychological and social functioning into its definition (Aaronson, 1988; Landgraf & Abetz, 1996). Equally important as the defining features of quality of life is the conceptual model from which one chooses to measure it. Several conceptual models have been proposed and have guided the development of functional (e.g., Health Status Measure for Children) and value-based measures (e.g., Quality of Well Being Scale) of childhood quality of life (Eisen, Ware, Donald, & Brook, 1979; Rosenbaum, Cadman, & Kirpalani, 1990; Torrence, 1987). Unfortunately, many authors reporting the development and use of quality of life instruments in the child health literature have not clearly specified the conceptual and definitional assumptions guiding measurement development. Given the relevance of these assumptions to the dimensions that are selected for measurement, child health clinicians and researchers interested in using quality of life indices in their work should evaluate carefully the instrument's conceptual foundation.

Quality of life instruments tend to be categorized as either generic or specific. Generic measures provide a global or summary rating of quality of life, usually across multiple areas of functioning (e.g., Quality of Well Being Scale), or health profiles that provide information about specific domains (e.g., Child Health and Illness Profile, Health Status Measure for Children). These instruments allow for quality of life comparisons to be made across different groups of children, although they have been criticized for lacking precision and sensitivity in detecting changes over time in certain populations (Spieth & Harris, 1996). Specific measures of quality of life examine domains that are most relevant to specific diseases, treatments, or populations (e.g., Pediatric Oncology Quality of Life Scale). These measures are considered to have greater clinical relevance than more generic instruments, although they tend not to be as comprehensive (Aaronson, 1988). We recommend the use of both generic and specific measures in clinical and research protocols whenever possible.

Another important feature on which quality of life measures may differ is the individual selected to make judgments about the child's functioning. Parents, health providers, and children themselves may be asked to respond to questions about health status and functioning. Research has found only moderate levels of agreement between parents and health providers in ratings of children's quality of life, and there is some evidence of low correlations between parents and children on ratings across certain domains (McCormick, Atreya, Bernbaum, & Charney, 1988; Pantell & Lewis, 1987). While different perspectives add a level of complexity to the assessment process, there clearly is a need for obtaining quality of life measures from multiple sources whenever possible. Indeed, some measures have been developed that permit quality of life assessment from both children and parents (e.g., Child Health Questionnaire).

The reviews that follow provide a sampling of the different types of quality of life measures that are available to child health professionals. We recognize that our list of included measures is not exhaustive, yet we attempted to provide examples of both generic and specific quality of life measures that have been developed specifically for use with children.

REVIEWS

Child Health and Illness Profile—Adolescent Edition (CHIP-AE)

B. Starfield, 1993

Manual and Address Information

There is a manual. Direct inquiries to: Barbara Starfield, 624 North Broadway, Baltimore, MD 21205, (410) 955-9725.

Purpose

The CHIP-AE is a generic adolescent health status questionnaire.

Format, Administration, and Scoring

The CHIP-AE is a self-administered questionnaire containing 107 items plus an additional 46 items that are specific to disease or injury. It is intended for use with adolescents from ages 11 through 17. The CHIP-AE comprises 6 domains and 20 subdomains that were conceptually derived and partially supported by factor analysis. The domains and subdomains include:

Domain	Subdomain
Satisfaction	Satisfaction with Health
	Self-Esteem
Discomfort	Physical Discomfort
	Emotional Discomfort
	Limitations of Activity
Disorders	Acute Minor Disorders
	Acute Major Disorders
	Recurrent Disorders
	Long-Term Medical
	Long-Term Surgical
	Psychosocial
Risks	Individual Risks
	Threats to Achievement
	Peer Influences

Resilience	Family Involvement
	Problem-Solving
	Physical Activity
	Home Safety and Health
Achievement	Academic Performance
	Work Performance

Symptoms and signs of illness and health protective behaviors are reported in terms of the number of days they occurred on a five-response format (no days to 15–28 days). Other scales are in a 4-point or 5-point Likert format. Scores for each domain are obtained by computing the average of the individual item responses. Domain scores are obtained by averaging the subdomain scores. Higher scores indicate more of the measured construct. The full CHIP-AE can be completed in about 30 minutes.

Psychometric Information

CHIP-AE items were generated on the basis of literature reviews, focus groups with children, adolescents, and parents, and consultation with several dozen health professionals and researchers. The initial measure was piloted, revised, and then administered to 3,451 urban and rural youths in four geographic locations (two predominantly Black urban Baltimore samples, one predominantly White rural Maryland sample, one predominantly Black rural Arkansas sample). Two samples of parents ($n = 400$) in Baltimore also completed the CHIP-AE.

Internal consistency reliability analyses yielded Cronbach's alphas exceeding .70 for all subdomains (except Academic Performance) in at least two out of four samples. Subdomain alphas for each of the domains ranged as follows: Satisfaction (.68–.87), Discomfort (.63–.93), Disorders (not computed), Risks (.70–.89), Resilience (.76–.85), and Achievement (.53–.78). Test-Retest reliability (1 week) with one of the Baltimore samples showed good stability (≥.60 intraclass correlation or Pi coefficients and ≥.60 Pearson correlation or Spearman's correlation coefficients) for 19 of 20 subdomains (exception was Home Safety and Health subdomain in Resilience domain).

To assess criterion validity, parent-adolescent correspondence on the CHIP-AE was examined. Intraclass correlation coefficients ranged from .11 (Physical Discomfort) to .45 (Home Safety and Health), Cohen's kappas ranged from .13 (Limitations of Activity) to .50 (Long-Term Medical Disorders), and Pearson's and Spearman's correlation coefficients ranged from .16 (Acute Minor Disorders) to .51 (Home Safety and Health). The correlations between Emotional Discomfort and scores on the State-Trait Anxiety Inventory-Children and the Children's Depression Inventory, as well as between Family Involvement and scores on the Family Assessment Device-General Functioning were provided as evidence for the convergent validity of these two subdomains (.59–.68). Hypothesized age, gender, and socioeconomic differences were found on the CHIP-AE and provided as evidence of discriminant validity.

Comment

The CHIP-AE is a potentially useful adolescent-specific measure of general health. Its evaluation on large, culturally and geographically diverse samples is a significant strength. The conceptually derived and empirically refined subdomains seem to be rather cohesive and demonstrate adequate levels of reliability and validity. The measure is rather long and time-consuming, and it may prove burdensome in some busy clinical settings. A shorter version is under development for situations where comprehensiveness is not critical. The authors noted that they are conducting additional studies to examine the measure's utility and psychometric properties with pediatric and psychiatric samples. The psychometric qualities of a child instrument and a parent version are currently being studied in a series of four large field tests for children ages 5 to 10. While they stated that the CHIP-AE will be particularly useful in evaluating community and health services programs, more careful evaluation of its predictive validity is necessary before using it as the sole or primary outcome measure in such investigations. The research group has developed a method for reporting health status of groups of adolescents that characterizes a youth in terms of 1 of 13 profiles or patterns of health. They report that these profiles may have utility in health resources planning and policy.

Relevant References

Riley, A. W., Forrest, C. B., Starfield, B., Green, B., Kang, M., & Ensminger, M. (in press). A taxonomy of adolescent health need: Reliability and validity of the adolescent health and illness profiles. *Medical Care.*

Riley, A. W., Green, B. F., Starfield, B., Forrest, C. B., Kang, M., & Ensminger, M. (1998). A taxonomy of adolescent health need: Development of the adolescent health and illness profiles. *Medical Care, 36,* 1228–1236.

Starfield, B., Bergner, M., Ensminger, M. E., Riley, A. W., Ryan, S. A., Green, B. F., McGauhey, P., Skinner, A., & Kim, S. (1993). Adolescent health status measurement: Development of the Child Health and Illness Profile. *Pediatrics, 91,* 430–435.

Starfield, B., Riley, A. W., Green, B. F., Ensminger, M. E., Ryan, S. A., Kelleher, K., Kim-Harris, S., Johnston, D., & Vogel, K. (1995). The Adolescent Child Health and Illness Profile: A population-based measure of health. *Medical Care, 33,* 553–566.

Child Health Assessment Inventory (CHAI)

M. S. Ulione, 1997

Manual and Address Information

No manual. Direct inquiries to: Margaret Smith Ulione, Barnes College of Nursing, University of Missouri-St. Louis, 8001 Natural Bridge Road, St. Louis, MO 63121.

Purpose

The CHAI is a biophysiological measure designed to assess children's health and injuries.

Format, Administration, and Scoring

This measure uses a combined structured observational and self-report format in which the child's health is assessed by physical examination and a series of interview questions. The CHAI has two sections: child's current illness symptoms and injuries and child's history of chronic illnesses, accident or injury patterns, and current medications. The severity of illness symptoms is rated by the nurse clinician using a 0- to 6-point scale, with lower scores indicating better health. No additional scoring information is provided.

Psychometric Information

The CHAI was used with 29 children (ages 6 weeks to 5 years) in a university child care center who were participating in a study examining the health benefits of a nurse-directed health promotion program. Examination of pre- and post-intervention CHAI scores showed that the intervention was effective in decreasing upper respiratory illness and accidental injury rates. Inter-rater reliability of the current and recent health of 15 children from the study was .92 (Pearson product-moment correlation).

Comment

The CHAI's very limited validity and reliability data should caution against its adoption as a primary measure of children's health and injury status. Furthermore, the inclusion of a physical examination of the child precludes its use by health professionals other than nurse clinicians or pediatricians. A more convenient, psychometrically sound, and culturally sensitive measure of preschoolers' health and injury status would seem more appropriate in future evaluations of child care health promotion programs.

Relevant References

Ulione, M. S. (1997). Health promotion and injury prevention in a child development center. *Journal of Pediatric Nursing, 12,* 148–154.

Child Health Questionnaire (CHQ) Child Form

J. M. Landgraf, 1996

Manual and Address Information

There is a manual. Direct inquiries to: Jeanne M. Landgraf, HealthAct, 205 Newbury Street, 4th Floor, Boston, MA 02116, (617) 375-7800, jml@healthact.com.

Purpose

The CHQ-Child Form (CF) is a paper-and-pencil measure completed by children at least 10 years old and is designed to assess their perceived physical and psychosocial health status. It was designed to be used for children with and without chronic health conditions.

Format, Administration, and Scoring

The CHQ-CF contains 87 items that are grouped according to the particular health dimension being assessed. Some questions require a simple yes or no response, whereas others ask parents to indicate the frequency of specific events using various scales. For the majority of questions, children are asked to respond with reference to the last 4 weeks.

The CHQ-CF measures 12 multidimensional health concepts. These health concepts include the following:

Global Health assesses child's perception of current health status.

Physical Functioning assesses whether the child has any physical limitations secondary to health-related problems and, if so, the degree of limitation.

Role/Social Limitations—Physical measures the presence and extent of any limitations in the child's school-related work and social activities due to physical health problems.

General Health Perceptions assesses perceived overall health (past, present, and future) and illness susceptibility.

Bodily Pain/Discomfort measures the intensity and frequency of child pain symptoms and discomfort.

Role/Social Limitations—Emotional assesses the presence and extent of any limitations in the child's school-related work and social activities due to emotional difficulties.

Role/Social Limitations—Behavioral assesses the presence and extent of any limitations in the child's school-related work and social activities due to behavioral difficulties.

Self-Esteem measures the child's satisfaction with school and athleticism, attractiveness and physical appearance, interpersonal relations, and life.

Mental Health assesses the frequency of anxiety, depression, and positive affect.

Behavior measures the frequency of behavior problems as well as the child's overall behavior.

Family taps the degree to which the family is impacted by the child's health and behavior. Two subscales are included that measure the extent of family disruption in activities (*Family Activities*) and family relationships in general (*Family Cohesion*).

In addition to these 12 scales, 1 additional 1-item scale (Change in Health) is included to measure the child's change in health over the past 12 months.

This measure can easily be administered across multiple settings (clinic, home) and there is an interview script in the manual that can be used for face-to-face administrations.

Psychometric Information

The primary standardization sample for the CHQ-CF was comprised of 263 children from a predominantly African American middle school who completed the instrument in the classroom setting. Additional standardization data are provided for three clinic-based samples: 55 children diagnosed with attention-deficit hyperactivity disorder, 30 children diagnosed with cystic fibrosis, and 19 children with end-stage renal failure.

Item internal consistency values exceeded the .40 standard in all but three scales. For the primary and clinical samples, the General Health, Mental Health, and General Behavior scales consistently yielded low item correlations. Very good item discriminant validity was reported for all scales across the different samples. Internal consistency estimates for the scales was very good, with 9 of the 10 multi-item scales exceeding .70 (range = .73–.97). The General Health scale showed the lowest internal consistency (.63).

Comment

The CHQ-CF is a very promising measure of child-reported health-related quality of life. It has a number of advantages over other child health questionnaires, including its conceptual underpinnings, comprehensiveness, ease of administration, and applicability to a wide range of child populations. The manual, which contains information about all versions of the CHQ, is very comprehensive; however, information specific to the CHQ-CF is often difficult to locate as it is embedded in sections focusing on the parent-report versions throughout the manual. At this time the CHQ-CF is not as well studied as its corresponding parent-report version (CHQ-PF). A nationally representative standardization sample is not currently available, and the primary norm reference group is predominantly African

American and from one middle school. Furthermore, two of the clinical samples were comprised primarily of African American and Hispanic American adolescents, thus raising the issue of generalization across culturally diverse groups of children and adolescents. While the CHQ-CF is for use with children ages 10 to 18, the manual does not specify what minimal reading level is necessary to complete the instrument; however, an interview script is available if a child's reading ability precludes self-completion. Unlike the parent-report version, summary scales are not currently available for the CHQ-CF. The authors note that studies are underway to recruit a national sample of adolescents, improve the reliability of some scales (e.g., General Health, Mental Health, General Behavior), develop a short-form, and develop summary measures like its parent-report version, all of which should make the CHQ-CF a solid choice for child health clinicians and researchers.

Relevant References

Kurtin, P., Landgraf, J. M., & Abetz, L. (1994). Patient-based health status measures in pediatric dialysis: Expanding the assessment of outcomes. *American Journal of Kidney Diseases, 24,* 376–382.

Landgraf, J. M., & Abetz, L. (1997). Functional status and well-being of children representing three cultural groups: Initial self-reports using the Child Health Questionnaire (CHQ-CF87). *Psychology and Health, 12,* 839–854.

Landgraf, J. M., Abetz, L., & Ware, J. E. (1996). *The CHQ user's manual.* Boston: The Health Institute, New England Medical Center.

Child Health Questionnaire (CHQ) Parent Form

J. M. Landgraf, 1996

Manual and Address Information

There is a manual. Direct inquiries to: Jeanne M. Landgraf, HealthAct, 205 Newbury Street, 4th Floor, Boston, MA 02116, (617) 375-7800, jml@healthact.com.

Purpose

The CHQ-Parent Form (PF) is a paper-and-pencil measure completed by parents and is designed to assess the physical and psychosocial health status of children ages 5 and older. It was designed to be used for children with and without chronic health conditions.

Format, Administration, and Scoring

There are three versions of the CHQ-PF, although the only difference among the versions is length (28 items, 50 items, 98 items) and time of completion (approximately 20 minutes for the 50-item version). Parents respond to questions that are grouped according to the particular health dimension being assessed. Some questions require a simple yes or no response, whereas others ask parents to indicate the frequency of specific events using various scales. For the majority of questions, parents are asked to respond with reference to the last 4 weeks.

The CHQ-PF measures 14 multidimensional health concepts. These health concepts include the following:

Physical Functioning assesses whether the child has any physical limitations secondary to health-related problems and, if so, the degree of limitation.

Role/Social Limitations—Physical measures the presence and extent of any limitations in the child's school-related work and social activities due to physical health problems.

General Health assesses perceived overall health (past, present, and future) and illness susceptibility.

Bodily Pain/Discomfort measures the intensity and frequency of child pain symptoms and discomfort.

Parental Impact is comprised of two subscales (*Parental Impact-Time, Parental Impact-Emotional*) that measure the degree to which the responding parent experiences time limitations and distress secondary to child health problems and behavior.

Role/Social Limitations—Emotional-Behavioral assesses the presence and extent of any limitations in the child's school-related work and social activities due to emotional or behavioral difficulties.

Self-Esteem measures the parent's perceptions of the child's satisfaction with school and athleticism, attractiveness and physical appearance, interpersonal relations, and life.

Mental Health assesses the frequency of anxiety, depression, and positive affect.

General Behavior measures the frequency of behavior problems as well as the child's overall behavior.

Family taps the degree to which the family is impacted by the child's health and behavior. Two subscales are included that measure the extent of family disruption in activities (*Family-Limitations in Activities*) and family relationships in general (*Family-Cohesion*).

In addition to these 14 scales, 1 additional 1-item scale (Change in Health) is included to measure the child's change in health over the past 12 months.

As previously noted, the CHQ-PF is a self-report paper-and-pencil questionnaire, and it can easily be administered across multiple settings (clinic, home). Moreover, the authors have developed an interview script that enable CHQ-PF users to efficiently conduct telephone or face-to-face administrations.

A computerized scoring program is provided with the purchase of the manual and is highly recommended due to the recoding, recalibrations, and transformations that are necessary in obtaining a CHQ-PF profile. Scores ranging from 0 to 100 are obtained for each of the 14 scales identified. Also, two summary measures, Physical Summary and Psychosocial Summary, are computed using a linear *t*-score transformation.

Psychometric Information

The CHQ-PF is the product of the Child Health Assessment Project, initiated in 1990 at the New England Medical Center's Health Institute. The original 98-item CHQ-PF was developed and tested in 1990. It was found to be quite sensitive to differences in children with varying levels of attention-deficit hyperactivity disorder and other conditions. Results of regression and item scaling analyses led to the 50-item version that has a large national normative database. A 28-item version was empirically developed and psychometrically examined in 1995.

Psychometric testing has been most extensive for the CHQ-PF version with 50 items. Its normative sample was nationally representative and comprised 391 children, ages 5 to 18 and their parent(s) who had participated in the 1990 National Survey of Functional Health Status conducted by the National Opinion Research Center. Detailed CHQ-PF norms are provided based on child age and gender, as well as several parent variables, including ethnicity, gender, education, and work status. In addition to the nationally representative general sample, normative data are available in the manual for six clinical samples (asthma, attention-deficit hyperactivity disorder, epilepsy, psychiatric condition, cystic fibrosis, and juvenile rheumatoid arthritis).

Reliability and validity data are provided in the manual for each of the standardization samples. Minimal criteria for item internal consistency was set at .40 and this was exceeded by 91% of all items for the national sample. The General Health scale yielded the lowest internal consistency (<.40) among its items, and the Mental Health and Behavior scales each had only one item that did not meet criteria. The median internal consistency reliability estimate across the 14 scales was .84 for the national sample and ranged from .69 to .89 for the clinical samples. The 2 summary scales have very high internal consistency (.93 for both scales for the national sample, .84–.97 for the clinical samples). In addition, item discriminant validity was very high, with a 95% success rate reported for the United States and clinical samples. Strong evidence for discriminant validity is also provided in the manual.

Comment

The CHQ-PF fills a significant void in child health assessment. The authors' conceptualization of child health is multifaceted and appropriately captures the dimensionality of health articulated by the World Health Organization and others. The methodological sophistication in the development and standardization of this measure is very impressive and should serve as the gold standard for test construction. The manual (571 pages) is well organized and extensive in its presentation of highly relevant information. Its section on how to handle problems and questions that may surface during administration of the CHQ is a useful added feature. A computerized scoring program (disk and written code) accompany the manual and their use is strongly recommended. Hand scoring instructions are provided in the manual, but this is very time-consuming and requires multiple levels of calculations that increase the likelihood of human error. The CHQ-PF 50-item version is strongly recommended for use over the other two versions. The 98-item version is too time-consuming for parents to complete and the 28-item version requires further psychometric validation with more representative samples. Internal consistency estimates for the 50-item version are not consistently high for three of the clinical samples (asthma, attention-deficit hyperactivity disorder, juvenile rheumatoid arthritis); however, additional studies are in progress with several clinical samples and their findings are made available to those who purchase the CHQ manual. Additionally, the authors are presently developing and standardizing a CHQ version that will permit the health assessment of children younger than 5 years old. Overall, this is an excellent measure of health-related quality of life and will prove very useful in multiple clinical and research settings.

Relevant References

Landgraf, J. M., Abetz, L., & Ware, J. E. (1996). *The CHQ user's manual.* Boston: The Health Institute, New England Medical Center.

Functional Disability Inventory (FDI)

L. S. Walker, 1991

Manual and Address Information

No manual. Direct inquiries to: Lynn Walker, Division of Adolescent Medicine, 436 Medical Center South, Vanderbilt University, Nashville, TN 37232, (615) 936-0252, walkerls@ctrvax.vanderbilt.edu.

Purpose

The FDI was designed to provide a global measure of how physical health status impacts children's everyday physical and psychosocial functioning in usual social roles.

Format, Administration, and Scoring

The 15-item FDI is a self-report paper-and-pencil measure that can be completed by school-age children and adolescents and their parents in a research or clinic setting. The authors noted that it can also be administered by telephone. The items tap several domains of physical and psychosocial functioning, including sleep and rest, eating, home management, school activities, general ambulation and mobility, and social interaction and recreation.

Adolescents respond to each item by indicating the degree of difficulty they experienced in the past few days completing the activity due to their physical health. Although the standard time frame for reporting disability on the FDI is the past few days, the authors have indicated that the time frame can be changed to reflect the particular needs of a study. Response options on the FDI include no trouble (0), a little trouble (1), some trouble (2), a lot of trouble (3), and impossible (4). A total score, ranging from 0 to 60, is obtained by summing item responses. Higher scores indicate greater functional disability. A thoughtful addition to the questionnaire is a statement at the midway point reminding adolescents that the questions ask them to indicate the difficulty due to physical health.

Examples of activities represented by the items include:

Walking up stairs.
Doing chores at home.
Doing activities in gym class (or playing sports).
Getting to sleep at night and staying asleep.

Psychometric Information

Two initial standardization samples collectively included 47 adolescents with minor physical complaints, 69 adolescents with abdominal pain (organic or functional), and 41 healthy adolescents and their mothers. In all instances, the FDI was administered verbally to the adolescents and mothers completed the written questionnaire independently. The adolescents were attending clinic appointments at a university medical center.

The FDI has high internal consistency (Cronbach's alpha = .85–.92 for the child form and .95 for the mother form) and very good test-retest reliability at 2 weeks (.80 for child form, .47 for mother form), 6 weeks (.70 for child form, .60 for child form), and 6 months (.63 for child form, .69 for mother form) for adolescents with recurrent abdominal pain.

Regarding concurrent validity, parent-child correspondence was mixed (.30–.71), although the child and parent FDI forms were strongly associated (.52 and .55, respectively) with a measure of disability (i.e., school days missed). Excellent construct validity was noted as the FDI was strongly associated with multiple indices of physical and emotional health (e.g., Children's Somatization Inventory, State-Trait Anxiety Inventory, Children's Depression Inventory, Child Behavior Checklist Internalization Factor). The FDI's predictive validity and sensitivity to changes in adolescents' health status following treatment for abdominal pain are good, as demonstrated by significant correlations between FDI scores and subsequent school absences, bed days, medication usage, and somatization symptoms even after controlling for child emotional distress, and significant decreases in FDI scores after medical intervention for organic abdominal pain. Finally, FDI scores were able to successfully discriminate between three diagnostic groups of adolescents (organic abdominal pain, functional abdominal pain, healthy).

Comment

The FDI is a useful global and subjective measure of functional disability in adolescents. A primary advantage the FDI holds over many other measures of functional disability is its moderately strong psychometric properties. Also, it is a brief measure that has been shown to be sensitive to clinical changes and, therefore, can be used by health professionals to monitor patient progress in an efficient manner. Like other generic measures, the FDI lacks specificity and health professionals are encouraged to add other disease-specific measures of functional disability if they are interested in targeting certain health conditions. Further validation of the FDI with a more heterogeneous patient population is needed. Finally, the FDI should not be used as a primary index of quality of life since it does not include several components considered essential in assessing quality of life (e.g., psychological functioning, social adjustment).

Relevant References

Walker, L. S., Garber, J., & Greene, J. W. (1993). Psychosocial correlates of recurrent childhood pain: A comparison of pediatric patients with recurrent abdominal pain, organic illness, and psychiatric disorders. *Journal of Abnormal Psychology, 102,* 248–258.

Walker, L. S., & Greene, J. W. (1991). The Functional Disability Inventory: Measuring a neglected dimension of child health status. *Journal of Pediatric Psychology, 16,* 39–58.

Functional Status Questionnaire (FSQ)

C. C. Lewis, 1989

Manual and Address Information

No manual. Direct inquiries to: Catherine C. Lewis, Department of Pediatrics and Psychiatry, University of California at San Francisco, 400 Parnassus Avenue, Room A 206, San Francisco, CA 94143-0314.

Purpose

The FSQ is a general health status measure developed as a brief self-report version of the Functional Status II(R).

Format, Administration, and Scoring

The FSQ is a parent-completed measure that contains 14 items from the FS II(R). The items selected from the FS II(R) were those that were applicable across the entire age range of the FS II(R) (i.e., ages 0 to 16). The questionnaire is divided into two sections in which the parent first indicates the frequency (never or rarely, some of the time, or almost always) of the item or symptom (e.g., sleep well, act moody) during the past 2 weeks and then, if the symptom has occurred, whether it was due to the child's illness (yes, sometimes, no). Only if the functional loss is directly attributable to the child's illness is the item scored.

The specific domains of functioning assessed by the FSQ include: eat well, sleep well, seem contented and cheerful, act moody, communicate what he/she wants, seem to feel sick and tired, occupy him/herself, seem lively and energetic, seem unusually irritable, sleep through the night, respond to your attention, seem unusually difficult, seem interested in what is going on around him/her, react to things by crying. Two scores are obtained for this measure: a specific score (FSQ-S = total items/problems endorsed that are specifically related to child's illness) and a general score (FSQ-G = total items/problems endorsed whether or not related to child's illness).

Psychometric Information

The FSQ was administered to 113 children (62% male) ages 4 to 16 who were participating in a randomized clinical trial examining methods to enhance children's understanding and management of their illness. The majority ($n = 100$) of children had asthma, although 13 children in the control group had other chronic physical conditions. The sample of parents completing the FSQ was culturally diverse (45% White, 21% Black, 19% Hispanic, 12% Asian).

Cronbach's alpha was .78 for the FSQ-S and ranged from .73 to .89 for the FSQ-G. Scores were not significantly correlated with sociodemographic variables. Construct validity was measured by correlating both the specific and general scores of the FSQ with another general health status measure; measures of asthma impact and severity. Both the FSQ-S and FSQ-G scores were positively correlated with the general health status measure (.47 and .27, respectively) and negatively correlated with one index of illness impact (acute clinic visits: −.24 and −.27, respectively), the FSQ-G was negatively correlated with the asthma severity index (−.22), the FSQ-S score was negatively correlated with school absences due to illness (−.27), and the FSQ-G score was negatively correlated with parents' telephone calls to clinic. Neither of the two FSQ scores were significantly correlated with number of child asthma attacks, number of hospital days, or number of days parent was absent from work due to the child's illness. Readministration of the FSQ with a smaller sample at 6 weeks and 3, 6, and 12 months following the intervention yielded only one significant time effect (baseline versus 6-month follow-up), thus indicating good stability across time.

Comment

The FSQ shows some promise as a brief parent-administered alternative to the more lengthy interviewer-administered FS II(R), although it requires more extensive psychometric evaluation prior to widespread use as a general health status measure. While its internal consistency is generally comparable to that of the FS II(R) (.78 versus .83), further validation of its construct and predictive validity are necessary. For instance, FSQ changes were not observed in children who participated in the randomized controlled clinical trial described by the authors and the FSQ scores were not consistently associated with indices of illness impact or severity. The relatively small and homogenous (i.e., asthma) sample limits its generalizability to other chronic health conditions. Furthermore, despite the culturally diverse sample, it is not known whether FSQ scores and their associations with indices of illness impact and severity differ as a function of ethnicity. The authors appropriately noted that the FSQ does not distinguish between functional loss secondary to illness and loss due to treatment effects, a consideration that should guide the development of future health status measures.

Relevant References

Lewis C. C., Pantell, R. H., & Kieckhefer, G. M. (1989). Assessment of children's health status: Field test of new approaches. *Medical Care, 27,* S54–S65.

Stein R. E. K., & Jessop, D. K. (1990). Functional Status II(R): A measure of child health status. *Medical Care, 28,* 1041–1055.

Functional Status II(R)

R. E. K. Stein, 1990

Manual and Address Information

There is a manual. Direct inquiries to: Ruth E. K. Stein, Department of Pediatrics, Albert Einstein College of Medicine, 111 East 210 Street, Bronx, NY 10461.

Purpose

The FS II(R) is a copyrighted revised generic health status measure used to assess the behavioral manifestations of health conditions that impact the activities of children and adolescents.

Format, Administration, and Scoring

There are several forms of the FSII(R): a 43-item version that provides a differentiated profile, a 14-item version, and a 7-item version. The 14-item version is the most commonly used and consists of one set of items across the entire age spectrum from infancy to 16 years. All versions are designed to be interviewer-administered to parents of children ages birth to 16 years with chronic health conditions or disorders. The items were designed to measure behavioral responses to health problems that interfere with otherwise normal role performance across leisure, work, and rest activities in three locations (home, neighborhood, and school). Each question is comprised of two parts. In the first part (Part 1), parents indicate whether their child engages in the identified activity or demonstrates the specified behavior (i.e., never or rarely, some of the time, or almost always). In the second part (Part 2), parents indicate the degree to which their child's functioning relative to items in Part 1 is due to a health condition (i.e., fully, partly, or not at all). The 43-item version takes about 20 minutes to administer, whereas the two shorter versions take about 5 minutes.

The measure is scored in such a manner to isolate dysfunction that is secondary to health conditions. Therefore, Part 1 scoring is based on responses provided to the probing question in Part 2. If a child is reported to exhibit some behavior that may reflect poor functioning in Part 1 (e.g., irritable), but on the probe in Part 2 it is determined that it is not related to the child's health condition, then the response in Part 1 is recoded according to the instructions in the manual. Based on the child's age, FS II(R) scoring of the 43-item version yields a total score and two or more factors scores:

Less than 2 years old: Total, General Health, Responsiveness
Ages 2 to 3 years old: Total, General Health, Activity
Ages 4 and older: Total, General Health, Interpersonal Functioning

The authors noted that a three-factor solution may be more appropriate for older children and adolescents (Total, General Health, Locomotion, and Interpersonal Functioning). The shorter versions contain only one score; a total score.

Psychometric Information

The FS II(R) represents a revision of the authors' original measure, the FS I, which was modeled after the Sickness Impact Profile (an adult health status measure). In the revision, the authors sought to improve item clarity, expand the age range, and improve the psychometric properties of the measure. The FS II(R) was administered to parents of 732 children ages 2 weeks to 16 years who were recruited from an inpatient hospital setting or an outpatient pediatric-clinic setting. The sample included White, Black, and Hispanic children with a chronic condition and those with no known chronic health condition.

Internal consistency estimates were .88 to .94 for the total score and .84 to .93 for factor scores across the different age groups.

The authors reported support for the measure's construct and concurrent validity. Scores for the FS II(R) were significantly lower (less functional) for children who experienced an exacerbation of their illness during the previous few weeks than those whose health had been the same as usual. FS II(R) scores were moderately correlated with physicians' ratings of the child's limitations in normal everyday activities. Correlational analyses further revealed that the total and factor scores on the FS II(R) were highly correlated with other indices or morbidity, including days in bed in the past 2 weeks, missed school days in the past 2 weeks, number of hospitalizations in the past 6 months, and hospital days in the past 6 months. Finally, the authors reported that FS II(R) was able to successfully differentiate those children with chronic health conditions from their healthy peers and these differences were statistically significant in the expected direction across all age categories.

Comment

The FS II(R) represents a significant psychometric improvement over its original version. It is internally consistent and demonstrates good construct validity. Further psychometric testing is needed to determine whether the FS II(R) is sensitive enough to detect changes in functional status following medical intervention. The measure is available in both English and Spanish versions, and its development and use with culturally diverse samples is noteworthy. It is an easily administered measure, although it requires the use of trained interviewers. The interview nature of the FS II(R) makes it a less cost-effective alternative to other self-administered health status instruments. While self-administered versions of the measure have been used in various research protocols, their psychometric properties are presently unknown and, therefore, their use is not recommended. To address the cost-effectiveness issue, the authors of the FS II(R) have developed two short-form versions consisting of 14 and 7 items, respectively. Psychometric data have been reported on the 14-item version that show that it is very comparable to the longer version in terms of its reliability and validity.

Relevant References

Silver E. J., Stein, R. E. K., & Dadds, M. R. (1996). Moderating effects of family structure on the relationship between physical and mental health in urban children with chronic illness. *Journal of Pediatric Psychology, 21*, 43–56.

Stein R. E. K., & Jessop, D. (1990). Functional Status II(R): A measure of child health status. *Medical Care, 28*, 1041–1055.

Stein, R. E. K., & Jessop, D. (1991). *Manual for the Functional Status II(R)*. Bronx, NY: Albert Einstein College of Medicine.

Health Status Measure for Children (HSMC)

M. Eisen, 1979

Manual and Address Information
There is a manual. Address unknown.

Purpose
The HSMC is a paper-and-pencil questionnaire originally designed to measure the impact of various health insurance plans on children's general health status.

Format, Administration, and Scoring
The HSMC is a parent-completed questionnaire comprised of 18 items for children ages birth to 4 years and 42 items for children ages 5 to 13. Parents use several different response categories (e.g., based on frequency, intensity, general perceptions, etc.) to respond to items tapping several core domains of health and that vary according to time frame (e.g., past 5 days, past 3 months, etc.). The core domains or scales for the two age groups include:

Ages birth to 4 years	Current Health
	Resistance/Susceptibility
	Prior Health
	General Health Ratings Index
	Satisfaction With Development
Ages 5 to 13	Current Health
	Resistance/Susceptibility
	Prior Health
	General Health Ratings Index
	Anxiety
	Depression
	Positive Well-Being
	Mental Health Index
	Social Relations

The General Health Rating Index includes questions about the child's physical activity (e.g., "Is the child unable to walk, unless assisted by an adult or by crutches, artificial limb, or braces?"), role activity (e.g., "Does this child's health keep him or her from going to school?"), self-care activity (e.g., "Because of health, does this child need help with eating, dressing, bathing, or using the toilet?"), and mobility (e.g., "Does this child have to stay indoors most or all of the day because of health?"). Scores are obtained for each scale by summing item scores.

Psychometric Information

The HSMC was developed as part of the Rand Corporation's Health Insurance Study, a multisite study examining the effects of different types of health care plans on health care utilization, patient satisfaction, and health status in the general population. Over 2,100 parents of children from five national sites were included in the psychometric evaluation of the HSMC. The samples were recruited in the mid-1970s, were predominantly White (except for the two sites in South Carolina that had large Black samples), healthy, and comprised nearly equal numbers of males and females. Normative data are not available for children with chronic health conditions.

Internal consistency estimates (Cronbach's alpha) ranged from .53 (Prior Health) to .77 (General Health Ratings Index) for the birth to 4 years HSMC version and .57 (Prior Health) to .87 (Mental Health Index) for the 5 to 13 years HSMC version. The internal consistency estimates from the heterogeneous samples approximate test-retest reliability. No inter-rater reliability estimates were obtained.

Comment

The HSMC is a useful generic measure of children's health status. Its development was guided by a multidimensional model of children's health, its basic psychometric properties are adequate, and its scoring system allows for the identification of specific domains of functional status. The HSMC was designed to assess the impact of health-care financing plans on children's health status and, consequently, it has not proven useful in distinguishing between children with different illness types. Additional research with pediatric populations is necessary to determine its usefulness and predictive validity with pediatric populations. Also, there is a need to further examine cultural differences in its application as well as its cost-effectiveness.

Relevant References

Eisen, M. Donald, C. A., Ware, J. E., & Brook, R. H. (1980). *Conceptualization and measurement of health for children in the Health Insurance Study* (R-2313-HEW). Santa Monica, CA: Rand Corporation.

Eisen, M., Ware, J. E., Donald, C. A., & Brook, R. H. (1979). Measuring components of children's health status. *Medical Care, 17,* 902–921.

Pediatric Oncology Quality of Life Scale (POQOLS)

D. A. J. Goodwin, 1994

Manual and Address Information

No manual. Direct inquiries to: Stephen R. Boggs, Department of Clinical and Health Psychology, P.O. Box 100165, University of Florida Health Science Center, Gainesville, FL 32610-0165, (352) 395-0490, sboggs@hp.ufl.edu.

Purpose

The POQOLS is a paper-and-pencil measure designed to measure cancer-specific quality of life in children and adolescents.

Format, Administration, and Scoring

The POQOLS is a brief, 21-item instrument completed by parents of children from preschool age through adolescence with cancer. Parents respond to each item, representing 21 observable behaviors, using a 7-point frequency scale ranging from 1 (*never*) to 7 (*very frequently*). Parents are instructed to respond on the basis of their child's behavior within the past 2 weeks. The measure is self-administered and can be completed in a variety of clinical settings or at home in about 10 minutes. Sample items include:

> My child has had less energy and has been easily tired out. (Factor 1)
> My child has expressed fear about the disease and its treatment. (Factor 2)
> My child has had nausea and/or vomiting due to treatment. (Factor 3)

In addition to a Total score, the POQOLS yields three empirically-derived factor scores: Factor 1 (restrictions in physical functioning and ability to maintain normal routine), Factor 2 (general emotional adjustment), and Factor 3 (physical discomfort associated with early-phase cancer treatment). Several items are reverse-scored and higher scores represent poorer quality of life.

Psychometric Information

Initially, parents of children with cancer, children and adolescents with cancer, and health professionals with pediatric oncology experience were asked to identify quality of life domains most affected by the cancer experience, as well as specific behavioral indices of such effects. An initial pool of 44 items was generated and administered to 210 parents of children with cancer at three separate cancer treatment facilities. Factor and item analyses supported a 21-item version that was then administered to a new sample of 107 parents of children with cancer at two separate facilities. The children of these parents displayed an appropriate range of demographic and disease characteristics, that is, age (preschool through older adolescence), gender (63% male), family income, disease duration (22% <6 months; 60% <2 years), and diagnosis (71% leukemia, 19% sarcoma).

Internal consistency reliability, using coefficient alpha, has been reported for the Total score (.85) and Factor scores (Factor 1 = .87, Factor 2 = .79, Factor 3 = .68). Inter-rater reliability was computed for 15 mother-father pairs (Total score = .87, Factor 1 = .91, Factor 2 = .87, Factor 3 = .75).

Regarding concurrent validity, the POQOLS is strongly associated with measures of similar constructs (e.g., Play Performance Scale for Children, Child Behavior Checklist, Multiattribute Health Status Questionnaire). Also, children receiving treatment and those in remission were correctly classified by Factor 1, Factor 3, and Total scores, indicating good discriminant validity.

Comment

The POQOLS represents an important advancement in the measurement of quality of life in children with cancer. Its multidimensional and developmental framework distinguishes it from other quality of life measures that lack a conceptual focus. The measure is psychometrically sound, having demonstrated excellent internal consistency, inter-parent reliability, and validity. Further psychometric studies with larger samples and longitudinal assessments of the same children over time are necessary next steps in evaluating the stability of its factor structure, clinical utility, and sensitivity over time. The POQOLS is a very practical instrument that can be used efficiently and with very little staff time in a busy pediatric oncology clinic. The 2-week time period of the instrument is adequate to allow for repeated assessment throughout the course of treatment and recovery, and will yield very useful information about child adaptation, symptom frequency, and treatment effects. A child self-report version would be a useful extension of this measure.

Relevant References

Boggs, S. R., & Durning, P. (1998). The Pediatric Oncology Quality of Life Scale: Development and validation of a disease-specific quality of life measure. In D. Drotar (Ed.), *Measuring health-related quality of life in children and adolescents: Implications for research and practice* (pp. 187–202). Mahwah, NJ: Lawrence Erlbaum Press.

Boggs, S. R., Graham-Pole, J., & Miller, E. M. (1991). Life-threatening illness and invasive treatment: The future of life assessment and research in pediatric oncology. In J. H. Johnson & S. B. Johnson (Eds.), *Advances in child health psychology* (pp. 353–361). Gainesville, FL: University of Florida Press.

Goodwin, D., Boggs, S. R., & Graham-Pole, J. (1994). Development and validation of the Pediatric Oncology Quality of Life Scale. *Psychological Assessment, 6,* 321–328.

Kazak, A. E., Penati, B., Waibel, M. C., & Blackall, G. F. (1996). The Perception of Procedures Questionnaire: Psychometric properties of a brief parent report measure of procedural distress. *Journal of Pediatric Psychology, 21,* 195–207.

Quality of Well-Being (QWB) Scale

R. M. Kaplan, 1978

Manual and Address Information

There is a manual. Direct inquiries to: Robert M. Kaplan, Department of Community and Family Medicine, Mail Code 0622, University of California at San Diego, La Jolla, CA 92093, (619) 534-6058, rkaplan@ucsd.edu.

Purpose

The QWB is a generic utility measure designed to assess the health-related quality of life of adults with physical illness, although it has recently been used with adolescents.

Format, Administration, and Scoring

Initially designed for use with adults to help guide health policy decision (i.e., General Health Policy Model), the QWB has been used extensively to examine health-related quality of life across many different disease populations. It is administered in the context of a structured interview and takes about 12 to 15 minutes to complete. In its more recent use with children, the structured interview is completed with the child's parent. Parents are asked to respond to a series of questions designed to elicit information about their child's functioning across dimensions of mobility, physical activity, social activity, and symptom presence (generated from a list of 27). Specific information is obtained about the child's functioning during each of the last 6 days and any impairments that are considered a function of the child's physical illness.

Administration of the QWB is complex and requires extensive training. The authors have developed audiotapes to assist users in practicing its administration.

Scoring the QWB is a complex task and the use of the authors' computerized scoring program is strongly encouraged. The QWB yields a single-index score ranging from 0 to 1 and is based on community surveys and relative preferences for dysfunction. A higher total score indicates better quality of life. Other users of the QWB with children have employed a different scoring system involving a combination of the functioning indices and symptoms over the preceding 6 days.

Psychometric Information

The QWB has been used with a large number of adult medical populations and has generally demonstrated good psychometric properties across most adult studies. Reliability over time (1 year) and inter-day reliability for index scores have been demonstrated. Moreover, sensitivity and specificity studies have shown the responsiveness of the QWB across several different diseases and injuries (.90–.99).

Also, construct validity has been shown, including significant positive correlations between the QWB and self-reported well-being (.42–.49), and significant negative correlations with number of chronic health conditions (–.75) and health resource utilization (physician visits, –.55).

The use of the QWB with child medical populations is limited to a few studies and its psychometric support is not as consistent as it is with adults. Good internal consistency across the scales and total score has been shown (>.90). Also, it has been shown that high interviewer reliability can be obtained (Symptoms = .70, Total = .85, Social Activity = .85, Mobility = 1.0, Physical Activity = 1.0), despite the complexity of its administration. Inter-respondent correspondence has been investigated in one study and results yielded low to moderate correlations (.23–.55) between parents and their adolescents with cystic fibrosis.

Regarding construct validity, the QWB has been found to be significantly associated with parents' and physicians' performance status ratings of the child, number of previous hospitalizations (–.41 for Total score, .37 for Physical Activity scale), and number of surgeries (.44 for Physical Activity scale) in a pediatric oncology sample. Studies examining evidence for its concurrent validity with important physiological measurements have not yielded consistent findings, and the QWB has been found to be insensitive in measuring the well-being of chronically ill children with low levels of impairment.

Comment

While not designed for use with pediatric populations, recent studies have attempted to examine its applicability to children and adolescents with chronic health conditions. However, the QWB continues to be used sparingly in pediatric populations and available data suggest that further examination of its psychometric properties and clinical utility with ill children is warranted prior to more widespread use. Current criticism of the QWB includes its insensitivity to variations in health, particularly in youths with low levels of impairment, low level of agreement between adolescent patients and their parents, and its practicality. The QWB may eventually prove quite useful in clinical trials research in which calculation of quality-adjusted life years is necessary to evaluate treatment effects. However, until additional studies are done to support its psychometric stability and utility with pediatric populations, it probably should be used only as a supplemental measure of health-related quality of life in research settings.

Relevant References

Bradlyn, A. S., Harris, C. V., Warner J. E., Ritchey, A. K., & Zaboy, K. (1993). An investigation of the validity of the Quality of Well-Being Scale with pediatric oncology patients. *Health Psychology, 12,* 246–250.

Czyzewski, D. I., Mariotte, M. J., Bartholomew, K., LeCompte, S. H., & Sockrider, M. M. (1994). Measurement of quality of well being in a child and adolescent cystic fibrosis population. *Medical Care, 32,* 965–972.

Hinds, P. (1990). Quality of life in children and adolescents with cancer. *Seminars in Oncology Nursing, 6,* 285–291.

Kaplan, R. M., Bush, J. W., & Berry, C. C. (1976). Health status: Types of validity and the Index of Well-Being. *Health Services Research, 11,* 478–507.

General Observations and Recommendations

Quality of life assessments have assumed greater prominence in understanding children's health and the impact of chronic conditions and medical intervention. The instruments reviewed in this chapter have clear conceptual and methodological strengths and adequately reflect the arduous process of measure development and validation. While the instruments share many similarities in their construction (e.g., item selection and reduction), there are important differences in questionnaire format, reproducibility, responsiveness, and validity. In general, however, their potential application in the three broad areas considered most relevant to quality of life assessment—discrimination, prediction, and evaluation—is high. Additional points that we have selected to highlight include:

1. There is relative inattention to developmental processes in the childhood quality of life assessment literature. Indeed, we agree with Rosenbaum and colleagues (1990) who appropriately noted that children are a "moving target" for quality of life assessments because of cognitive and language developmental changes. Measures developed initially for use with adults are not appropriate for use with children or adolescents. Further evaluation of the instruments reviewed in this chapter with children in varying stages of development is needed to advance the childhood quality of life measurement.
2. The degree to which quality of life instruments attend to issues of cultural diversity warrants improvement. Few measures have been validated with children of color.
3. Disease-specific quality of life measures are less likely to yield representative validation samples because of the demographic characteristics of certain disease types (e.g., cancer, diabetes). Despite the greater opportunity, however, generic measures as a group have not sufficiently assessed their clinical utility with more culturally diverse groups of children.
4. Many researchers have developed their own disease-specific quality of life measures, although they have not provided ample information about their construction or validation. We encourage those considering the development of disease-specific measures to review the excellent methodological framework provided by Jaeschke and Guyatt (1990).
5. Although excellent disease-specific measures exist for certain chronic health conditions (e.g., cancer, diabetes), there are other illnesses for which pediatric quality of life measures have not been developed or validated (e.g., sickle cell disease).

References

Aaronson, N. K. (1988). Quality of life: What is it? How should it be measured? *Oncology, 2,* 69–74.

Eisen, M., Ware, J. E., Donald, C. A., & Brook, R. H. (1979). Measuring components of children's health status. *Medical Care, 17,* 902–921.

Jaeschke, R., & Guyatt, G. H. (1990). How to develop and validate a new quality of life instrument. In B. Spilker (Ed.), *Quality of life assessments in clinical trials* (pp. 47–57). New York: Raven Press.

Landgraf, J. M., & Abetz, L. N. (1996). Measuring health outcomes in pediatric populations: Issues in psychometrics and application. In B. Spilker (Ed.), *Quality of life and pharmacoeconomics in clinical trials* (2nd ed.) (pp. 793–802). Philadelphia: Lippincott-Raven Publishers.

McCormick, M. C., Atreya, B. H., Bernbaum, J. C., & Charney, E. B. (1988). Preliminary observations on maternal rating of health of children: Data from three subspecialty clinics. *Journal of Clinical Epidemiology, 41,* 323–329.

Pantell, R. H., & Lewis, C. C. (1987). Measuring the impact of medical care on children. *Journal of Chronic Diseases, 40* (Suppl. 1), 99S–108S.

Rosenbaum, P., Cadman, D., & Kirpalani, H. (1990). Pediatrics: Assessing quality of life. In B. Spilker (Ed.), *Quality of life and pharmacoeconomics in clinical trials* (2nd ed.) (pp. 205–215). Philadelphia: Lippincott-Raven Publishers.

Spieth, L. E., & Harris, C. V. (1996). Assessment of health-related quality of life in children and adolescents: An integrative review. *Journal of Pediatric Psychology, 21,* 175–193.

Torrence, G. W. (1987). Utility approach to measuring health-related quality of life. *Journal of Chronic Diseases, 40,* 593–600.

Chapter 9

Health-Related Knowledge and Adherence to Medical Regimens

GARY R. GEFFKEN
JAMES R. RODRIGUE

Adherence to medical regimens covers a variety of diverse behaviors including initiating and maintaining a treatment program, keeping appointments with health care providers, correct consumption of prescribed medications, following appropriate lifestyle changes (e.g., diet and exercise), and avoidance of health-risk behaviors (e.g., smoking, alcohol and drugs) (Meichenbaum & Turk, 1987). The scope of nonadherence ranges across all age groups and medical domains (Cramer, 1991). The importance of adherence to health regimens in youngsters with chronic health conditions is paramount. For example, national attention has been given to the recent Diabetes Complication and Control Trials findings that intensive treatment for IDDM fostering better adherence is associated with better metabolic control and decreased long-term complications.

Assessing the level of patient adherence and causes for nonadherence has been a substantial research concern. However, examining the sources and consequences of medical adherence in children is an understudied subject. Nonadherence in children involves more than refusal to cooperate with the treatment programs. Problems arise from children adhering to regimens incorrectly, exceeding medications dosages, inadequate knowledge, and other errors. Often children with diabetes have been found to perform blood glucose monitoring incorrectly and to misread or misrecord the results almost 80% of the time (Rapoff & Barnard, 1991). Furthermore, health care providers may be unaware of such nonadherence factors, resulting in providing even stricter regimens and more medications. The effects of nonadherence in children can result in adverse health-related events. For instance, children who were nonadherent with asthma medications were more likely than adherent patients to experience more days of wheezing (Rapoff & Barnard, 1991). An additional concern created through nonadherence is cost. Unused medications, physician visits, superfluous diagnostic tests, and preventable hospitalizations place wasteful costs on families, insurance companies, and taxpayers. Clearly, the analysis of adherence in children is important.

Recent research has examined many personal and environmental variables thought to be associated with adherence. These include family support and involvement, the patient's intent to comply, the quality of the physician-patient relationship, and the details of the treatment regimen, just to name a few (Cromer, 1991). Moreover, research has found that with many childhood health conditions, adherence in one aspect of a regimen does not predict adherence in another. For example, patients with renal disease who adhere to their fluid regimen do not necessarily adhere to their dietary or medication regimen (Symister & Friend, 1996). Furthermore, diabetes or asthma adherence in children is not a single construct. Adherence to a diabetes regimen involves diet, exercise, blood-glucose and urine monitoring, and insulin administration. It has been found that adherence to a given aspect of the diabetes regimen does not predict adherence with other aspects of the regimen (Geffken & Johnson, 1994; Glasgow, 1991). Consequently, measures of adherence to medical regimens for use with children and adolescents may require complex models with multiple assessment dimensions.

In this chapter, we review measures for assessing adherence to medical regimens in children and adolescents. Chronic health conditions sampled by these measures include diabetes, asthma, and cystic fibrosis. The methods are mostly similar in structure, consisting of interviews or questionnaires that involve direct face-to-face or telephone contact. Informants include children, parents, or both. We also include a few instruments designed to tap knowledge of disease and/or health problems because a large body of research has examined the relationship between knowledge and adherence behaviors. Indeed, most programs designed to enhance adherence behaviors (either in response to a complex medical regimen or better health promotion) include a teaching component to increase knowledge about the short- and long-term risks and benefits of adherence or nonadherence. Generally, education to enhance knowledge is considered to be a necessary, but insufficient, component of adherence-focused interventions.

REVIEWS

Adaptiveness Rating Scale (ARS)

A. V. Deaton, 1985

Manual and Address Information

No manual. Direct inquiries to: Ann V. Deaton, Children's Hospital, 2924 Brook Road, Richmond, VA 23220.

Purpose

The ARS was devised to rate children's (ages 6 to 14) decisions of compliance or noncompliance to medical regimen.

Format, Administration, and Scoring

There are eight 5-point dimensions to this scale, including two related to the activeness and clarity of the compliance choice, two regarding knowledge of the child and its role in decision-making, two relating to knowledge of the regimen itself, and two relating to how compliance decisions are evaluated. It is from the total score on these dimensions that an "adaptiveness rating" is derived.

Psychometric Information

Participants in the original study utilizing this measure were 30 (17 male, 13 female) 6- to 14-year-old children who had been given a diagnosis of asthma by a pediatric allergist and were under treatment for control of their illness.

Inter-rater reliability using this scale was assessed using six randomly selected tapes (20%) and an independent rater. The correlation between the two raters was .94 for scores summed across the eight dimensions and ranged from .70 to .97 for individual dimensions. With the exception of the dimension "knowledge of side effects" (.70), inter-rater reliability was at least .80. In addition, when the two raters disagreed on exact ratings, the difference in their ratings, in all cases but one, was a single point on the rating scale.

Medication adherence (but not adherence with behavioral recommendations) was correlated with parents' rated adaptiveness, however, this relationship was not always consistent. Several of the parents who were rated as adaptive were nonadherent with many aspects of their child's regimen, and some of the parents who were low on this measure of adaptiveness were relatively adherent.

While adaptiveness was not significantly correlated with amount of time a child was hospitalized or the number of physician contacts during a 9-month period, the correlations were in the hypothesized direction. Adaptiveness was correlated with quality of life, with children of more adaptive parents experiencing less disruption and other negative effects of their illness. Adaptiveness also was negatively correlated with the number of school absences.

Comment

The ARS appears to have adequate inter-rater reliability. Additional work on this scale is needed to further assess its validity as well as other forms (e.g., test-retest, split-halves) of reliability. Moreover, a larger, more representative standardization sample would be useful in developing the empirical basis of this measure.

Relevant References

Deaton, A. V. (1985). Adaptive noncompliance in pediatric asthma: The parent as expert. *Journal of Pediatric Psychology, 10,* 1–14.

Diabetes Mismanagement Questionnaire (DMQ)

J. Weissberg-Benchell, 1995

Manual and Address Information

No manual. Direct inquiries to: Jill Weissberg-Benchell, Children's Memorial Medical Center, 2300 Children's Plaza, Box 10, Chicago, IL 60614, (773) 880-4818.

Purpose

The DMQ is intended to document the existence and prevalence of diabetes mismanagement, the reasons for engaging in this mismanagement, and the impact of the mismanagement on metabolic control.

Format, Administration, and Scoring

This is a 10-item multiple-choice questionnaire. The questions on the DMQ address three areas of diabetes care: blood glucose testing, insulin injections, and diet. The questionnaire asks subjects how many times within the past 10 days they had engaged in various behaviors. Items are scored on a 5-point Likert-type scale with responses ranging from 1 (*never*) to 5 (*frequently*). Sample items include:

> In the past 10 days, how often did you miss your shots?
>
> In the past 10 days, how often did you make up blood test results because the real ones were too high?
>
> In the past 10 days, how often have you eaten something you know you really should not have eaten?

Psychometric Information

The measure was standardized using 144 children and adolescents (72 males, 72 females) with insulin-dependent diabetes mellitus attending consecutive diabetes clinic outpatient appointments. The range for diabetes duration was 1 to 16 years ($m = 5.34$, $sd = 3.62$).

A factor analysis of the DMQ indicated that the measure had two factors: blatant mismanagement and covering up, and faking illness and faking test results. Internal consistency for the two factors of the DMQ were .74 and .60, respectively. Furthermore, the items on the questionnaire appear to have face validity.

Comment

The DMQ appears to measure the prevalence and reasons for diabetes mismanagement. While initial examination of the psychometric properties, specifically construct validity, are encouraging, more information is needed on the reliability and validity of the measure. Specifically, concurrent validity, such as independent ratings of adherence to medical regimen, would be helpful in assessing the usefulness of this tool. Furthermore, a more geographically diverse standardization sample would improve the generalizability of the findings of initial studies that utilize the DMQ. With additional psychometric support for its utility, the DMQ offers the clinician a brief and efficient means of assessing adolescents' mismanagement of their diabetes regimen.

Relevant References

Weissberg-Benchell, J., Glasgow, A. M., Tynan, W. D., Wirtz, P., Turek, J., & Ward, J. (1995). Adolescent diabetes management and mismanagement. *Diabetes Care, 18,* 77–82.

Family Asthma Management System Scale (FAMSS)

M. D. Klinnert, 1997

Manual and Address Information

No manual. Direct inquiries to: Mary Klinnert, National Jewish Medical and Research Center, 1400 Jackson Street, Denver, CO 80206, (303) 398-1231, klinnertm@njc.org.

Purpose

The FAMSS was designed to evaluate how families manage the asthma treatment regimen.

Format, Administration, and Scoring

The FAMSS is a semistructured interview that lasts about 1 hour in which a primary caregiver of a child with asthma is interviewed. During the semistructured interview, the family's behavior in 11 domains critical to asthma management are assessed. These domains include:

> Family's perceived alliance with medical caregiver
> Collaborative relationship between family and medical caregiver
> Knowledge of asthma and medications
> Adherence with asthma medications
> Adherence with environmental recommendations
> Knowledge and assessment of child's symptoms
> Balance of responsibility between parent and child
> Appropriateness of action plan and emotional response to asthma symptoms
> Parent-child interactions in domain of asthma care
> Parental resources
> Balanced integration of asthma into family life.

Psychometric Information

Presently, the authors report only one study in which the FAMSS was used. In this study, the mothers of 30 children with mild to moderate asthma severity were interviewed using the FAMSS. The children ranged in age from 6 to 9 and were predominantly Whilte (67%; 17% African American, 17% Hispanic). Children in the study were recruited from the outpatient clinic at the National Jewish Center for Immunology and Respiratory Medicine and from an urban pediatric practice in Denver, Colorado.

Inter-rater reliability for the domains ranged from .67 to .93, and the intraclass correlation for the FAMSS Summary Score was found to be .97. All subscales of the FAMSS were found to correlate significantly with the Summary Score (.45–.85), and internal consistency for the scale was reported to be .91.

The validity of the FAMSS scale was assessed by determining the relationship between the FAMSS Summary Score and the functional severity of the children's asthma. To this end, the FAMSS Summary Score and the Functional Severity of Asthma Summary Score were found to be moderately negatively correlated (–.39), indicating an inverse relationship between effective asthma management and functional impairment due to asthma.

Comment

The FAMSS appears to be a reliable and valid measure of family asthma measurement, however, future research is needed on the standardization of the measure. Due to the relatively small sample size and limited geographic location employed in this study, generalization of the results may be questionable. Also, whether the findings of the current study apply to children with severe asthma (as opposed to mild to moderate asthma) remains to be tested. Factor analysis would be helpful in assessing the validity of each of the subscales of the FAMSS.

Relevant References

Klinnert, M. D., McQuaid, E. L., & Gavin, L. A. (1997). Assessing the Family Asthma Management System. *Journal of Asthma, 34*, 77–88.

Medical Compliance Incomplete Stories Test (MCIST)

G. Koocher, 1990

Manual and Address Information

There is a manual. Direct inquiries to: Gerald P. Koocher, Ph.D., Department of Psychiatry, Children's Hospital, 300 Longwood Avenue, Boston, MA 02115-5737, (617) 355-6699, koocher@a1.tch.harvard.edu.

Purpose

The MCIST was designed to assess the attitudes of school-age children and adolescents toward situations involving medical adherence, based on a competency/coping skills model.

Format, Administration, and Scoring

The MCIST is an individually administered test composed of five incomplete stories that are expressively read aloud to the participant in a quiet setting. Each of the stories depict the main character as having to choose a specific course of action regarding his/her health in response to medical advice. The participant is asked to complete the story and predict what will happen to the main character in each situation. Responses are recorded verbatim. The test administrator needs to be familiar enough with the scoring criteria to ensure that sufficient information is obtained in order to score the narrative. If needed, nondirective probes may be used to obtain the additional data, that is, "What do you think the future holds for that person?"

Each story is scored separately along three dimensions representative of a competent individual according to a set of objective criteria. These areas include: compliance (C), optimism (O), and self-efficacy (SE). For each area, responses are scored from 0 to 2 based on their meeting previously defined criteria. For example, to obtain a score of "2" in Health Optimism, the participant must have included a statement that indicates affirmation of positive outcome in the future.

Higher scores reflect more positive indicators for each category. The sum of the three subscales also provides a "competency/compliance" score that may range from 0 to 30.

A parent form of the MCIST (MCIST-PF) is an extension of the MCIST intended to measure the attitudes of parents toward medical compliance in situations concerning their children. The format of the MCIST-PF is similar to that of the MCIST, in that it is comprised of five incomplete stories. Parents are asked to complete each of the stories, and in doing so predict the outcome of the main character of each scenario. Scores for the MCIST-PF are computed using the same procedure as that of the MCIST.

Psychometric Information

The initial study to use the MCIST focused on 40 youth with cystic fibrosis ranging in age from 13 to 23. Internal consistency was found to be low for two of the three domains (Compliance coefficient alpha = .28, Health Optimism coefficient alpha = .43; Self-efficacy coefficient alpha = .76). The three subscales did correlate highly with the MCIST total score (.74, .91, and .86, respectively).

Evidence for criterion validity was reported, as the MCIST scores on all three subscales and the total score were highly correlated with observed medical adherence. Regarding discriminant validity, MCIST scores were found to correlate significantly with medical adherence and discriminate significantly between those who were adherent and those identified as nonadherent.

Comment

The MCIST provides an interesting format for youngsters in assessing medical adherence, and preliminary research shows that its scores are significantly correlated with actual adherence behaviors. Additional work on the internal consistency of the compliance and health optimism domains would be of value, as would research with more diverse groups of children with chronic health conditions. It is noteworthy that ongoing research by the authors is examining the relationship between parents' attitudes and children's adherence behaviors.

Relevant References

D'Angelo, E. J., Woolf, A., Bessette, J., Rappaport, L., & Ciborowski, J. (1992). Correlates of medical compliance among hemophilic boys. *Journal of Clinical Psychology, 48,* 672–680.

Gudas, L. J., Koocher, G. P., & Wypij, D. (1991). Perceptions of medical compliance in children and adolescents with cystic fibrosis. *Journal of Developmental and Behavioral Pediatrics, 12,* 236–242.

Koocher, G. P., Czajkowski, D. R., & Fitzpatrick, J. R. (1990). *Manual for the Medical Compliance Incomplete Stories Test (MCIST).* Boston: Children's Hospital and Harvard Medical School.

Koocher, G. P., McGrath, M. L., & Gudas, L. J. (1990). Typologies of non-adherence in cystic fibrosis. *Journal of Developmental and Behavioral Pediatrics, 11,* 353–358.

Preschool Health and Safety Knowledge Assessment (PHASKA)

C. E. Mobley, 1996

Manual and Address Information

There is a manual. Address inquiries to: Caryl E. Mobley, College of Nursing, Texas Woman's University, 1810 Inwood Road, Dallas, TX 75235-7299, (214) 689-6510.

Purpose

The PHASKA was designed to measure health and safety knowledge in children of preschool age.

Format, Administration, and Scoring

The PHASKA is comprised of 53 picture cards that are administered to the child by a trained researcher or clinician. Children are asked to look at each card and choose whether the activity reflected in the picture represents a particular health or safety concept. The first 3 cards are administered to familiarize the child with the task demands. The remaining 50 cards are then administered to the child and used to score the instrument. All of the cards show situations that are familiar to many, if not all, children. When children are incorporated into the pictures, they are depicted by simple black and white line drawings of features and hairstyles that are not ethnicity-specific. Approximately half of the pictures depict boys and half girls. Color has been added to clothing or objects in the pictures to help the child focus on the concept represented in the picture. Children can respond to the task demands verbally or nonverbally.

There are four content areas reflected in the picture cards that correspond to topics typically addressed in preschool health and safety education programs: household, playground, bicycle, and motor-vehicle safety and accident prevention (31 items; e.g., using a car seatbelt, not playing with poisons, stranger safety), nutrition (6 items; e.g., drinking milk versus soda, eating balanced meals), general hygienic measures (5 items; e.g., washing hands before eating, brushing teeth), and health recognition and promotion (8 items; e.g., covering mouth sneezing). A total score is derived by summing the number of correct responses.

Psychometric Information

Standardization sample characteristics included 315 children (137 boys, 178 girls) ages 28 to 80 months who were 69% White, 16% Black, and 11% Hispanic. Family income ranged from lower (28% with annual income less than $20,000) to upper (36% with income greater than $60,000) class. Daycare centers, preschools, and community programs were the primary recruitment sites.

Internal consistency was calculated to be .51 (Cronbach's alpha). Two-hour test-retest reliability with 43 children was .88.

This instrument is a revision of a previous instrument, the Preschool Health Knowledge Assessment (PHKA). Based on the results and observations made when using the PHKA, more advanced items were added, wording was changed to clarify meaning, and color was added to highlight specific concepts. Content validity was then reexamined by four pediatric/child development experts and a few changes in wording were made. No other validity data were reported. However, older children obtained higher PHASKA scores than younger children, which would be expected given the rapid changes in cognitive development during the preschool years.

Comment

Assessing preschoolers' knowledge of health and safety concepts is very difficult, although the PHASKA provides a creative and useful method for acquiring such information. The authors report that the measure is attractive to young children and adequately captures their attention. There are concerns about its low internal consistency overall and the lack of reliability data for the individual scales or content areas. Also, reliability and validity information by age would be helpful to better assess its psychometric stability across the rapidly progressing developmental transitions that occur between ages 2 and 6. Overall, in light of the movement toward more early-childhood and school-based health promotion programs, this instrument warrants further development and refinement so it potentially can be used to evaluate the effectiveness of early-childhood health education programs.

Relevant References

Banks, E. (1990). Concepts of health and sickness of preschool- and school-aged children. *Children's Health Care, 19*, 43–48.

Mobley, C. E. (1996). Assessment of health knowledge in preschoolers. *Children's Health Care, 25*, 11–18.

Robinson, C. A. (1987). Preschool children's conceptualizations of health and illness. *Children's Health Care, 16*, 89–96.

Self-Care Adherence Interview (SCAI)

C. L. Hanson, 1987

Manual and Address Information

There is a manual. Direct inquiries to: Cindy L. Hanson, Department of Psychology, University of Central Florida, P.O. Box 161390, Orlando, FL 32816-1390, chanson@pegasus.cc.ucf.edu.

Purpose

The SCAI provides an assessment of the adherence to the treatment regimen for youngsters with insulin-dependent diabetes mellitus. Dimensions of assessment include diet, glucose testing, insulin adjustment, and hypoglycemia preparedness.

Format, Administration, and Scoring

The SCAI is intended to be administered as a semistructured interview by an interviewer familiar with the requirements of the diabetic regimen. Allow approximately 15 minutes to complete the interview. It should immediately be emphasized that there are "no right or wrong answers" and that the interviewer is interested only in finding out how they typically handle things and what works best for them as individuals. They also are told that their answers will not be seen by medical personnel or parents. The interview begins with the question, "Do you ever test your urine or blood for sugar?" and proceeds in order.

Items are scored on 2- to 5-point scales, which are then summed to provide a total score. The maximum total score is 41 points. Higher scores are indicative of good adherence or positive self-care behaviors. For each of the content areas, the possible points range from 0 to 8 for glucose testing, 0 to 23 for dietary behaviors, 0 to 3 for insulin adjustment, and 0 to 7 for hypoglycemia preparedness.

Psychometric Information

Standardization data comes from several samples of children and adolescents across varying geographic regions. The adherence scores have been demonstrated to relate significantly to glycemic control and these behaviors remain stable over time (.70 at 3 months, .71 at 1 year).

Validity studies also have supported convergent, discriminant, and predictive validity of the SCAI. For example, the SCAI was found to relate most highly with the youth's overall quality of nutritional intake while not significantly associating with factors not assessed by the SCAI, such as physical activity levels. In addition, the SCAI was able to prospectively predict glycemic levels at 6 months and 1 year, controlling for age and illness duration.

Comment

While additional psychometric research with diverse samples is indicated for the SCAI, it appears to be a valid measure for evaluating self-care behaviors in youngsters with diabetes. Unlike specific, point-in-time measures of dietary intake, the SCAI provides a summary of dietary measures over a longer period of time, which the authors suggest may be an improvement in methodology for the assessment of the relationship between adherence behavior and more long-term measures of glycemic control such as HbA1c.

Relevant References

Hanson, C. (1989). *Protocol for the administration and scoring of the Adherence and IDDM Questionnaire-R.* Orlando, FL: University of Central Florida.

Hanson, C. L., DeGuire, M. J., Schinkel, A. M., Kolterman, O. G., Goodman, J. P., & Buckingham, B. A. (1996). Self-care behaviors in insulin-dependent diabetes: Evaluation tools and their associations with glycemic control. *Journal of Pediatric Psychology, 21,* 467–482.

Hanson, C. L., Henggeler, S. W., & Burghen, G. A. (1987). Social competence and parental support and mediators of the link between stress and metabolic control in adolescent with insulin-dependent diabetes mellitus. *Journal of Consulting and Clinical Psychology, 55,* 529–533.

Hanson, C. L., Schinkel, A. M., De Guire, M. J., & Kolterman, O. G. (1995). Empirical validation for a family-centered model of care. *Diabetes Care, 18*(10), 1347–1356.

Skin Cancer Knowledge Questionnaire (SCKQ) for Parents

T. J. Mickler, 1997

Manual and Address Information

No manual. Direct inquiries to: James R. Rodrigue, Department of Clinical and Health Psychology, P.O. Box 100165, University of Florida Health Science Center, Gainesville, FL 32610-0165, (352) 395-0490, jrodrigu@hp.ufl.edu.

Purpose

The SCKQ was designed to assess parents' knowledge of the seriousness and prevalence of skin cancer, skin cancer risk factors, and sun protective behaviors.

Format, Administration, and Scoring

The SCKQ is a paper-and-pencil measure that is completed by parents of children ages 6 months to 10 years. The SCKQ can be administered in either an individual or group format. It contains 20 items, 8 are worded in a multiple choice format and 19 are true or false. There is an additional item that asks parents to indicate their perceived skin cancer knowledge on a 5-point Likert scale (1 = poor to 5 = excellent), but this item is not included in the total knowledge score. A total knowledge score is derived by summing the correct responses, thus yielding a possible score ranging from 0 to 20. A computer analysis found the measure to be written at a sixth-grade reading level. Sample items include:

> What percentage of skin cancers are curable? (a) 20% (b) 50% (c) 75% (d) 90%
>
> Almost all wrinkling of the skin that is common in adulthood can be attributed to the normal aging process. (True or False)

Sun tanning in a tanning salon or booth is a safer way to tan than direct exposure to the sun. (True or False)

The majority of sun damage to a person's skin occurs in the first 18 years of life. (True or False)

Psychometric Information

The SCKQ was adapted from a previously published knowledge questionnaire for adults as well as from the clinical and scientific literature. Twenty-seven items were derived from materials published by various organizations (e.g., American Cancer Society), professional groups (e.g., American Academy of Dermatology), and researchers who have specified what parents should know about sun exposure health hazards and appropriate sun protection behaviors. A licensed dermatologist reviewed the items for accuracy. Based on the dermatologist's recommendations as well as factor analysis findings, 7 items were dropped from the initial pool.

The standardization sample included 216 primary caregivers of children ages 6 months to 10 years who were recruited from several school-based daycare programs in one community. Also, a sample of 101 health professionals (nurses and physicians) were recruited to complete the measure.

Internal consistency was .73. Two-week test-retest reliability using a subset ($n = 32$) of the sample was .74. Health professionals answered 79% of the items correctly, and the authors concluded that this provided partial support of the measure's content validity.

Comment

The SCKQ represents an improvement over knowledge questionnaires that have typically been used in the skin cancer research literature. It is easily administered in any setting (e.g., school, clinic, home) and can be completed in less than 15 minutes. While the preliminary psychometric data are promising, further assessment of reliability and validity, especially with more diverse populations is needed. Efforts to examine SCKQ scores and their relationship to actual sun protection behaviors are reportedly in progress by the authors of this measure.

Relevant References

Lescano, C. M., & Rodrigue, J. R. (1997). Skin cancer prevention behaviors among parents of young children. *Children's Health Care, 26,* 107–114.

Mickler, T. J., & Rodrigue, J. R. (1997). Knowledge of sun exposure and skin cancer among parents of young children. *Children's Health Care, 26,* 97–106.

Rodrigue, J. R. (1996). Promoting healthier behaviors, attitudes, and beliefs toward sun exposure in parents of young children. *Journal of Consulting and Clinical Psychology, 64,* 1431–1436.

Test of Diabetes Knowledge (TDK)

S. B. Johnson, 1982

Manual and Address Information

No manual. Direct inquiries to: Suzanne B. Johnson, Center for Pediatric Psychology and Family Studies, P.O. Box 100165, University of Florida Health Science Center, Gainesville, FL 32610-1065, (352) 395-0490, sjohnson@hp.ufl.edu.

Purpose

The TDK was developed to assess what children, adolescents, and parents know about diabetes.

Format, Administration, and Scoring

The self-administered TDK consists of 74 multiple-choice items broken down into two components: General Information (38 items) and Problem Solving (36 items). The TDK can be administered to children 10 years old and older and to parents of children with diabetes. The General Information component taps knowledge about various diabetes facts, whereas the Problem Solving component assesses knowledge about how these facts are used in different situations. Sample items include:

When giving insulin injections you should: (General Information)
  a. inject into the same area
  b. inject into a different area every time
  c. inject only in the leg
  d. I don't know.

You are going to prom night and there will be a lot of food. Which of the following should you do: (Problem Solving)
  a. tell a friend you have diabetes and what to do for low blood sugar
  b. take some extra NPH insulin before you go to the prom
  c. don't dance much so you won't go low
  d. I don't know.

Each item contains four response choices, including an "I don't know" alternative to discourage guessing and to more accurately assess what the child or parent knows about diabetes. Scores are obtained for Total Knowledge, General Information, and Problem Solving. Administration time is approximately 20 to 30 minutes.

Psychometric Information

TDK items were generated from previous diabetes literature and various diabetes educational materials, and subsequently reviewed by two physicians and a nurse for accuracy. The initial, predominantly White (80%) normative sample comprised 151 children with diabetes (ages 6–18 years) and 179 parents. Several additional studies have been reported in the literature. Overall, internal consistency reliability (split-half Spearman-Brown) ranges from .86 to .90 for General Information and .84 to .85 for Problem Solving for the Child version, and ranges from .80 to .88 for General Information and .75 to .85 for Problem Solving for the Parent version. Children and parents tend to score lower on Problem Solving compared to General Information, and child age is positively associated with scores on both test components.

The two TDK components are only moderately correlated with each other (.62–.72) across studies, which suggests that they may be conceptually distinct dimensions. TDK scores have been found to be sensitive to change following educational programs. For instance, in a sample of 93 children with diabetes, Harkavy and colleagues (1983) found that both General Information and Problem Solving scores improved significantly by the end of a 2-week diabetes summer camp. However, these knowledge changes were found only for older children (ages 12 and older).

Comment

The development and validation of the TDK has served as a model for researchers who study knowledge acquisition in other chronic conditions. Its developers have repeatedly evaluated its content (i.e., to maintain up-to-date diabetes information), psychometric properties, and clinical utility, and they have made modifications as needed. Indeed, the current TDK is a fourth-generation measure. It has excellent content validity, evidence for predictive validity with adolescents, and its clinical utility has been demonstrated with children as young as 6. However, TDK scores of young children may be less impacted by diabetes educational programs, and there is a need to evaluate the predictive validity of the TDK Parent version. The inclusion of a problem-solving component and an "I don't know" response choice allows clinicians to more accurately assess diabetes knowledge and targets for educational intervention. While it may be a time-consuming questionnaire to administer in a clinic setting, its cost-effectiveness may be realized in the more efficient targeting of diabetes education to specific knowledge and problem-solving deficits. Further examination of its applicability to more culturally diverse groups of children is needed.

Relevant References

Harkavy, J., Johnson, S. B., Silverstein, J., Spillar, R., McCallum, M., & Rosenbloom, A. (1983). Who learns what at diabetes summer camp? *Journal of Pediatric Psychology, 8,* 143–153.

Johnson, S. B. (1995). Managing insulin-dependent diabetes mellitus in adolescence: A developmental perspective. In J. L. Wallander & L. J. Siegel (Eds.), *Adolescent health problems: Behavioral perspectives* (pp. 265–288). New York: Guilford Press.

Johnson, S. B., Pollak, R. T., Silverstein, J. H., Rosenbloom, A. L., Spillar, R., McCallum, M., & Harkavy, J. (1982). Cognitive and behavioral knowledge about insulin-dependent diabetes among children and parents. *Pediatrics, 69,* 708–713.

The 24-Hour Recall Interview

S. B. Johnson, 1986

Manual and Address Information

There is a manual. Direct inquiries to: Suzanne B. Johnson, Center for Pediatric Psychology and Family Studies, University of Florida Health Science Center, P.O. Box 100165, Gainesville, FL 32610-0165, (352) 395-0210, sjohnson@hp.ufl.edu.

Purpose

The 24-hour recall interview, a long-standing method of dietary assessment was modified to assess not only dietary information but also information regarding all diabetes management behaviors.

Format, Administration, and Scoring

The interview is intended to be administered in a conversational format to the child and a parent, usually taking place over the phone. Child and parent are interviewed separately. Respondents are asked to recall the events of the previous day in temporal sequence, beginning with the time the child woke up and ending with the time the child went to bed. All diabetes-specific behaviors are recorded. In order to obtain a more extensive and representative sample of daily diabetes management behavior, at least three independent interviews (two concerning weekdays, one concerning a weekend day) are conducted with the child and parent over a time frame of 2 weeks.

Two versions of the 24-Hour Recall Interview exist. The first is a standard interview sheet on which the responses of the subject are recorded, and the second is an interview program on disk. The disk version is particularly practical as the data is simultaneously recorded and entered into a format from which it may be converted into a statistical analysis package.

Thirteen measures of treatment compliance or adherence may be calculated from the 24-Hour Recall Interview. Higher scores indicate relative noncompliance with lower scores indicative of relative compliance. The measures of adherence include: frequency, duration, and type of exercise; injection regularity, injection interval, injection-meal timing, and regularity of injection-meal timing; testing frequency and eating frequency, average amount of daily concentrated sweets consumed, percentage of calories from carbohydrates, percentage of calories from fat, and deviation from ideal total calories consumed. In order to obtain an estimate of the parents' daily supervision of the child, the percent of diabetes-related behaviors observed by the parent may be calculated.

Psychometric Information

The initial standardization sample consisted of 168 parent-child pairs attending summer camps. Children ranged in age from 6 to 19 with a diabetes duration between 1 and 17 years. On 8 of the 13 measures of adherence, the younger children were significantly more adherent than were the older children. The younger children tended to eat more often, check their blood more frequently, and exercise more often than adolescents, and adolescents were found to show more variable injection times, deviate from the ideal injection interval, and often take their insulin at the same time as, or even after, eating a meal. In addition, their diet consisted of too much fat and not enough carbohydrates.

Parent-child agreement in the standardization sample was initially used as a measure of reliability. Although perfect agreement between parent and child reports was not expected, all of the Pearson product-moment correlations for the 13 adherence measures were statistically significant, ranging from .42 (for regularity of injection-meal timing) to .78 (for glucose testing frequency), with a mean of .62. Parent-child agreement tended to differ according to the age of the child, with the youngest children (ages 6 to 9) evidencing the poorest agreement for measures involving time, although this group only showed moderate agreement for diet composition and high agreement for calories consumed, exercise type, and the frequency measures. The children ages 10 to 15 showed the most consistent parent-child concordance across all measures, while the children ages 16–19 showed great variability in their parent-child agreement. Another study found estimates of parent-child agreement to be as high or higher than reported in the original study for all 13 adherence measures.

Exploratory factor analysis of the 13 different diabetes adherence behaviors initially identified five components of adherence, accounting for over 70% of the variance. However, when confirmatory factor analysis was applied across two independent samples in order to test the equality of this factor pattern, six adherence measures emerged. Factors 1 through 4 (Exercise, Injection, Diet Type, and Eating/Testing Frequency) were confirmed. However, Factor 5 (Diet Amount) was discovered to be too complex. The adherence measures composing this factor (total calories and concentrated sweets consumed) should instead be viewed as separate constructs.

Comment

One strength of the 24-Hour Recall Interview is that it is extremely simple to administer. However, it can become time-consuming when administering the interview to both a parent and a child over three administrations. In addition, the method seems to exhibit adequate reliability and to present a reasonably accurate and nonreactive picture of the child's adherence behavior, particularly when three or more interviews are conducted. When the interview is also conducted with the parent, the reliability and validity of the 24-Hour Recall Interview increases. It is an extremely useful measure to administer in order to gain an estimate of a child's adherence to each of the domains encompassed by the diabetes treatment regimen.

Relevant References

Freund, A., Johnson, S. B., Silverstein, J., & Thomas, J. (1991). Assessing daily management of childhood diabetes using 24-hour recall interviews: Reliability and stability. *Health Psychology 10,* 200–208.

Johnson, S. B., & Carmichael, S. K. (1997). *A preliminary manual for the 24-hour recall interview.* Unpublished manuscript, University of Florida.

Johnson, S. B., Silverstein, J., Rosenbloom, A., Carter, R., & Cunningham, W. (1986). Assessing daily management in childhood diabetes. *Health Psychology, 5,* 545–564.

Johnson, S. B., Tomer, A., Cunningham, W., & Henretta, J. (1990). Adherence in childhood diabetes: Results of a confirmatory factor analysis. *Health Psychology, 9,* 493–501.

Reynolds, L. A., Johnson, S. B., & Silverstein, J. (1990). Assessing daily diabetes management by 24-hour recall interview: The validity of children's reports. *Journal of Pediatric Psychology, 15,* 493–509.

General Observations and Recommendations

La Greca (1990) has noted that how to measure adherence behaviors of children and adolescents is perhaps one of the most difficult questions facing pediatric researchers and clinicians. Treatment outcome and health status, drug assays, self-reports, behavioral observations, monitoring devices, and ratings by health professionals are the most commonly used methods for assessing adherence behaviors (La Greca & Schuman, 1995). In this chapter, we reviewed several techniques that have been developed to assess adherence with a focus on self-report measures because they are the most commonly used, least expensive, and efficiently implemented in the context of busy clinical practices. It is important to remember, however, that such self-reports tend to overestimate adherence and are subject to social desirability effects.

In general, it is our impression that the development of adherence measurement models is in its infancy. Given the association between nonadherence and subsequent health outcomes, it is essential that pediatric researchers continue to develop and evaluate the utility of measurement tools for assessing adherence behaviors across both chronic and acute health conditions. Existing child health measures of regimen adherence are strongest in the area of diabetes. Indeed, there is a relative absence of illness-specific measures of adherence for most childhood chronic health conditions. The measurement techniques developed to assess adherence to diabetes regimens (e.g., 24 Hour Recall) might serve as a model for researchers interested in developing measurement tools in other areas (e.g., asthma, sickle cell disease). Furthermore, few tools exist to assess adherence in more acute medical settings and this may prove to be an important domain for scientific inquiry.

Knowledge of disease and its management is considered essential to maintaining good adherence to complex treatment protocols. However, few knowledge measures exist to specifically assess both children's and parents' understanding of disease processes and problem-solving skills related to its management. In light of the fact that most intervention programs designed to enhance adherence behaviors include educational components, it would seem wise to develop and validate disease-specific knowledge questionnaires that can be used efficiently in pediatric clinics.

Standardization and sample diversity are important issues in the development of adherence and knowledge measures. While samples are well described for some measures, other published reports reveal little about variables such as ethnicity, socioeconomic status, or developmental considerations. Replication of findings in geographically diverse areas and across cross-cultural samples would strengthen the empirical basis of many of these measures.

References

Cramer, J. A. (1991). Overview of methods to measure and enhance patient compliance. In J. A. Cramer & B. Spilker (Eds.), *Patient compliance in medical practice and clinical trials* (pp. 3–10). New York: Raven Press.

Cromer, B. A. (1991). Behavioral strategies to increase compliance in adolescents. In J. A. Cramer & B. Spilker (Eds.), *Patient compliance in medical practice and clinical trials* (pp. 99–106). New York: Raven Press.

Geffken, G. R., & Johnson, S. B. (1994). Diabetes: Psychological issues. In R. A. Olsen, L. L. Mullins, J. B. Gillman, & I. M. Chaney (Eds.), *A sourcebook of pediatric psychology*. Boston: Allyn and Bacon.

Glasgow, R. E. (1991) Compliance to diabetes regimes: Conceptualization, complexity, and determinants. In J. A. Cramer & B. Spilker (Eds.), *Patient compliance in medical practice and clinical trials* (pp. 209–224). New York: Raven Press.

La Greca, A. M. (1990). Issues in adherence with pediatric regimens. *Journal of Pediatric Psychology, 15,* 423–436.

La Greca, A. M., & Schuman, W. B. (1995). Adherence to prescribed medical regimens. In M. C. Roberts (Ed.), *Handbook of pediatric psychology* (2nd ed.) (pp. 55–83). New York: Guilford Press.

Meichenbaum, D., & Turk, D. C. (1987). *Facilitating treatment adherence.* New York: Plenum Press.

Rapoff, M. A., & Barnard, M. U. (1991). Compliance with pediatric medical regimes. In J. A. Cramer & B. Spilker (Eds.), *Patient compliance in medical practice and clinical trials* (pp. 73–98). New York: Raven Press.

Symister, P., & Friend, R. (1996). Quality of life and adjustment in renal disease: A health psychology perspective. In R. J. Resnick & R. H. Rozensky (Eds.), *Health psychology through the life span* (pp. 265–288). Washington: American Psychological Association.

Chapter 10

Parent, Family, and Health Care Professional

GARY R. GEFFKEN

This chapter includes reviews of measures typically completed by parents, other family members, and health care professionals that did not fit neatly into any of our other content categories or domains. Within this framework, we review measures that are disease-specific, such as those focusing on diabetes (e.g., Diabetes Family Behavior Checklist, Diabetes Family Responsibility Questionnaire), cancer (e.g., Bereaved Extended Family Member Support Group), and cystic fibrosis (e.g., Interview Schedule on Impact of Cystic Fibrosis on Families). Other measures reviewed include those that are setting-specific (e.g., pediatric or neonatal intensive care units). Moreover, more general or non-disease specific measures also are reviewed (e.g. Chronicity Impact and Coping Instrument: Parent Questionnaire).

Chronic health conditions in children affect more than the child. Parents must modify their roles and activities, supervise or manage complex medical regimens, and maintain the aspects of the household or family that extend beyond the affected child. Consequently, child health professionals have called for greater attention to a systems-based assessment of children's health and its associated consequences (Kazak, 1989; Rodrigue, 1994). In this context, the perspectives of the parents, siblings, peers, and health providers are equally important to obtain in child health assessments and the psychological adjustment of these individuals has been the focus of many studies.

The measures reviewed in this chapter reveal the importance of parents and families (e.g., Health Resources Inventory for Parents) as sources to assess in evaluating children's health and its impact on family functioning. While parents and family members have long been recognized as being impacted by childhood illness, some measures (e.g., Pediatric Oncology Nurse Questionnaire) reveal a recognition that health care professionals dealing intensely with conditions having significant morbidity and mortality risks are critical in the health care equation and deserving of attention. Other measures reviewed use physicians as informants (e.g., Family APGAR-Revised) in assessing family functioning.

The measures reviewed in this chapter use varying formats and methods, ranging from paper-and-pencil questionnaires to interviews with varying degrees of structure. While the content of this chapter is unified by the inclusion of measures of subsystems of persons involved in the care of children, at times there is overlap with content areas reviewed in other chapters. For example, the Health Resources Inventory for Parents may also be used to examine parents' perceptions of children's adjustment in terms of social competence. However, as with the other chapters in this handbook, this chapter reviews a collection of clinical and research tools designed to assess a set of issues organized around a theme in child health care.

REVIEWS

Bereaved Extended Family Members Support Group Evaluation (BEFMSGE)

S. Heiney, 1993

Manual and Address Information

No manual. Direct inquiries to: Sue P. Heiney, Richland Memorial Hospital, 7 Richland Medical Park Drive, Columbia, SC, 29203.

Purpose

The BEFMSGE is a paper-and-pencil measure used to evaluate satisfaction with participation in a support group for family members of children with cancer.

Format, Administration, and Scoring

This specific version of the BEFMSGE is completed by family members of a child who has died from cancer. Other versions include evaluation rating forms for children and adolescents with cancer, and their parents. The BEFMSGE was designed to help investigate the effects of participation in such a support group on various parameters of psychosocial functioning.

The BEFMSGE consists of both forced-choice and open-ended questions focusing on three main points: opinions about the group, usefulness of topics, and ease in discussing topics. Open-ended questions also include items related to suggestions for improving the group. The first section focusing on opinions about the group contains four Likert-scale items (1 = strongly disagree to 4 = strongly agree). For example, one item states "I am glad I participated." Other sections on utility and ease of discussing topics ask respondents to rank each topic from most to least helpful, and easiest to hardest to discuss. Scores are obtained by summing the responses to the Likert-scale questions. Open-ended questions are used qualitatively.

Sample items include:

I could share thoughts in the group that I could not share with most people.
I felt less alone when learning that other people felt similar to me.
I felt that I could cope because I saw that other people were coping too.

Psychometric Information

Items on the BEFMSGE were rationally derived. The scale was administered to a group of five parents who participated in a support group. Earlier versions of the support group evaluation, focusing on children with cancer or parents of surviving children, also utilized small samples. The mean on the BEFMSGE was 3.75 indicating high satisfaction with the group. No other psychometric data have been reported.

Comment

The BEFMSGE represents an initial look at empirically evaluating support group experience in bereaved parents. It has been used with parents whose children died of cancer. The measure is relatively simple to complete, and its open-ended section can provide useful information to group leaders. Aside from descriptive data, no psychometric tests of the measure have been performed. While other measures were reported in studies utilizing the BEFMSGE, findings related to concurrent or divergent validity have not been reported. Also, there have not been any investigations of its reliability. The use of support groups in medical settings is widespread, and there has been very little effort to evaluate their effectiveness or participants' satisfaction with them. Therefore, it would seem wise to further develop and validate instruments for use in such contexts. Although the BEFMSGE may provide useful clinical information, its psychometric properties must be further evaluated before it can be recommended for adoption in clinical practice.

Relevant References

Heiney, S. P., Ruffin, J., Ettinger, R. S., & Ettinger, S. (1988). The effects of group therapy on adolescents with cancer. *Journal of Pediatric Oncology Nursing, 5,* 20–24.

Heiney, S. P., Ruffin, J., & Goon-Johnson, K. (1995). The effects of a support group on selected psychosocial outcomes of bereaved parents whose child died from cancer. *Journal of Pediatric Oncology Nursing, 12,* 51–58.

Heiney, S. P., Wells, L. M., & Gunn, J. (1993). The effects of group therapy on bereaved extended family of children with cancer. *Journal of Pediatric Oncology Nursing, 10,* 99–104.

Chronicity Impact and Coping Instrument: Parent Questionnaire (CICI:PQ)

D. P. Hymovich, 1983

Manual and Address Information

No manual. Direct inquiries to: Debra P. Hymovich, School of Nursing, University of Pennsylvania, Philadelphia, PA.

Purpose

The CICI:PQ was developed to assess parents' perceptions of the impact of having a chronically ill child in their family. This measure also assesses parental coping styles in dealing with their child's illness.

Format, Administration, and Scoring

The CICI:PQ is a closed-ended self-administered questionnaire consisting of 160 items. This measure consists of six sections: the child, the parent, the parent's spouse, the child's brothers and sisters, hospitalization, and other. The entire scale breaks down into three subscales: stressors, coping strategies, and values/attitudes/beliefs. These subscales are based on information provided in 63 interviews with parents of chronically ill children.

Psychometric Information

Standardization of the most recent revision of this measure is underway. However, earlier versions have been standardized on 29, 33, and 44 parents for each of three revisions, respectively. Only reliability data for the stressor and coping strategies subscales are reported. Hoyt's coefficient for these are .94 and .93, respectively.

Evidence for content validity is suggested by the author. Items were reviewed by a clinical psychologist, three master's-level nurses who cared for families of children with chronic illness, and a doctoral nurse faculty member who worked with chronically ill children. As a second measure of content validity, parents were asked to report whether they felt that the instrument covered things that they felt were important. The majority of parents indicated that this was so, and that they felt that the instrument should be helpful to their caretakers.

Comment

While initial psychometric properties of the CICI:PQ are encouraging, more information is clearly needed. Initial investigation of the reliability has suggested adequacy in this area; however, test-retest reliability for all subscales and for the measure as a whole would be useful. More studies on the validity of the instrument would strengthen its empirical underpinnings, specifically, factor analysis of the measure, and examination of the six sections would provide useful information. A larger, more diverse (both ethnically and geographically) standardization sample is needed to improve the generalizability of the initial findings.

Relevant References

Hymovich, D. P. (1983). The chronicity impact and coping instrument: Parent questionnaire. *Nursing Research, 32,* 275–281.

Hymovich, D. P. (1984). Development of the chronicity impact and coping instrument: Parent questionnaire (CICI:PQ). *Nursing Research, 33,* 218–222.

Coping Health Inventory for Parents (CHIP)

H. I. McCubbin, 1981

Manual and Address Information

There is a manual. Direct inquiries to: H. I. McCubbin, Center for Excellence in Family Studies; Family, Stress, Coping, and Health Project, University of Wisconsin-Madison, 1300 Linden Drive, Madison, WI 53706, manual@macc.wisc.edu

Purpose

This instrument was developed to assess parents' appraisal of their coping responses when they have a child who is seriously and/or chronically ill.

Format, Administration, and Scoring

This is a 45-item self-report checklist. Parents respond to the helpfulness of each of 45 coping behaviors on a 4-point Likert-type scale (0 = not helpful to 3 = extremely helpful). For each of the coping strategies not employed by parents, they are asked to report (1) if they chose not to use it or (2) it was not possible to use it. Sample items include:

> Believing that my child(ren) will get better.
> Trusting my spouse (or former spouse) to help support me and my child(ren).
> Investing time and energy in my job.
> Talking with other individuals/parents in my same situation.

Psychometric Information

The CHIP was initially standardized with a sample of 100 families who had one or more children with cystic fibrosis who were seen at the Cystic Fibrosis Center, Pediatric Outpatient Clinic at the University of Minnesota Hospitals. Factor analysis of the CHIP revealed three factors (labeled coping patterns) that account for 71.1% of the variance. The first of these coping patterns (Coping I) is labeled Maintaining Family Integration, Cooperation, and an Optimistic Definition of the Situation, and centers around strengthening family life, relationships, and the parents' outlook on life and the child with a chronic illness. The second coping pattern (Coping II), labeled Maintaining Social Support, Self-Esteem, and Psychological Stability, focuses on the parents' efforts to maintain their own sense of well-being through social relationships. It also involves participating in activities to enhance self-esteem and doing things to manage stress and tension. The third coping pattern (Coping III), Understanding the Health Care Situation Through Communication With Other Parents and Consultation With the Health Care Team, represents the relationship between the parents and the health care team to develop more knowledge and understanding of the illness and to master the care of the child at home. Internal consistency reliabilities for each of the coping strategies are .79, .79, and .71, respectively.

Construct validity has been reported through its use in several large studies of parents with children who have congenital heart disease, cystic fibrosis, leukemia, cerebral palsy, and childhood cancer. In each of these studies, the CHIP revealed differences in hypothesized directions, and subsequent samples were found to have score distributions similar to that of the standardization sample. Concurrent validity has been reported for all three coping patterns as they have been found to be significantly correlated with various subscales on the Family Environment Scale. For mothers, Coping I is associated with family cohesiveness (.21), Coping II is related to family expressiveness (.19), and Coping III is related to family cohesiveness (.19). For fathers, Coping II was correlated with family cohesiveness (.36), and inversely related to family conflict (−.21). Coping I was also positively associated with family organization (.32) and Coping III was positively associated with both family organization (.22) and family control (.19).

Comment

The CHIP has been demonstrated to be a reliable and valid measure with multiple culturally diverse samples of children and their parents. Furthermore, it has been used successfully with parents of children who have a variety of chronic health conditions, including cancer, diabetes, developmental disorders, asthma, liver disease, and kidney disease, among others. Consequently, it has developed a strong empirical foundation through an extensive body of research. It is useful in assessing the coping skills that parents find most useful in dealing with life as the parent of a child with a chronic health condition.

Relevant References

Brown, R. T., Kaslow, N. J., Hazzard, A. P., Madan-Swain, A., Sexson, S. B., Lambert, R., & Baldwin, K. (1992). Psychiatric and family functioning in children with leukemia and their parents. *Journal of the American Academy of Child and Adolescent Psychology, 31*, 495–502.

McCubbin, H. I., McCubbin, M. A., Nevin, R., & Cauble, E. (1981). Coping-Health Inventory for Parents (CHIP). In H. I. McCubbin, A. I. Thompson, & M. A. McCubbin (1996). *Family assessment: Resiliency, coping and adaptation—Inventories for research and practice.* (pp. 407–453). Madison: University of Wisconsin System.

McCubbin, H. I., McCubbin, M. A., Patterson, J. M., Cauble, A. E., Wilson, L. R., & Warwick, W. (1983). CHIP-Coping Health Inventory for Parents: An assessment of parental coping patterns in the care of the chronically ill child. *Journal of Marriage and the Family, May*, 359–370.

Svavarsdottir, E., & McCubbin, M. A. (1996). Parenthood transition for parents of an infant diagnosed with a congenital heart condition. *Journal of Pediatric Nursing, 11*, 207–216.

Diabetes Family Behavior Checklist (DFBC)

L. C. Schafer, 1986

Manual and Address Information

No manual. Direct inquiries to: Lorraine C. Schafer, 1000 North Oak Avenue, Mashfield, WI 54449, (715) 387-5182, schaferl@mfidclin.edu.

Purpose

The DFBC was developed to assess the frequency of both supportive and nonsupportive behaviors in families of adolescents with diabetes.

Format, Administration, and Scoring

The DFBC consists of 16 questions (9 positive/supportive, 7 negative/nonsupportive) designed to tap how often family members do things related to the patient's diabetes regimen. Responses for each item ranges from 1 (never) to 5 (at least once a day). There are two forms, one for the patient and one for "other" (usually a parent or caretaker). A positive summary score ranges from 9 to 45, and a negative summary score ranges from 7 to 35. Sample items include:

Praise you/the person with diabetes for following your/their diet.

Encourage you/the person with diabetes to participate in sports activities.

Criticize you/the person with diabetes for not recording the results of blood tests.

Psychometric Information

Schaefer has collected sample data on 71 children (ages 10–18) with type I diabetes and their parents. These data indicate internal consistency coefficients ranging from .67 to .80 on the supportive subscale and .74 to .82 on the nonsupportive subscale. Other published data by the original author show internal consistency estimates for the supportive and nonsupportive subscales as .63 and .60, respectively. Test-retest reliability (6 months) have been reported to be .60 to .84 for the supportive subscale and .28 to .77 for the nonsupportive subscale, with variations being largely a function of time interval (i.e., shorter time intervals yielding lower correlations). Correspondence between adolescents and their parents has ranged from .01 to .27.

Adolescents' DFBC scores have not consistently been shown to be significantly correlated with adherence to a diabetes regimen, although more recent data suggest a significant relationship between DFBC subscale items and certain regimen behaviors in adolescents (.28–.57). Evidence of convergent validity is demonstrated by the correlation between mother-supportive behavior (as measured by the DFBC) and scores on the Diabetes Social Support Interview; unsupportive behavior scores correlated significantly with Family Environment Scale (FES) conflict scores (.26–.39), and supportive scores correlated with FES cohesion scores (.26–.39). Supportive scores also were positively correlated with the Shared Responsibility subscale of the Diabetes Family Responsibility Questionnaire (DFRQ) (.25–.38) and negatively correlated with the Child Takes Responsibility subscale of the same measure (–.29 — –.37).

Comment

The DFBC has shown improved psychometric properties for adolescents in recent, as yet unpublished data. Complex findings warrant that the reader examine the research carefully in identifying the empirically validated uses of the DFBC. This measure can be useful in assessing supportive and nonsupportive behaviors in families of adolescents with diabetes, and how they are related to regimen adherence in the adolescent. Further study of the DFBC will be of value to those with interests in the youngsters with diabetes and their families.

Relevant References

La Greca, A. M., Auslander, W. F., Greco, P., Spetter, D., Fisher, E. B., & Santiago, J. V. (1995). I get by with a little help from my family and friends: Adolescents' support for diabetes care. *Journal of Pediatric Psychology, 20,* 449–476.

Schafer, L. C., McCaul, K. D., & Glasgow, R. E. (1986). Supportive and nonsupportive family behaviors: Relationships to adherence and metabolic control in persons with type I diabetes. *Diabetes Care, 9,* 179–185.

Diabetes Family Responsibility Questionnaire (DFRQ)

B. J. Anderson, 1990

Manual and Address Information

No manual. Direct inquiries to: Barbara J. Anderson, Joslin Diabetes Center, 1 Joslin Place, Boston, MA 02215, (617) 732-2594, banderso@joslin.harvard.edu.

Purpose

The DFRQ was developed to fill the need for a measure with good psychometric properties that can be used clinically with families concerning the issue of family sharing responsibility for diabetes treatment tasks.

Format, Administration, and Scoring

This measure consists of 17 statements describing various tasks or situations that relate to diabetes management. It is a self-report measure and the respondent is asked to indicate which family member is responsible for various diabetes management tasks, that is, child's responsibility, shared responsibility, or parents' responsibility. This 17-item measure describes patterns of agreement and disagreement between mothers and children concerning their perceptions of the division of responsibility across a broad range of diabetes management tasks. Measurement is based on the responses of each mother-child dyadic score. Factor analysis revealed three domains: general health management tasks, regimen tasks, and social presentation of diabetes. Sample items include:

> Remembering to take morning or evening injection.
> Telling friends about diabetes.
> Remembering when blood sugar should be checked.

Psychometric Information

The initial standardization sample consisted of 121 mother-child dyads. The children were diagnosed as having insulin-dependent diabetes mellitus (IDDM) for at least 1 year and also were receiving treatment at a medical center. The three subscales determined by factor analysis had internal consistency reliabilities ranging from .69 to .85. The authors reported as evidence of concurrent validity the significant correlations between DFRQ scores and subscales on the Family Environment Scale. Higher reports of independence as a priority for individual family members as measured by the FES Independence Subscale were correlated with mothers' report of child assumption of greater responsibility for regimen tasks on the DFRQ (.27), and for the total tasks of the DFRQ scale (.21).

Comment

The DRFQ appears to be a useful tool in assessing the perceptions of responsibility of various family members for the compliance with the diabetes regimen. While the reliability of the measure appears adequate, more information on the validity of the subscales of the DFRQ (general health management tasks, regimen tasks, and social presentation of diabetes) would be useful. Also, data on more ethnically diverse samples would strengthen the empirical basis of this measure.

Relevant Reference

Anderson, B. J., Auslander, W. F., Jung, K. C., Miller, J. P., & Santiago, J. V. (1990). Assessing family sharing of diabetes responsibilities. *Journal of Pediatric Psychology, 15,* 477–492.

Family APGAR-Revised

J. K. Austin, 1989

Manual and Address Information

No manual. Direct inquiries to: Joan K. Austin, Indiana University School of Nursing, 1111 Middle Drive, Indianapolis, IN, 46202-5107, (317) 274-8254, iszd100 @iupui.edu.

Purpose

The Family APGAR-Revised was developed as a rapid assessment tool for measuring family functioning.

Format, Administration, and Scoring

Intended for use by physicians, this measure consists of five items, written at the second-grade reading level, to which patients and family members respond using a 5-point Likert-type scale (0 = never to 4 = always). These five items each measure one of five aspects of family functioning: adaptation, partnership, growth, affection, and resolve. *Adaptation* assesses the family's resources for dealing with the problem. *Partnership* measures the sharing of decision making and sharing of problems by the family. *Growth* is the support for and acceptance of change in individual family members. *Affection* is family members' response to expressions of emotions. Finally, *Resolve* assesses satisfaction with the quality of time that the family members spend together. Sample items include:

> When something is bothering me, I can ask my family for help.
> I like what my family does when I feel mad, happy, or loving.
> I like the way my family talks over things and shares problems with me.

Psychometric Information

The Family APGAR-Revised was standardized in two studies. In the first of these studies, 50 children (ages 8–12; Mean age = 9.88 years) were administered the measure. The children were all outpatients at a large medical center and were diagnosed with either epilepsy or asthma. Approximately half of the participants also had learning disorders. In the second study, 250 children (128 with epilepsy, 122 with asthma) were administered the measure. The sample consisted of 109 girls and 141 boys, ages 8–12 (mean age = 10.35). Approximately half of the children were from a large medical center, and the remaining children were from private physicians. One-third of the sample had learning disabilities.

Internal consistency (coefficient alpha) of the Family APGAR-Revised was reported as .70. Test-retest reliability (2 weeks) was .73, and item-to-total score correlations ranged from .32 to .52. Correlations between the Family APGAR-Revised and the Family APGAR (original version) were given as support for concurrent validity. The correlation was .79 for the first of two administrations, and .72 for the second administration.

Comment

The Family APGAR-Revised would benefit from further validation studies. While the correlation between the original and revised versions of this measure was acceptable, this finding reflects the relatively small change in the measure (rewording of the items to the second-grade reading level without changing the meaning). The standardization sample is acceptably sized, however, no socioeconomic data was reported.

Relevant References

Austin, J. K., & Huberty, T. J. (1989). Revision of the family AGPAR for use by 8-year-olds. *Family Systems Medicine, 7*, 323–327.

Family Coping Scale (FCS)

M. J. Kupst, 1984

Manual and Address Information

No manual. Direct inquiries to: Mary Jo Kupst, P.O. Box 118, Ringwood, IL 60072, (414) 456-4170, mkupst@post.its.mcw.edu.

Purpose

The FCS was designed to assess the current responses of family members to a crisis.

Format, Administration, and Scoring

The FCS is completed by a nurse or physician who assesses all family members on each of three coping criteria: (a) the family works toward a cognitive understanding of the realities of the illness and its implications, (b) family members are able to deal with the emotional aspects of the illness, and (c) the family works toward a constructive action plan that involves care of the child, care of other responsibilities, and support and communication among family members. Raters give a score ranging from 10 (not constructive or appropriate) to 40 (very constructive or supportive). A score of 30 indicates constructive or appropriate behavior, but raters may give any score between 10 and 40. Scores may be averaged within each member of the family or across members, depending on variables of interest.

Psychometric Information

The sample used in the original study was comprised of 60 families of children with diabetes. The average duration since diagnosis was 22.8 months (SD = 5.3 months). Seven mental health professionals rated families based on audiotaped interviews at diagnosis and at 1-year follow-up. At least three separate raters judged each tape. At diagnosis, the mean correlation across all raters was .72, and at 1 year the mean correlation was .73. No information on the validity of this measure was reported.

Comment

Further development of psychometric information on this measure could strengthen its empirical basis. While inter-rater reliability was sufficient, further measures of reliability would be useful. As no information on the validity of the scale is offered, research examining the factor structure of the scale, as well as other measures of construct and concurrent validity would be useful. Also, data on more diverse samples would be of interest.

Relevant Reference

Kupst, M. J., Schulman, J. L., Maurer, H., Honig, G., Morgan, E., & Fochtman, D. (1984). Coping with pediatric leukemia: A two year follow up. *Journal of Pediatric Psychology, 9,* 149–163.

Family Inventory of Resources for Management (FIRM)

McCubbin, 1987

Manual and Address Information

There is a manual. Direct inquiries to: Hamilton I. McCubbin, Center for Excellence in Family Studies, University of Wisconsin-Madison, 1300 Linden Drive, Madison, WI 53706, manual@macc.wisc.edu.

Purpose

The FIRM was developed to assess the family's basic resources and how well the family adapts to stressful events and strains.

Format, Administration, and Scoring

The FIRM consists of 69 self-report items, in which the respondent reports how well items describe their family on a 4-point Likert-type scale (0 = not at all to 3 = very well). Items were originally selected on the basis of literature reviews and typology theory of family adaptation in three primary domains: personal resources, family system internal resources, and established social support systems. There are four major subscales for the FIRM:

1. Family Strengths I: Esteem and Communication—looks at the presence of a combination of personal resources, family system internal resources, and community support in six areas: (a) family esteem, (b) communication, (c) mutual assistance, (d) optimism, (e) problem solving ability, and (f) encouragement of autonomy among family members.
2. Family Strengths II: Mastery and Health—assesses the presence of a combination of personal resources, family system internal resources, and community support in three areas: (a) sense of mastery over family events and outcomes, (b) family mutuality, and (c) physical and emotional health of family members.
3. Extended Family Support—examines how much mutual support and help is received from and given to relatives.
4. Financial Well-Being—measures the family's perceived financial status along four dimensions: (a) ability to meet financial commitments, (b) adequacy of financial reserves, (c) ability to financially help others, and (d) optimism about the family's financial future.

In addition to the four primary subscales, two factors (Financial Support and Social Desirability) have been added to the original scale but are not considered major dimensions. Scores are obtained by summing the items within subscales. The FIRM takes about 30 minutes to complete. Sample items include:

Being physically tired much of the time is a problem in our family.

We have money coming in from our investments (such as rental property, stocks, bonds, etc.).

We do not plan too far ahead because many things turn out to be a matter of good or bad luck anyway.

Psychometric Information

The FIRM was standardized on two separate groups of people. The first of these groups was a sample of 322 families having a child with either cerebral palsy or myelomeningocele. The second sample was comprised of 2,000 Midwest families. Cronbach alphas were .89 for the entire measure, .62 for Extended Family Support, and .85 for Family Strengths I, Family Strengths II, and Financial Well-Being. The intercorrelations among the four subscales range from .19 to .37, and overall FIRM scores are correlated with measures of family organization (.25), cohesion (.46), conflict (−.30), and expressiveness (.27).

Comment

The FIRM appears to have adequate reliability; however, further examination of its validity would strengthen the empirical basis of this measure. Factor analysis appears to support the model suggested by the author. Further information on criterion-related validity would be an asset. While the size of the standardization sample was reasonable, information based on a more culturally diverse population would be useful. The FIRM has demonstrated utility as a measure of adaptation among families with children who have chronic health conditions, and its continued use in such family-based child health research appears warranted.

Relevant References

McCubbin, H. I., & Comeau, J. (1987). FIRM: Family Inventory of Resources for Management. In H. I. McCubbin & A. I. Thompson (Eds.), *Family assessment inventories for research and practice* (pp. 145–160). Madison: University of Wisconsin-Madison, Family Stress, Coping and Health Project.

McCubbin, M. A., & McCubbin, M. I. (1988). Family Systems Assessment. In P. Karoly (Ed.), *Handbook of child health assessment: Biopsychosocial perspective* (pp. 252–253). New York: John Wiley & Sons.

Rodrigue, J. R., MacNaughton, K., Hoffmann, R. G., Graham-Pole, J., Andres, J. M., Novak, D. A., & Fennell, R. S. (1997). Transplantation in children: A longitudinal assessment of mothers' stress, coping, and perceptions of family functioning. *Psychosomatics, 38,* 478–486.

Health Resources Inventory for Parents (HRIP)

E. L. Gesten, 1976

Manual and Address Information

No manual. Direct inquiries to: Ellis L. Gesten, 3653 Elk Grove Court, Land O'Lakes, FL 34639-4656, (813) 974-0390.

Purpose

The HRIP is a paper-and-pencil measure that is completed by parents of either healthy or ill children and was designed to measure parents' perceptions of children's social competence.

Format, Administration, and Scoring

The HRIP is based largely on the Health Resources Inventory for Teachers (HRIT), which was designed to assess teachers' perceptions of the social competence of children. On the HRIT teachers respond to 51 items describing the child using a 5-point Likert scale (1 = not at all to 5 = very well). Item examples include: "Is interested in schoolwork" and "Is trustworthy." The HRIT has five factors that are combined to yield one Sum Factors score. Specific items or format of the HRIP have not been reported.

Psychometric Information

The HRIP was standardized on parents of elementary school-age children. It has also been used with pediatric samples, and in one investigation in particular, was used with a heterogeneous sample of children with several different chronic illnesses. Children in this sample were between the ages of 7 and 18. Psychometric data have been reported on the HRIT, on which the HRIP is based. The HRIT was evaluated through factor analyses that yielded five internally consistent factors accounting for 71% of the variance. Test-retest reliability of the HRIT has ranged from .72 to .91 for each of the five factors. Discriminant validity of the original scale also was established in that teachers' responses on the HRIT correctly discriminated between healthy and clinic-referred children. Descriptive data for the HRIT have been reported.

Comment

The HRIP is a relatively easy to complete self-report measure that can be used for a broad age range of children. It has been used with a sample of parents of children with varying degrees of illnesses (healthy through chronic illness affecting the brain). Standardization samples of both the HRIT and the HRIP have been heterogeneous, suggesting the HRIP's potential use with a wide range of populations. The measure on which the HRIP is based, the HRIT, has been found to have very acceptable reliability and validity. However, psychometric data for the HRIP have not been reported. More data on children with chronic health conditions is warranted prior to the HRIP's use in evaluating children's social competence.

Relevant References

Gesten, E. L. (1976). A health resources inventory: The development of a measure of the personal and social competence of primary grade children. *Journal of Consulting and Clinical Psychology, 44,* 775–786.

Perrin, E. C., Ayoub, C. C., & Willett, J. B. (1993). In the eyes of the beholder: Family and maternal influences on perceptions of adjustment of children with a chronic illness. *Journal of Developmental and Behavioral Pediatrics, 14,* 94–105.

Impact on Family Scale (IFS)

R. E. K. Stein, 1980

Manual and Address Information

There is a manual. Direct inquiries to: Ruth E. K. Stein, Department of Pediatrics, Albert Einstein College of Medicine, 1300 Morris Park Avenue, Bronx, NY 10461.

Purpose

The IFS was originally developed to measure the impact of a child's chronic illness on the family system. Revisions of the IFS have been used to measure the impact of children generally, as well as with behavior problems and developmental disabilities on family adjustment.

Format, Administration, and Scoring

The original self-administered IFS contains 24 statements to which parents indicate their agreement or disagreement using a 4-point Likert-type scale (0 = strongly agree to 3 = strongly disagree), as well as whether the item is currently impacting the family (yes or no). Factor analysis yielded four factors or subscales for which scores are derived: Financial Burden (4 items), Familial/Social Burden (9 items), Personal Strain (or Caretaker Burden) (6 items), and Coping/Mastery (5 items). A total score also is obtained. Sample items include:

> The illness is causing financial problems for the family. (Financial Burden)
> We see family and friends less because of the illness. (Familial/Social Burden)
> It is hard to find a reliable person to take care of my child. (Personal Strain)
> Because of what we have shared we are a closer family. (Coping/Mastery)

A recent, unpublished revision of the IFS by a separate group of researchers contains 73 items and two factors for which scores are obtained: Family Burden (62 items) and Family Adaptation (11 items).

Psychometric Information

Items for the original IFS were generated from field interviews with mothers of chronically ill children being treated at a university medical center and with health care providers. A pool of 190 items was reduced to 24 items following expert panel reviews and item analyses. The normative sample comprised 100 mothers of chronically ill children who were predominantly ethnic minority (66% Hispanic, 22% Black), low income (75%), unemployed (84%), and nonmarried

(65%). Internal consistency reliability (Cronbach's alpha) for the total score and four factors were: Total (.88), Financial Burden (.72), Familial/Social Burden (.86), Personal Strain (.81), and Coping/Mastery (.60). In an unpublished study by the authors, the original four-factor solution was not replicated and coefficient alphas for two factors were below .70.

The standardization sample for the recent revision of the IFS included 303 parents (mothers and fathers) of children with a medical condition (34%), behavioral condition (12%), medical and behavioral condition (12%), and who were healthy (41%). Unlike the Stein and Jessop sample (1985), this sample was predominantly White (76%), married (68%), employed (74%), and lower middle-class. The two factors (Family Burden and Family Adaptation) were negatively correlated (–.30) and yielded alpha coefficients of .92 and .77, respectively. Families of children with behavioral problems showed more family burden than those of children with medical conditions, and there was a trend for families of children with less severe medical conditions (e.g., hearing and visual impairments, obesity) to report less family burden compared to those with more serious medical conditions (e.g., cancer, cerebral palsy, diabetes).

Comment

The degree to which a family system is affected (negatively or positively) by a child's chronic health condition is an important area of inquiry in any child health assessment. The original IFS represented a crucial first step toward a comprehensive assessment of the family system, and it has been used in several studies that have documented family impact as a consequence of children's physical and/or behavioral conditions. However, several issues, including its homogenous normative sample, inattention to fathers, unstable factor structure, and lack of validity data, raise questions about its clinical utility and continued use in child health studies. The revised IFS may provide a more promising measure of family burden and adaptation than its predecessor. Nevertheless, further examination of its factor structure stability and psychometric properties across various samples is needed before its clinical utility can be appropriately assessed.

Relevant References

Edwards, D., Johnson, S. B., Cunningham, W., & Fennell, E. (1998). *Toward a better measure of family adjustment: The Revised Impact on Family Scale.* Unpublished manuscript.

Sheebler, L. B., & Johnson, J. H. (1992). Applicability of the Impact on Family Scale for assessing families with behaviorally difficult children. *Psychological Reports, 71,* 155–159.

Stein, R. E. K., & Jessop, D. J. (1985). *Tables documenting the psychometric properties of a measure of impact of chronic illness on a family.* Unpublished manuscript.

Stein, R. E. K., & Riessman, C. K. (1980). The development of an Impact-on-Family Scale: Preliminary findings. *Medical Care, 18,* 465–472.

Interview Schedule on Impact of Cystic Fibrosis on Families

S. Phillips, 1985

Manual and Address Information

No manual. Direct inquiries to: Sheridan Phillips, University of Maryland School of Medicine, Child and Adolescent Psychiatry, 701 West Pratt Street, 4th Floor, Baltimore, Maryland 21201.

Purpose

This interview addresses potential problem areas for families with children who have cystic fibrosis.

Format, Administration, and Scoring

This semistructured parent interview schedule is comprised of 62 items addressing parents' perceptions of cystic fibrosis on the marital relationship, child-parent relationships, family activities, the ill child's relationship with his/her siblings and peer group, the relationship between the family and the community, family planning, finances, employment, and home therapy. The interview also contains items to assess the parents' interactions with their physician and sources of information the parents found most helpful. The interview takes about 2 hours to complete. Each response is categorized according to criteria defining it as being a major problem, a minor problem, or no problem. A major problem is defined by frequency and intensity of occurrence (i.e., "I frequently cannot accept my child's illness"). A minor problem is defined as being less emotionally demanding, or as occurring less often or with a more limited focus. For example, "I restrict the child's activities so that he does not become overtired" is coded as a major problem because of the broad array of activities this affects, whereas a report of "I don't allow him to play sports or games" would be considered to be a minor problem. No problem was defined as no stated problems or difficulties.

Psychometric Information

This interview schedule was initially developed for use with 43 families of children with cystic fibrosis. Forty-three mothers and 29 fathers were interviewed independently. Inter-rater reliability for this instrument was reported to exceed 95% agreement by two independent raters. While no explicit validity information has been provided, there is some evidence of face validity of the items assessed in this interview.

Comment

This interview format warrants further psychometric establishment and validation as a screening measure for potential problems that may emerge in families of children with cystic fibrosis. However, it does have obvious utility in helping clinicians and families to identify potential problems as well as strengths, and gives the clinician the opportunity to aid the family in understanding, acceptance, and coping with having a chronically ill child. Its primary drawback is the length of time it takes to complete.

Relevant Reference

Phillips, S., Bohannon, W. E., Gayton, W. F., & Friedman, S. B. (1985). Parent interview findings regarding the impact of cystic fibrosis on families. *Journal of Developmental and Behavioral Pediatrics, 6,* 122–127.

Parent Perception Inventory (PPI)

J. J. Samuelson, 1992

Manual and Address Information

No manual. Direct inquiries to: Martha J. Foxall, University of Nebraska Medical Center, College of Nursing, 600 South 42nd Street, Omaha, NE 68198.

Purpose

The PPI is a modification of the Chronicity Impact and Coping Instrument: Parent Questionnaire (CICI:PQ) and was designed to measure family health-related stressors.

Format, Administration, and Scoring

The PPI is comprised of two components. The Needs component is an 18-item Likert scale (1 = do not need now to 3 = would like) and is intended to measure parental needs related to their child's care. The Concerns component is a 34-item Likert scale (0 = no/does not apply to 4 = a great deal). It is designed to measure parents' health-related concerns resulting from the child's condition.

Psychometric Information

The standardization sample for this measure involved a convenience sample of 17 mothers and 17 fathers with preschool to eighth-grade children diagnosed with myelomeningocele. All families were white. The parents had been married 13.1 years. The majority of parents had some post-high school education. The average income was $30,000.

No reliability data are reported for the two components separately; however, Hoyt's coefficient for the total score was .93. The authors suggest that the content validity of the items is similar to that of the CICI:PQ. Other analyses related to the validity of the PPI are yet to be conducted.

Comment

This measure appears very similar to the CICI:PQ, and is likely therefore to demonstrate the good psychometric properties of that measure; however, examination of this assumption is needed, specifically, information on the reliability of the separate components. The authors of this measure suggest that the validity of the PPI is supported by the validity of the CICI:PQ; however, no direct evidence of this claim is given. Such information is necessary to assess the validity of the scale. A more ethnically, geographically, and socioeconomically diverse standardization sample would strengthen this measure.

Relevant References

Samuelson, J. J., Foltz, J., & Foxall, M. J. (1992). Stress and coping in families of children with myelomeningocele. *Archives of Psychiatric Nursing, 6,* 287–295.

Hymovich, D. P. (1983). The chronicity impact and coping instrument: Parent Questionnaire. *Nursing Research, 32,* 275–281.

Parent Protection Scale (PPS)

M. Thomasgard, 1995

Manual and Address Information

No manual. Direct inquiries to: Michael Thomasgard, Children's Hospital, 700 Children's Drive, Columbus OH 43205-2696, (614) 722-2435, mthomasgard@chi.osu.edu.

Purpose

The PPS is a paper-and-pencil measure that is completed by parents of children 2 to 10 years old. It was designed to examine specific parenting behaviors related to child autonomy, individuation, and separation.

Format, Administration, and Scoring

The PPS contains 25 items to which parents respond on a 4-point scale (0 = never to 3 = always). Parents are instructed to read each item and to respond based on how they raise their children. A total score is derived by summing all 25 items, thus yielding a range of scores from 0 to 75. Seven items are reverse scored. Factor analysis of the PPS revealed a four-factor solution: supervision (7 items), separation problems (7 items), dependence (5 items), and control (9 items). To convert factors into subscales, a cutoff point of .3 was used to identify salient loadings. Subscale scores are obtained by summing the raw responses for the items on each subscale. The factors share little common variance and appear to measure independent dimensions. Higher scores reflect greater levels of protection. Age norms, determined by cut-off points corresponding to 1 standard deviation above the mean, were used to identify "overprotective" behavior. Sample items include:

> I blame myself when my child gets hurt.
> I have difficulty leaving my child with a babysitter.
> I encourage my child to play with other children.
> I allow my child to do things on his/her own.

Psychometric Information

The authors developed items for the PPS from relevant research literature and from their own clinical experiences. An initial pool of 27 items were generated; however, 2 items were dropped after initial pilot testing revealed low item-to-total correlations. During the initial phases of scale development, several different groups of parents were sampled to examine reliability and validity. Specifically, the reliability sample included 29 parents of children ages 2 to 5 who were being seen in a university-based pediatric clinic, and the validity sample included 34 parents of children ages 2 to 10 who had been referred to a mental health professional. Two clinical samples also were included in the initial standardization of the measure: 892 parents of children ages 2 to 5 and 280 parents of children ages 5 to 10. The clinical samples were recruited from one pediatric HMO site and two pediatric private practice sites, and they were predominantly White and middle- to upper-middle class. Total PPS scores for the clinical samples were normally distributed, with a linear decline in protection scores as the age of the child increased.

Coefficient alpha for the reliability sample was .73, and test-retest reliability over a 3- to 5-week period was .86 for the total score. For the four subscales, internal consistency ranged from .50 to .64, and test-retest reliability ranged from .70 to .96. A 2-year follow-up study ($n = 114$) revealed a high degree of stability for the PPS, particularly for parents with initially low total scores.

To assess criterion validity, the authors asked mental health professionals to classify parents in therapy on the presence or absence of parental overprotectiveness. Parents then completed the PPS independently. Clinical history of overprotectiveness and PPS scores were then compared. Using this criterion-referenced clinical history approach, there was evidence for sensitivity, specificity, and positive predictive value.

To assess concurrent validity, parents were asked to respond to questions focused on child safety and personal autonomy to elicit the degree of parental control and supervision during each activity. Logistic regression yielded a correct prediction rate of .76 for parental overprotection.

Comment

The PPS is a useful instrument that might add significantly to any clinical assessment of the parent-child relationship. Its brevity and ease of administration allow it to be used efficiently in a primary or ambulatory care setting. While the PPS is copyrighted, the authors provide permission for its reproduction. Considering that ethnic and cultural variables may play a role in parenting practices, it is essential to further examine the PPS with a more diverse population. Furthermore, while reliability and validity estimates are adequate, sample sizes used in the initial development of the measure were very small. Given the orthogonal nature of the four factors, it is surprising that alpha coefficients and test-retest reliability analyses were not provided separately for each of the four subscales.

Relevant References

Thomasgard, M., & Metz, W. P. (1996). Differences in health care utilization between parents who perceive their child as vulnerable versus overprotective parents. *Clinical Pediatrics, 35,* 303–308.

Thomasgard, M., & Metz, W. P. (1996). The 2-year stability of parental perceptions of child vulnerability and parental overprotection. *Journal of Developmental and Behavioral Pediatrics, 17,* 222–228.

Thomasgard, M., & Metz, W. P. (in press). Parent-child relationship disorders: What do the Child Vulnerability Scale and the Parent Protection Scale measure? *Clinical Pediatrics.*

Thomasgard, M., Metz, W. P., Edelbrock, C., & Shonkoff, J. P. (1995). Parent-child relationship disorders. Part I: Parental overprotection and the development of the Parent Protection Scale. *Journal of Developmental and Behavioral Pediatrics, 16,* 244–250.

Thomasgard, M., Shonkoff, J. P., Metz, W. P., & Edelbrock, C. (1995). Parent-child relationship disorders. Part II: The vulnerable child syndrome and its relation to parental overprotection. *Journal of Developmental and Behavioral Pediatrics, 16,* 251–256.

Parental Coping Scale: Pediatric Intensive Care Unit (PCS:PICU)

M. S. Miles, 1985

Manual and Address Information

No manual. Direct inquiries to: Margaret Shandor Miles, School of Nursing, Carrington Hall CB 7460, University of North Carolina, Chapel Hill, North Carolina 27599-7460, (919) 966-3620, mmiles.uncson@mhs.unc.edu.

Purpose

The intent of this measure is to assess the helpfulness of the various parental coping strategies as well as the helpfulness of the ICU staff during a child's hospitalization.

Format, Administration, and Scoring

The PCS:PICU was developed to be used as a retrospective self-report method by parents with children recently discharged from pediatric ICU. Information is collected relevant to both staff behaviors and parental coping responses. Parents fill out this 40-item questionnaire using a four-point Likert scale, judging each of the items as 1 = not helpful, to 4 = extremely helpful. Parents also have the option of judging "0," indicating that the behavior referred to in that item was not used.

Staff behaviors were identified from the literature and interviews with parents. The behaviors identified were related to four parental needs in particular: assistance with the parenting role for the ill child, providing adequate information and communication about the child's condition and the ICU environment, providing emotional support to the family, and the quality of their nursing care. Parents are asked to assess their perception regarding the use and helpfulness of a number of staff behaviors, as well as whether or not these staff behaviors are experienced. If the desired action was not performed, parents were asked to estimate how helpful they believed the behavior would have been to them if it had been implemented. Parents also are requested to indicate the three staff behaviors they found to be the most beneficial as well as other behaviors they found helpful. The staff behaviors portion of the PCS:PICU contains 19 items.

Parent-coping responses were derived from literature and other instruments used in assessing coping. Inclusion in the final version of the scale required that the items be relevant to the situation (parental responses to a sudden, critical, and relatively short-term experience with an ill child). Parents are asked to respond to the items to indicate whether certain coping strategies were useful and helpful in their coping with their child's illness. The parent-coping scale section of the PCS:PICU contains 21 items.

Psychometric Information

Participants in the initial study using the PCS:PICU included 21 mothers and 15 fathers of 27 children who had recently been discharged (within 5 days) from one of two Midwestern pediatric ICUs. Mean age of the parents was 31 years. Nine children were represented by both parents. The mean age of the children was 4 years, and they had been in the ICU a mean of 6 days with a range of 1 to 33 days.

The authors refer to the literature in addition to two previous pilot studies with the PCS:PICU as support for content validity. In addition, they cite some support for the construct validity of the PCS:PICU's coping section as they based the measure on a well-defined conceptual framework. No reliability data was reported for the measure.

Comment

More investigations establishing the reliability and validity of the PCS:PICU with larger and more diverse samples of families and children are indicated before conclusions regarding the utility of this instrument can be drawn.

Relevant Reference

Miles, M. S., & Carter, M. C. (1985). Coping strategies used by parents during their child's hospitalization in an intensive care unit. *Children's Health Care, 14,* 14–21.

Parental Stressor Scale: Neonatal Intensive Care Unit (PSS:NICU)

M. S. Miles, 1993

Manual and Address Information

No manual. Direct inquiries to: Margaret Shandor Miles, School of Nursing, Carrington Hall CB 7460. University of North Carolina, Chapel Hill, North Carolina 27599-7460, (919) 966-3620, mmiles.uncson@mhs.unc.edu.

Purpose

The PSS:NICU was intended to assess the level of stress experienced by the mothers that is related to various aspects of their infant's stay in the neonatal intensive care unit. It is suggested that NICU environmental stress may be an important factor contributing to overall parental distress.

Format, Administration, and Scoring

The PSS:NICU is a 47-item questionnaire adapted from the Parental Stressor Scale: Pediatric Intensive Care Unit (PSS:PICU). Four major changes were made to the PSS:PICU in the development of the PSS:NICU in order to reflect stressors related to (a) the appearance and behavior of the premature infant, (b) changes in the parental role that differ for parents of sick infants, (c) differences in the routines and environment of the NICU, and (d) parental relationships with the staff on the NICU.

Parents are asked to rate the stressfulness of each item on the PSS:NICU using a Likert-type scale (1 = not at all stressful to 5 = extremely stressful). Parents are only asked to rate those items that are relevant to situations they have experienced. The scale can then be scored in two ways: the Stress Occurrence Level and the Overall Stress Level. For the Stress Occurrence Level score, any item that is scored as N/A or is missing is not computed in the score. Means are computed using the number of items scored. For the Overall Stress Level, any item that is scored as N/A is coded as a "1" indicating no stress and mean scores are computed using all items on the tool. The Stress Occurrence Level is the level of stress experienced by parents that is related to their particular situation. The Overall Stress Level is the overall level of stress engendered by the NICU environment. The results of the test can be examined in terms of subscales including infant behavior and appearance, parental role alterations, and sights and sounds.

Psychometric Information

The instrument was standardized on 190 parents (115 mothers and 75 fathers) of premature infants in five NICUs in the United States and Canada. Most parents (79.8%) were White and married (87.1%). Average parental age was 27.5 years. The average infant gestational age was 30.8 weeks. Cronbach's alpha coefficients were calculated for each of the subscales, as well as for the total instrument, furthermore, the coefficients were calculated using both the Stress Occurrence Level and the Overall Stress Level. For the Stress Occurrence Level, the Cronbach alpha levels for the infant behavior and appearance, parental role alterations, and sights and sounds subscales were .92, .90, and .80, respectively. Cronbach's alpha for the total score was .94. For the Overall Stress Level, the Cronbach alpha levels for the three subscales were .83, .83, and .73, respectively, and .89 for the overall score.

The authors report the scales are supported by factor analysis. Also, correlations between this scale and a measure of state anxiety were in the hypothesized directions, that is, higher perceived levels of environmental stress were significantly associated with anxiety as measured by the State-Trait Anxiety Inventory (STAI).

Comment

The PSS:NICU appears to be a reliable measure of parental stress for parents with children in neonatal intensive care units. The ease of use and comprehensive nature of the PSS:NICU are an asset of the measure. Data collection at five sites represents a strength of the PSS:NICU, though minority representation is low. The PSS:NICU has psychometric data to support its use in both research and clinical settings.

Relevant References

Cobiella, C. W., Mabe, P. A., & Forehand, R. L. (1990). A comparison of two stress-education treatments for mothers of neonates hospitalized in a neonatal intensive care unit. *Children's Health Care, 19,* 93–100.

Miles, M. S., & Carter, M. C. (1989). The Parental Stressor Scale: Pediatric Intensive Care Unit. *Maternal Child Nursing Journal, 18,* 187–198.

Miles, M. S., Funk, S. G., & Carlson J. (1993). Parental Stressor Scale: Neonatal Intensive Care Unit. *Nursing Research, 42,* 148–152.

Miles, M. S., Funk, S., & Kasper, M. A. (1992). The stress response of mothers and fathers of preterm infants. *Research in Nursing and Health, 15,* 261–269.

Miles, M. S., Funk, S. G., & Kasper, M. A. (1991). The neonatal intensive care unit environment: Sources of stress for parents. *AACN Clinical Issues in Critical Care Nursing, 2,* 346–354.

Parents of Children with Disabilities Inventory (PCDI)

A. B. Noojin, 1996

Manual and Address Information

No manual. Direct inquiries to: Jan Wallander, University of Alabama-Birmingham, SC-313/UAB Station, Birmingham, AL 35294-0017, (205) 934-2452, jwalland.civitan@civmail.civc.uab.edu.

Purpose

The PCDI was developed to measure both the amount and perception of stress experiences by mothers with respect to having a child with a disability.

Format, Administration, and Scoring

Parents respond to each of the 40 items of the PCDI regarding frequency of worry about the listed concerns on a 6-point scale (almost always to hardly ever). Items included in the measure were selected from 125 items from four domains: Medical and Legal Concerns, Concerns for the Child, Concerns for the Family, and Concerns for the Self. Final items were selected based on response distribution, item-total correlation, and inter-item correlations. Sample items include:

My child has accidents as a result of his/her disability.
My child cannot play sports or games with the other children.
I think about things that my child will never be able to do.
It is hard to find a sitter who can be with my child.

Psychometric Information

This measure was examined using mothers of 63 families. Internal consistency reliabilities for the four domains were .67 for Medical and Legal Concerns, .77 for Concerns for the Child, .65 for Concerns for the Family, and .84 for Concerns for the Self. Test-retest reliability for the total score was .60, and test-retest reliability for the domains was .66 for Medical and Legal Concerns, .53 for Concerns for the Child, .41 for Concerns for the Family, and .52 for Concerns for the Self.

The authors of the PCDI examined construct and concurrent validity of the scale. The PCDI total score was moderately correlated to the parent ratings of stressors on the Questionnaire on Resources and Stress-Short Form. This was expected due to the intended use of the PCDI as a measure of stress as opposed to a checklist of occurrence on problems. Among the subscales, Medical and Legal Concerns was the only scale to be significantly related to the QRS-SF. Construct validity was supported through significant findings for several hypothesized relationships. Severity of child disability was significantly correlated to the PCDI total score, Medical and Legal concerns, Concerns for the Child, and Concerns for the Self. Child behavior problems, as measured by the Conners Parent Rating Scale was significantly related to Concerns for the Child scale (.39). Concerns for the Family was found to be moderately correlated (.24) with maternal level of dissatisfaction with the family (as measured by the Family Adaptability and Cohesion Evaluation Scales). When compared to the QRS-SF, the PCDI accounted for a greater proportion of the variance in mental and physical health (R^2 increase = .17 for mental health and .06 for physical health).

Comment

Initial results support that the PCDI may be a useful and informative instrument for assessing mothers of children with physical disabilities regarding perceived disability-related stress. More work on the psychometric properties of the PCDI is warranted. Specifically, a larger and more diverse standardization sample would strengthen the PCDI as would further development of the reliability the instrument.

Relevant References

Noojin, A. B., & Wallander, J. L. (1996). Development and evaluation of a measure of concerns related to raising a child with a physical disability. *Journal of Pediatric Psychology, 21*, 483–498.

Noojin, A. B., & Wallander, J. L. (1997). Perceived problem-solving ability, stress, and coping in mothers of children with physical disabilities: Potential cognitive influences on adjustment. *International Journal of Behavioral Medicine, 4*, 415–432.

Pediatric Oncology Nurse Stressor Questionnaire (PONSQ)

J. E. Emery, 1991

Manual and Address Information

No manual. Direct inquiries to: Janet Emery, 7755 East Bridgewood Drive, Anaheim Hills, CA, 92808, Janetcfnp@aol.com.

Purpose

The PONSQ is a paper-and-pencil measure that is completed by nurses with at least 2 years' experience working in a pediatric oncology unit. The purpose of the scale is to assess the perceived sources of stress among pediatric oncology nurses.

Format, Administration, and Scoring

The PONSQ consists of 50 items that are on a 5-point Likert scale. Nurses are asked to circle the number that best corresponds to their own personal feelings about the stressfulness of the item in the past 6 months. Answers range from 0 to 5, with 1 meaning not stressful, 5 meaning extremely stressful, and 0 representing not experienced in the past 6 months. In addition to the 50 Likert-scale items, 2 open-ended questions ask nurses to indicate the most stressful aspects of their job with possible solutions to the stress, and their greatest source of job satisfaction. Five areas or domains are represented in the PONSQ: management issues (7 items), professional communications (10 items), working conditions (22 items), moral and ethical dilemmas (6 items), and death and dying concerns (5 items). Sample items include:

> Working with a nurse I do not feel is competent.
> Floating to another unit.
> Enforcing unit rules with patients and families.

Psychometric Information

The PONSQ was originally comprised of 75 questions. Items on the original questionnaire were rationally derived from the author's review of relevant literature and personal clinical experience. The 75 items were somewhat modified after review of the instrument by 6 nurses. The PONSQ's test-retest reliability was then examined using a sample of 14 pediatric oncology nurses (.66). Following this pilot study, 25 questions were eliminated and others were reworded and revised. Personal communication from the author indicated the final version of the PONSQ was not tested but was evaluated by 2 additional pediatric oncology nurses each with a graduate degree and then content validity was estimated by an additional 3 master's-prepared pediatric oncology nurses.

In an early investigation that included the PONSQ, 398 registered nurses were asked to complete the measure, in addition to the State-Trait Anxiety Inventory (STAI); 155 were returned and used for analysis. Subjects were recruited through using mailing lists of the Association of Pediatric Oncology Nurses. Descriptive data for each of the items and the five domains are reported by the author. Personal communication from the author indicated state anxiety scores among the nurses were lower than the reference mean (white-collar female working adult) and were equal to the trait anxiety scores. The five categories were positively correlated with the state-trait anxiety inventory as well as with eight separate demographic factors.

Comment

The PONSQ is one of few paper-and-pencil instruments designed to assess nurses' perceived sources of stress. The measure appears to be face-valid, and has undergone content validity reviews from pediatric oncology nurses. In addition to the 50 Likert-scale questions, the PONSQ provides subjective data related to the most difficult and most satisfying aspects of a nurses' duties. It has shown satisfactory test-retest reliability. Further development of psychometric properties of the PONSQ could have significant value for the system in pediatric oncology.

Relevant Reference

Emery, J. E. (1993). Perceived sources of stress among pediatric oncology nurses. *Journal of Pediatric Oncology Nursing, 10,* 87–92.

Perceived Illness Experience Scale (PIE)

C. Eiser, 1995

Manual and Address Information

No manual. Direct inquiries to: C. Eiser, Department of Psychology, University of Exeter, Exeter Devon, U.K. EX4 4GQ, ceiser@exeter.ac.uk.

Purpose

The parent version of the PIE was designed to measure the quality of life, or perceived illness experience, of adolescents with cancer, as indicated by their parents. The PIE (child version) was created to provide a rating based on the adolescent's own experience, rather than that of either the parent or health care professional, with the parent version serving as an additional respondent.

Format, Administration, and Scoring

The child and parent versions of the PIE both consist of 40 5-point Likert scale (i.e., five boxes with disagree and agree as endpoints) statements. Parents are asked to respond in a similar fashion as their children, and separate versions for referring to daughters and sons exist. The most recent parent version of the PIE consists of 10 subscales including physical appearance, interference with activity, disclosure, school, peer rejection, parental behavior, manipulation, preoccupation with illness, food, and treatment. Questions related to the adolescent's physical symptoms or health status have been purposefully omitted from the scale. Sample statements are:

> My son/daughter only tells people about his/her illness if he/she really has to.
> My son/daughter can't see his/her friends as often as he/she would like.

Scores are calculated separately for each of the 10 subscales, with each item's score ranging from 1 to 5. A PIE total score is also calculated.

Psychometric Information

Items for both the child and parent versions of the PIE were generated from semi-structured interviews with children and adolescents. Children either in the midst of, or recently completed treatment for cancer, were asked to describe areas in their life that were most difficult for them. Specific statements of the parent version of the PIE scale were then generated based on these responses, totaling 78 items. The standardization sample included 35 parents. Analyses supported nine subscales with internal consistencies ranging from .40 to .85. Test-retest reliabilities have ranged from .51 to .92. Adolescent and parent ratings were significantly correlated with one another for seven of the nine subscales. Descriptive data for the standardization sample on each subscale of the PIE, and the total PIE score, are provided by the authors.

Satisfactory construct validity was demonstrated in correlating the PIE with other measures of psychological symptomatology; four of the nine subscales had significant correlations with the other measure. According to the authors of the PIE, six items were added subsequent to the initial analyses; four items yielding an additional "treatment" subscale, and two items added to the physical appearance subscale.

Comment

The parent version of the PIE is a paper-and-pencil instrument of an adolescent's perception of his/her illness across 10 domains, as reported by the adolescent's parent. Statements related to the child's physical health status or symptoms have been purposefully omitted. Analysis of the measure, including the resulting 10 subscales and psychometric information, have been provided by the authors. Similar to the child version of the PIE, specific description of item and scale analyses have not been reported for the parent version. In addition, items were added after initial analyses, and it is unclear if these items have also been tested psychometrically. Although descriptive statistics of the standardization sample exist, one should use caution when comparing other parents' data to those provided given the small number of parents ($n = 35$) in the initial sample. Furthermore, if this scale is administered to parents of adolescents who have not undergone treatment, four items must be removed from the scale. Strengths of this measure are its compatibility to the child version of the PIE, and its subscales' high internal consistencies. Adolescent and parent report have been found to be correlated, indicating the potential use of only one respondent in situations in which that may be necessary. Test-retest reliabilities have been found to be adequate. Although the measure was designed for use with parents of adolescents with cancer, its general wording allows for it to be applied to most chronic illness populations. Given the recency of the development of the PIE, future research incorporating its parent version will likely help discern the appropriate spectrum of its use.

Relevant Reference

Eiser, C., Havermans, T., Craft, A., & Kernahan, J. (1995). Development of a measure to assess the perceived illness experience after treatment for cancer. *Archives of Disease in Childhood, 72,* 302–307.

General Observations and Recommendations

The relevance of approaching child health assessment from a larger contextual perspective cannot be understated. The measures reviewed in this chapter are quite diverse and, collectively, consider the multiple perspectives that likely are useful in assessing the factors associated with adaptation to chronic health conditions. In general, our impressions of the measures reviewed in this chapter can be summarized as follows:

1. There is considerable variability in the degree to which the measures covered in this chapter have been subjected to psychometric study. Some measures are outlines of clinical interviews with very little empirical foundation while others are very well researched.
2. Many measures would benefit from further development of their standardization sample. More diverse samples in terms of geography, ethnicity, and socioeconomic status would be useful.

3. Some of the general non-disease-specific measures would become more useful by developing a broader empirical foundation through data collection on more diverse pediatric conditions.
4. Conceptual frameworks about what is therapeutically important for subsystems of persons involved with pediatric conditions are inherent in the measures (e.g., DFBC and DRFQ).
5. Some measures would benefit from factor-analytic study of rationally derived domains.
6. Sibling issues are assessed in some measures though no measure reviewed was devoted exclusively to issues of siblings of patients with pediatric conditions.
7. Measures like the PONSQ, which studies pediatric oncology nurses, recognize the importance of the emotional adaptation of subsystems of persons outside the patient and family.

References

Kazak, A. E. (1989). Families of chronically ill children: A systems and social ecological model of adaptation and challenge. *Journal of Consulting and Clinical Psychology, 57,* 25–30.

Rodrigue, J. R. (1994). Beyond the individual child: Innovative systems models of service delivery in pediatric psychology. *Journal of Clinical Child Psychology, 23* (Suppl.), 32–39.

Chapter 11

Reflections and a Glance Toward the Future

JAMES R. RODRIGUE

As we reflect on our experience in preparing reviews for inclusion in this handbook, we have identified several common themes that cut across the various content domains presented. We have now had the opportunity to review several hundred manuscripts reporting the development, validation, and/or use of a particular measurement tool designed to tap some aspect of children's health, and we have read the comments of many of our psychologist, pediatrician, and nursing colleagues who have addressed issues relevant to child health assessment. The statements that follow reflect our perceptions of the current state of child health assessment and our recommendations for its future advancement. Many of these observations are not unique nor are they necessarily shared by other experts in the field.

Until recently, there were few measures specifically developed for use with children who have chronic health conditions or their family members. Questions concerning the relevance, generalizability, and utility of more general measures designed for use with healthy children, in large part, has contributed to the recent influx of assessment techniques designed for more specialized child populations. It is clear from our review of the literature, that the development of child health instruments has proceeded at a rather uneven pace, both in terms of the content domains that are assessed and the sophistication of the instruments themselves. For instance, measures developed to examine some aspect of children's stress and coping have exceeded, in number, those designed to tap disease-related knowledge or adherence behaviors. Moreover, the application of sophisticated measurement technology has emerged in some areas (e.g., pain assessment) but not others (e.g., family-based assessments), and there has been uneven application of measurement techniques within some domains (e.g., stress and coping).

The increased number of instruments now accessible to child health professionals has its benefits and its drawbacks. On the one hand, clinicians and researchers are able to select an instrument that best meets their needs within a particular domain of functioning (e.g., quality of life), a luxury not previously available to child health professionals. On the other hand, the growing interest in measurement development has simultaneously contributed to fewer and less sophisticated validation studies on existing, promising assessment tools. Indeed, we have spoken to many colleagues who, as researchers, struggle with the decision to design their own instrument for measuring particular construct of interest or to use existing measures and provide additional psychometric data on them. While there are some notable exceptions, one consequence of the proliferation of new child health instruments is that the burden of appropriate validation studies is assumed almost solely by the instrument's original developers. There is a need for validation studies to be conducted by researchers other than the original developers. As we discovered in correspondence regarding the instruments reviewed for this handbook, a change of career, research interests, or professional responsibilities by the developer of a particular instrument often leads to the instrument's early retirement or, in some instances, untimely death. Clearly, more coordinated instrument development work is needed for the field of child health assessment to progress beyond its current state.

As clinicians, we work in an era when rapid assessments are necessary and, consequently, we must use assessment tools that are brief, cost-effective, highly relevant to the population with whom we work, and culturally sensitive. Unfortunately, it is our assessment that most of the instruments reviewed in this handbook fall short of the mark across each of these dimensions. While some of the instruments can be used efficiently in the context of a busy pediatric setting, their cost-effectiveness has rarely been examined and existing normative data often are restricted along dimensions of diversity (i.e., developmental level, ethnicity, geography, socioeconomic status). Furthermore, measures must have a high degree of relevance to the specific population with whom the clinician works. While we are not aware of any large-scale survey data, there is anecdotal evidence indicating that the majority of child health clinicians do not regularly use instruments designed specifically for children with chronic health conditions in their practices. Why not? In addition to the issues noted previously, clinicians make a determination about the instrument's relevancy to assessing the construct of interest. If the pediatric psychologist or pediatrician works predominantly with children who have sickle cell disease, general measures of stress may not adequately address his or her concerns about the child's perceived illness-specific stressors. One consequence of not attending to the relevancy issue is that clinicians in child health care settings continue to use measures that have been developed to assess more traditional child clinical problems (i.e., with healthy children) and that are ill-suited for children with chronic health conditions. Adapting or extending existing instruments for use with specific child health populations to increase its utility and relevancy across conditions appears necessary.

Child Health Assessment: Recommendations for Instrument Development

We readily acknowledge that standards and guidelines for instrument development already exist. Nevertheless, it is apparent from our review of the literature that there is less uniformity in the use of such guidelines than is desirable for the advancement of child health assessment. The recommendations that follow represent our current assessment of the field of child health assessment and our assessment of what we need to do differently or better in the future.

1. We need to focus less on developing new instruments and more on validating, adapting, and extending existing child health instruments for use with children who have other health conditions. If new instruments are developed, a clear rationale should be provided along with an assessment of its strengths or advantages relative to existing measures.
2. If one takes the time to develop an instrument, it would be wise to maintain a long-term commitment to its validation and refinement, if at all possible. In the absence of such commitment or responsibility, there is no coordination of effort and the measure tends to take on a slightly different look with each published reference.
3. There is a need for authors to provide a more complete theoretical or conceptual rationale for the development of their measures. Many of the measures reviewed in this handbook lacked the conceptual foundation one would expect to find in the context of an instrument's design, evaluation, and eventual clinical use.
4. Greater attention must be given to the comprehensive evaluation and presentation of an instrument's reliability and validity. Too often, the internal structure of the measure is inadequately examined and there is an overwhelming need for more information about construct and criterion validity. Specification of the criteria employed to conclude that construct validity has been demonstrated is also needed since these criteria tend to vary across studies.
5. We echo the sentiments of many notable experts in the field that more careful reporting of measurement information is necessary in published studies. Indeed, we reviewed several measures for which basic reliability and validity data were not reported, reported incorrectly, or reported in insufficient detail to allow for appropriate assessment of the instrument's psychometric stability. It has also been suggested by some child health professionals that the instruments be listed in all journal abstracts to facilitate more comprehensive computer-generated literature searches. This is an excellent suggestion, and we too encourage authors (and journal editors) to adopt this practice.
6. We recommend less reliance on convenience samples and the inclusion of greater diversity in the development and validation of child health instruments. The issue of diversity (broadly defined) must be underscored here and represents perhaps our greatest criticism of the child health assessment litera-

ture to date. Much like the child health literature in general, measurement tools in this area have been developed using predominantly White, lower- to middle-class children receiving health services at large university-based medical centers. Moreover, parent-report measures have been developed and validated mostly with mothers serving as study participants, largely because they are more readily accessible to researchers. The inclusion of fathers in the instrument development and validation process is an import goal for future research, particularly as we focus more on systems-level assessments.

7. Developers should be encouraged to use caution in presenting preliminary versions of their instruments. Publishing very preliminary (even though promising) data opens the door for confusion when revised versions are subsequently published, outdated versions being used unknowingly, and wasting valuable time and resources conducting validation studies on outdated versions. Moreover, the psychometric data presented in a preliminary manner typically do not hold up after further empirical scrutiny with larger, more representative samples.

8. A manual should be provided for each child health instrument. Contained in the manual should be a comprehensive description of the rationale for the instrument's development, the manner in which the items or questions were generated, scoring and interpretation guidelines, specific sample characteristics, complete psychometric information, and relevant references. An excellent example of such a manual is that developed for the Child Health Questionnaire, although such comprehensiveness is not necessary for each instrument developed. The overwhelming majority of instruments reviewed in this handbook do not have a manual. It is not always possible to provide sufficient detail about an instrument's development and validation in a published article, and we found instances in which different scoring criteria were reported in separate published articles describing the same instrument.

9. Instruments developed with an eye toward future use in actual clinical situations or settings should be practical, sensitive, nonreactive, appropriate, and cost-effective. Measures that require 45 minutes to complete, are not able to detect change over time, and require a significant amount of time to administer (e.g., complex behavioral observations), score, and interpret, will not be easily integrated into clinical practice in most pediatric settings. Perhaps most relevant to child health clinicians are instruments that are relatively brief and that can be used to evaluate the effects of intervention and/or the recovery of function following illness and/or injury and its treatment.

10. A more sophisticated consideration of child development is warranted in the design and description of instruments. Few developers of the instruments we reviewed commented specifically on the developmental level of the child for whom the measure was most appropriate. While age ranges are typically provided, the reading level of most instruments was never formally assessed. With the increasing availability of computer software programs designed to assess the reading grade level of written material, provision of this information should be required in all descriptions of an instrument.

11. Since self-report instruments are the primary source of information for child health clinicians and researchers, it seems appropriate to identify those cognitive processes and contextual factors that underlie children's reports of events, attitudes and beliefs, emotional states, and symptoms. Better understanding of such processes (e.g., comprehension, memory, belief structure, social context, cultural influences) may facilitate the development of techniques for improving the reliability and validity of self-report instruments.
12. We strongly encourage the use of interdisciplinary teams in the development of new instruments. The majority of measures reviewed may have been developed by several individuals, but typically they represented one profession. There are several potential benefits of a more interdisciplinary approach to instrument development and validation, including the unique strengths and perspectives that each discipline brings to the table, easier identification of what measures may already exist in a particular profession, and more rapid dissemination of validation study findings across discipline boundaries. As psychologists, for instance, we were struck by the number of pain assessment techniques published in the nursing literature of which we had little or no knowledge, and we have been consulted on several occasions during the past few years by pediatricians interested in developing "new" quality of life instruments that already exist in the psychological literature.

Overall, it is our contention that the field of child health assessment is moving in the right direction, although we offer the preceding recommendations to ensure that its growth continues in a most helpful and coordinated manner. While the task is arduous and time-consuming, we look forward to the time when new child health instruments and new study findings on existing assessment tools necessitate the revision of this handbook.

Index

Acceptance of Illness Scale (AIS), 29–30
Adaptiveness Rating Scale (ARS), 198–199
adherence to medical regimens
  Adaptiveness Rating Scale (ARS), 198–199
  Diabetes Mismanagement Questionnaire (DMQ), 199–200
  Family Asthma Management System Scale (FAMSS), 200–202
  Medical Compliance Incomplete Stories Test (MCIST), 202–203
  Self-Care Adherence Interview (SCAI), 205–206
AIDS prevention
  Attitudes for AIDS Prevention, 95–97
  Intentions to Engage in AIDS-Risk Situations, 119–120
alternate-form reliability, 10
assessment issues
  reliability of test, 9–11
  validity of test, 11–12
assessment
  future needs for, 251–253
  information gained in, 17
  multiple respondents, benefits of, 18
  research-based, 22–25
assessment methods
  choosing appropriate instrument, 16–22
  informal assessment, 14
  interviews, 12–13
  norm-referenced tests, 7–9
  observational assessment, 13–14
asthma
  Asthma Attitudes Questionnaire (AAQ), 93–94
  Family Asthma Management System Scale (FAMSS), 200–202
  Perceptions of Asthma Medication Scale (PAM), 125–127
attitude assessment
  Asthma Attitudes Questionnaire (AAQ), 93–94
  Attitudes for AIDS Prevention, 95–97
  Attitude Toward Disabled Persons Scales (ATDP), 94–95
  Body Attitude Scale (BAS), 97–98
  Chedoke-McMaster Attitudes Toward Children with Handicaps (CATCH) Scale, 99–101

Child Attitude Toward Illness Scale (CATIS), 101–103
Children's Eating Attitude Test (ChEAT), 107–108
Children's Health Care Attitudes Questionnaire (CHCAQ), 109–110
Children's Health Locus of Control Scale (CHLC), 111–112
Children's Hope Scale (CHS), 112–113
Child Satisfaction Questionnaire (CSQ), 103–104
Child Vulnerability Scale (CVS), 105–106
Death Anxiety Questionnaire (DAQ), 114–115
Diabetes Opinion Survey (DOS), 115–117
Enuresis Nuisance and Tolerance Scales, 118–119
Intentions to Engage in AIDS-Risk Situations, 119–120
Parental Attitudes Toward Children with Handicaps (PATCH) Questionnaire, 122–124
Parental Health Belief Scale, 124–125
Parent Participation Attitude Scale (PPAS), 121–122
Perceptions of Asthma Medication Scale (PAM), 125–127

Behavioral Approach-Avoidance and Distress Scale (BAADS), 134–135
Behavioral Profile Rating Scale (BPRS), 30–31
Behavioral Upset in Medical Patients-Revised (BUMP-R), 32–33
beliefs. *See* Attitude assessment
Bereaved Extended Family Members Support Group Evaluation (BEFMSGE), 218–219
Body Attitude Scale (BAS), 97–98

cancer
  Pediatric Oncology Quality of Life Scale (POQOLS), 190–191
  Skin Cancer Knowledge Questionnaire (SCKQ), 207–208
Charleston Pediatric Pain Pictures (CPPP), 135–137

Chedoke-McMaster Attitudes Toward Children with Handicaps (CATCH) Scale, 99–101
Child-Adult Medical Procedure Interaction Scale-Revised (CAMPIS-R), 137–140
Child Attitude Toward Illness Scale (CATIS), 101–103
Child Behavior Observation Rating Scale (CBORS), 140–141
Child Health Assessment Inventory (CHAI), 174–175
Child Health and Illness Profile-Adolescent Edition (CHIP-AE), 172–174
Child Health Questionnaire (CHQ) Child Form, 176–178
Child Health Questionnaire (CHQ) Parent Form, 178–181
Children's Concern Scale (CCS), 67–68
Children's Eating Attitude Test (ChEAT), 107–108
Children's Eating Behavior Inventory (CEBI), 34–35
Children's Health Care Attitudes Questionnaire (CHCAQ), 109–110
Children's Health Locus of Control Scale (CHLC), 111–112
Children's Hope Scale (CHS), 112–113
Children's Hospital of Eastern Ontario Pain Scale (CHEOPS), 142–143
Children's Pain Inventory (CPI), 143–145
Children's Physical Self-Concept Scale (CPSS), 35–37
Children's Somatization Inventory (CSI), 37–39
Child Satisfaction Questionnaire (CSQ), 103–104
Child Vulnerability Scale (CVS), 105–106
Chronicity Impact and Coping Instrument: Parent Questionnaire (CICI:PQ), 219–220
coefficient alpha, 11
compliance. *See* Adherence to medical regimens
construct validity, 12
content validity, 11–12
convergent validity, 12
Coping Health Inventory for Children (CHIC), 68–69

254

Index   255

Coping Health Inventory for Parents (CHIP), 221–222
Coping Strategies Inventory (CSI), 70–71
criterion-related validity, 12
cystic fibrosis, Interview Schedule on Impact of Cystic Fibrosis on Families, 234–235

Deasy-Spinetta School Behavior Questionnaire (DSBQ), 40–41
death and dying
  Bereaved Extended Family Members Support Group Evaluation (BEFMSGE), 218–219
  Death Anxiety Questionnaire (DAQ), 114–115
diabetes
  Diabetes Adjustment Scale (DAS), 41–42
  Diabetes Family Behavior Checklist (DFBC), 223–224
  Diabetes Family Responsibility Questionnaire (DFRQ), 224–225
  Diabetes Mismanagement Questionnaire (DMQ), 199–200
  Diabetes Opinion Survey (DOS), 115–117
  Test of Diabetes Knowledge (TDK), 209–210
discriminant validity, 12

eating behavior
  Children's Eating Attitude Test (ChEAT), 107–108
  Children's Eating Behavior Inventory (CEBI), 34–35
Enuresis Nuisance and Tolerance Scales, 118–119

Faces Pain Scale (FPS), 145–146
face validity, 11
family assessment, 122–124
  Bereaved Extended Family Members Support Group Evaluation (BEFMSGE), 218–219
  Chronicity Impact and Coping Instrument: Parent Questionnaire (CICI:PQ), 219–220
  Coping Health Inventory for Parents (CHIP), 221–222
  Diabetes Family Behavior Checklist (DFBC), 223–224
  Diabetes Family Responsibility Questionnaire (DFRQ), 224–225
  Family APGAR-Revised, 226–227
  Family Asthma Management System Scale (FAMSS), 200–202
  Family Coping Scale (FCS), 227–228, 228–230
  Family Inventory of Resources for Management (FIRM), 228–230
  Health Resources Inventory for Parents (HRIP), 230–231
  Impact on Family Scale (IFS), 232–233
  Interview Schedule on Impact of Cystic Fibrosis on Families, 234–235
  Parental Coping Scale: Pediatric Intensive Care Unit (PCS:PUCU), 239–240
  Parental Health Belief Scale, 124–125
  Parental Stressor Scale: Neonatal Intensive Care Unit (PSS:NICU), 240–242

Parent Participation Attitude Scale (PPAS), 121–122
Parent Perception Inventory (PPI), 235–236
Parent Protection Scale (PPS), 236–238
Parents of Children with Disabilities Inventory (PCDI), 242–243
Perceived Illness Experience Scale (PIE), 245–247
Fear Faces Scale (Fear Self-Report Scale-Fear SR), 72–73
fear. See Stress/coping assessment
financial factors, research-based assessment, 25
Functional Disability Inventory (FDI), 181–183
Functional Status II(R), 185–187
Functional Status Questionnaire (FSQ), 183–185

guessing, impact on reliability, 9

Headache Symptom Questionnaire-Revised (HSQ-R), 146–148
health-knowledge assessment
  health-knowledge assessment
  Preschool Health and Safety Knowledge Assessment (PHSKA), 204–205
  Skin Cancer Knowledge Questionnaire (SCKQ), 207–208
  Test of Diabetes Knowledge (TDK), 209–210
  The 24-Hour Recall Interview, 211–213
Health Resources Inventory for Parents (HRIP), 230–231
Health Status Measure for Children (HSMC), 188–189
height of child, Negative Events Related to Short Stature (NERSS), 47–48
Hospital Fears Questionnaire (HFQ), 73–74
Hospital Fears Rating Scale (HFRS), 75–76
Hospitalization Self Report Instrument (HSRI), 42–44
Hospital Stress Scale (HSS), 76–77

Impact on Family Scale (IFS), 232–233
informal assessment, 14
injury
  Injury Behavior Checklist (IBC), 148–149
  Minor Injury Severity Scale (MISS), 150–151
  See also Pain assessment
Intentions to Engage in AIDS-Risk Situations, 119–120
internal consistency, as reliability, 11
inter-rater reliability, 11
interviews, 12–13
  pros/cons of, 13
Interview Schedule on Impact of Cystic Fibrosis on Families, 234–235

Kiscope, 78–80
Kuder-Richardson formula, 11

Life Events Checklist (LEC), 80–81
Living with a Chronic Illness (LCI), 44–46

Medical Compliance Incomplete Stories Test (MCIST), 202–203
Medical Experiences Questionnaire (MEQ), 82–83
Medical Fear Questionnaire (MFQ), 83–85
Memories of Hospitalization Questionnaire (MHQ), 42–44
Minor Injury Severity Scale (MISS), 150–151
Modified Behavioral Pain Scale (MBPS), 152–153

Negative Behavioral Changes (NBC), 46–47
Negative Events Related to Short Stature (NERSS), 47–48
Neonatal Infant Pain Scale (NIPS), 153–155
norm-referenced tests, 7–9
  percentile rankings, 8
  raw scores, 8
  standardization of, 7–8
  standardized scores, 8
  z-scores, 8–9
nurse assessment
  Nurse's Rating Form (NRF), 49–50
  Pediatric Oncology Nurse Stressor Questionnaire (PONSQ), 244–245

observational assessment, 13–14
  recording/coding in, 14
Observation Scale of Behavioral Distress (OSBD)-Revised, 155–157
Oucher Scale, 157–159

pain assessment
  Behavioral Approach-Avoidance and Distress Scale (BAADS), 134–135
  Charleston Pediatric Pain Pictures (CPPP), 135–137
  Child-Adult Medical Procedure Interaction Scale-Revised (CAMPIS-R), 137–140
  Child Behavior Observation Rating Scale (CBORS), 140–141
  Children's Hospital of Eastern Ontario Pain Scale (CHEOPS), 142–143
  Children's Pain Inventory (CPI), 143–145
  Faces Pain Scale (FPS), 145–146
  Headache Symptom Questionnaire-Revised (HSQ-R), 146–148
  Injury Behavior Checklist (IBC), 148–149
  Minor Injury Severity Scale (MISS), 150–151
  Modified Behavioral Pain Scale (MBPS), 152–153
  Neonatal Infant Pain Scale (NIPS), 153–155
  Observation Scale of Behavioral Distress (OSBD)-Revised, 155–157
  Oucher Scale, 157–159
  Pediatric Pain Questionnaire (PPQ), 159–161
  Perception of Procedures Questionnaire (PPQ), 161–163
  Scare Scale (SS), 164–165
  Toddler-Preschooler Postoperative Pain Scale (TPPPS), 165–167
  Waldron/Varni Pediatric Pain Coping Inventory (PPCI), 87–89

Index

Parental Attitudes Toward Children with Handicaps (PATCH) Questionnaire, 122–124
Parental Coping Scale: Pediatric Intensive Care Unit (PCS:PUCU), 239–240
Parental Health Belief Scale, 124–125
Parental Stressor Scale: Neonatal Intensive Care Unit (PSS:NICU), 240–242
Parent Participation Attitude Scale (PPAS), 121–122
Parent Perception Inventory (PPI), 235–236
Parent Protection Scale (PPS), 236–238
Parents of Children with Disabilities Inventory (PCDI), 242–243
Pediatric Behavior Scale (PBS), 50–53
Pediatric Inpatient Behavior Scale (PIBS), 53–55
Pediatric Oncology Nurse Stressor Questionnaire (PONSQ), 244–245
Pediatric Oncology Quality of Life Scale (POQOLS), 190–191
Pediatric Pain Questionnaire (PPQ), 159–161
Pediatric Symptom Checklist (PSC), 55–57
Perceived Illness Experience Scale (PIE), 245–247
Perceived Illness Experience Scale (PIE)-Child Version, 58–59
percentile rankings, norm-referenced tests, 8
Perception of Procedures Questionnaire (PPQ), 161–163
Perceptions of Asthma Medication Scale (PAM), 125–127
Personal Adjustment and Role Skills Scale (PARS-III), 59–61
physically/medically impaired adjustment
  Acceptance of Illness Scale (AIS), 29–30
  Behavioral Profile Rating Scale (BPRS), 30–31
  Behavioral Upset in Medical Patients-Revised (BUMP-R), 32–33
  Children's Eating Behavior Inventory (CEBI), 34–35
  Children's Physical Self-concept Scale (CPSS), 35–37
  Children's Somatization Inventory (CSI), 37–39
  Deasy-Spinetta School Behavior Questionnaire (DSBQ), 40–41
  Diabetes Adjustment Scale (DAS), 41–42
  Hospitalization Self Report Instrument (HSRI), 42–44
  Living with a Chronic Illness (LCI), 44–46
  Memories of Hospitalization Questionnaire (MHQ), 42–44
  Negative Behavioral Changes (NBC), 46–47
  Negative Events Related to Short Stature (NERSS), 47–48
Nurse's Rating Form (NRF), 49–50
Pediatric Behavior Scale (PBS), 50–53
Pediatric Inpatient Behavior Scale (PIBS), 53–55
Pediatric Symptom Checklist (PSC), 55–57
Perceived Illness Experience Scale (PIE)-Child Version, 58–59
Personal Adjustment and Role Skills Scale (PARS-III), 59–61
Post-Hospitalization Behavior Questionnaire (PHBQ), 61–62
Post-Hospitalization Behavior Questionnaire (PHBQ), 61–62
predictive validity, 12
Preschool Health and Safety Knowledge Assessment (PHSKA), 204–205

quality of life assessment
  Child Health Assessment Inventory (CHAI), 174–175
  Child Health and Illness Profile-Adolescent Edition (CHIP-AE), 172–174
  Child Health Questionnaire (CHQ) Child Form, 176–178
  Child Health Questionnaire (CHQ) Parent Form, 178–181
  Functional Disability Inventory (FDI), 181–183
  Functional Status II(R), 185–187
  Functional Status Questionnaire (FSQ), 183–185
  Health Status Measure for Children (HSMC), 188–189
  Pediatric Oncology Quality of Life Scale (POQOLS), 190–191
  Quality of Well-Being (QWB) Scale, 192–193

raw scores, norm-referenced tests, 8
reliability of test, 9–11
  affecting factors, 9
  alternate-form reliability, 10
  and choosing instrument, 18–19
  internal consistency, 11
  inter-rater reliability, 11
  meaning of, 9
  reliability coefficient, 9
  research-based assessment, 23
  split-half reliability, 10–11
  and test construction, 9–10
  test-retest reliability, 10
research-based assessment, 22–25
  choosing instruments, 23
  financial factors, 25
  interpretations, 24
  reliability of test, 23
  sample population, 22
  sensitivity of test, 23–24
  time factors, 24–25
  validity of test, 23
Role-Play Inventory of Situations and Coping Strategies (RISCS), 85–87

sample population, research-based assessment, 22

Scare Scale (SS), 164–165
Self-Care Adherence Interview (SCAI), 205–206
self-concept
  Body Attitude Scale (BAS), 97–98
  Children's Physical Self-Concept Scale (CPSS), 35–37
  Negative Events Related to Short Stature (NERSS), 47–48
self-reports, 19
sensitivity of test, research-based assessment, 23–24
Skin Cancer Knowledge Questionnaire (SCKQ), 207–208
Spearman-Brown formula, 11
split-half reliability, 10–11
standardized scores, norm-referenced tests, 8
stress/coping assessment
  Children's Concern Scale (CCS), 67–68
  Coping Health Inventory for Children (CHIC), 68–69
  Coping Strategies Inventory (CSI), 70–71
  Fear Faces Scale (Fear Self-Report Scale-Fear SR), 72–73
  Hospital Fears Questionnaire (HFQ), 73–74
  Hospital Fears Rating Scale (HFRS), 75–76
  Hospital Stress Scale (HSS), 76–77
  Kiscope, 78–80
  Life Events Checklist (LEC), 80–81
  Medical Experiences Questionnaire (MEQ), 82–83
  Medical Fear Questionnaire (MFQ), 83–85
  Role-Play Inventory of Situations and Coping Strategies (RISCS), 85–87
  Waldron/Varni Pediatric Pain Coping Inventory (PPCI), 87–89

Test of Diabetes Knowledge (TDK), 209–210
test-retest reliability, 10
time factors, research-based assessment, 24–25
Toddler-Preschooler Postoperative Pain Scale (TPPPS), 165–167
The 24-Hour Recall Interview, 211–213

validity of test, 11–12
  and choosing instrument, 18–19
  construct validity, 12
  content validity, 11–12
  convergent validity, 12
  criterion-related validity, 12
  discriminant validity, 12
  face validity, 11
  meaning of, 11
  predictive validity, 12
  research-based assessment, 23

Waldron/Varni Pediatric Pain Coping Inventory (PPCI), 87–89

z-scores, norm-referenced tests, 8–9